The Story of
The Milford Haven
Waterway

An early 1900s photo of Haverfordwest looking down on the back of the riverside warehouses. To the right of the New Bridge is Lewis's Furniture Warehouse which was demolished in the later 1930s and replaced by the County Theatre and Cavendish Furniture store which have also now disappeared to make way for council offices. Immediately opposite Lewis's is Picton House, at that time the town house of the Philipps family of Picton Castle. It is now occupied by the offices of Haverfordwest Town Council

The Story of
The Milford Haven Waterway

by
Sybil Edwards

Logaston Press

LOGASTON PRESS
Little Logaston Woonton Almeley
Herefordshire HR3 6QH
logastonpress.co.uk

First published by Logaston Press 2001
This revised edition published by Logaston Press 2009
Copyright text © Sybil Edwards 2009
Copyright illustrations © as acknowledged 2009

ISBN 978 1 906663 10 0

Typeset by Logaston Press
and printed in Great Britain by
Bell & Bain Ltd., Glasgow

Front cover photograph by Toby Driver, © RCAHMW

Contents

Acknowledgements

When I began this book it was with the support and encouragement of my husband Jim McBrearty whose ever enquiring mind had given him an exceptionally wide-ranging knowledge of the county of Pembrokeshire from its earliest times. His sudden death in 1999 has been the greatest loss in every way.

I have, however, been fortunate in the help very readily given yet again for this second edition by so many people who are experts in their field and those with far reaching memories of living and working on the waterway.

Since the first edition was published in 2001 an enormous amount has happened in the area and their assistance has been invaluable in what has been a fascinating year of research. While the county retains the wild beauty of areas where time stands still it has truly moved industrially into the 21st century with the promise of good times ahead.

I am indebted to Mariam Moazzen and Mike Ashworth of the Milford Haven Port Authority; John Evans, Sunderland Trust; Gerallt Nash, National Museum of Wales, St Fagans; staffs of Pembrokeshire County Record Office and Haverfordwest Reference Library; Phil Thomson, Chevron; Len Mullins and Ceri Jones, Pembrokeshire County Council; Simon Rickaby and Diana Warlow, Braemar Howells; Terry John; Roger Worsley; George Geear, Chapel Bay Fort; Roger Thomas, English Heritage Military Support Officer; David James and West Wales Maritime Heritage; Neil Fairburn, National Grid project manager; Jamie Gordon, National Grid; Laverick Breeze; Gordon Pilot; Peter James; Martin Caveney; Linda Asman, Pembroke 21C; Simon Hancock; Paul Lucas; David Lort Philipps and Adrian Lort Philipps — and very especially to Alan Robinson for his mostly patient, but always unstinting, technical support.

Above all my thanks to Andy Johnson of Logaston Press for his patience and understanding and the expertise and meticulous care he brought to editing *The Story of the Milford Haven Waterway*.

1847 Chart of the Milford Haven waterway

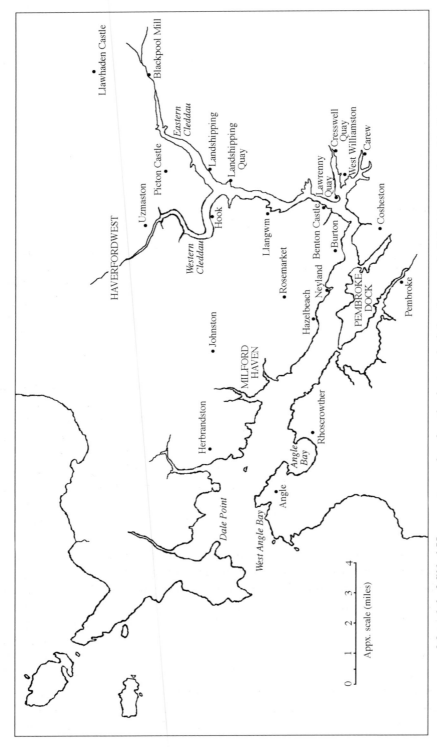

Map of the Milford Haven waterway based on the chart overleaf, showing several of the places mentioned in the text

Chapter 1

Early Days

Today's maps show Milford Haven as a wide, deep estuary, bounded by low banks on its southern side and by higher ground to the north, its seaward end dominated by the cliffs of St. Ann's Head. In the Stone Ages the geography of this area was vastly different. Huge quantities of water were still locked away in the glaciers which had retreated from this latitude not many millennia earlier, making the sea level hereabouts some 200 feet lower than it is today. There would have been wide plains of forest and scrub where St. Bride's Bay is now, making all the islands part of the mainland which stretched out as far as the Smalls.

The people who lived there would have been fisher folk, living off the huge shoals of codfish and haddock which abounded offshore and came into shallow water to breed. Remains of encampments of such people have been found across northern Europe, but those in Pembrokeshire long ago sank beneath the ocean. Travel overland was hard going with few, if any, tracks, so inshore waters and rivers were their highways, which accounts for the main centres of early settlement all over the world being along river valleys. Both the Eastern and Western Cleddau would have been rushing torrents, carrying the meltwater from glaciers to the north, scouring out deep channels in the rock. The shape of their course can still be seen in the submarine contours of Milford Haven. Settlements would have been on the low cliffs on either side.

The study of the prehistory of Pembrokeshire indicates human activity from late in the Old Stone Age. Over the years scores of artefacts from that period have been picked up along the ridge of high ground that runs from Haverfordwest Racecourse, through Mount Airey to Priory Mount. Most of these were flint microliths — stone tools and implements hardly larger than a finger nail. These were cutting blades, scrapers and awls, each one flaked from a stone core and shaped to its own purpose. Some of these microliths were found grouped together, suggesting that the people who made and used them stayed in one place for a period of time.

One prehistoric event which is generally reckoned to have taken place on the Haven is the passage along it of the bluestones of Stonehenge. This bluestone, or Spotted Dolerite, came from Carn Meini in the Preseli Hills, although it is found over a wide area of north Pembrokeshire. It was highly sought after as raw material for stone axes and the prestige possessions of people described by an English Heritage archaeologist as 'neolithic yuppies'. It was possibly valued as a sacred stone in its own right, the white spots of quartz in their blue/grey bed resembling stars in the sky. The 80 stones that went to Stonehenge may well have already been a sacred monument in Pembrokeshire which

A selection of finds from the collection of Miss Joan Rees who discovered them in fields near Haverfordwest, finds 1 to 9 at Priory Farm after the area was bulldozed prior to the building of the Priory Housing Estate, 10 and 11 from the prolific Palmerston area. Both sites are on high ground above Merlin's Brook. In all the artefacts the selective use of the most appropriate materials for the purpose to which they were put indicates that these early tribes were familiar with the properties of the local stone.

1. An abraded pebble or hammerstone from the Mesolithic periods — cracks and scars on the stone indicate that it has been subjected to a vigorous hitting motion.

2. A flint core from which blades have been struck — probably now too small for chipping further blades.

3, 4, 5, 6 and 7. Small blades used to form composite projectile points (such as arrow barbs), awls and other tools.

8. Flint likely to have been notched for shaping an instrument such as a bone needle. The Mesolithic tribespeople had to create not only their tools but also the tools with which to make the various implements.

9. A barbed and tanged arrow head from the Neolithic or Bronze age. This would have been attached to a wooden shaft with gut and/or resin. Shafts could be securely held by the use of wet rawhide which shrank as it dried to hold the implement in a firm grip.

10 and 11. Two scrapers which would have been used to clean skins. No. 10 is shaped at both ends.

(Photograph by Martin Cavaney)

was shipped as a complete assemblage to be incorporated into the bigger monument in Wiltshire. (Some years ago some Americans bought one of London's bridges and had it dismantled and re-erected in one of the southern states — purely as a prestige project to show the world how wealthy and important they were. Technology may have advanced during the past 4,000 years but maybe human nature is basically unchanged.)

Diligent research by renowned Stonehenge experts Professors Timothy Darvill and Pembrokeshire-born Geoffrey Wainwright culminated in March 2008 in the first dig on site for 40 years and has shed potential new light on the mysterious history of the iconic monument. The professors have long believed that the smaller bluestones of the Carn Meini area of Preseli, rather than the huge sarsen stones, hold the key to the purpose of Stonehenge. They now contend that the bluestones were credited with healing powers, a part of the Celtic mythology of the curative properties of the prolific sacred springs at the base of the Preseli outcrop.

Their dig concentrated on just one of the bluestones and resulted in forensic testing, dating the arrival of the stones at 2300 BC, the same as given as the death of a man buried in nearby Amesbury. The skeleton, unearthed in 2002, became known as the Amesbury Archer and tests indicated that he was from the Alpine area — 600 miles from Stonehenge. He had been buried with flint arrowheads and a treasure trove of gold and copper, making this the richest Neolithic grave in the country. He had suffered what would have been painful long term injuries, including a dental abscess that had burst through his jaw bone which would have caused him excruciating pain, leading Darvill and Wainwright to speculate that he was a wealthy man who had travelled to Stonehenge in search of healing.

As further evidence for their theory Darvill comments 'There's an amazing and unnatural concentration of skeletal trauma in the bones that were dug up around Stonehenge, 50% of them those of people from far away. This was a place of pilgrimage for people coming to get cured — a Bronze age equivalent of Lourdes.'

Whatever their purpose these stones (six or eight feet long and each weighing up to four tons) would have been dragged down the boggy slopes of the hills, sliding over beds of cut green branches with poles bound round to support and protect them, until they arrived at the

Plan of Stonehenge showing the Bluestone Circle and Bluestone Ellipse, the latter probably being formed from an earlier structure

3

headwaters of the Eastern Cleddau. Enough poles, quite quickly cut, even with stone axes, would be added underneath until each stone floated, then they would be dragged downstream, singly or in convoy, to the open waters of the Haven. Out in the open sea the coast may or may not have been as rugged as it is today, but once round the western promontory a long haul lay ahead hugging the Bristol Channel coast to the mouth of the Avon. Then it was up the river and a short portage overland to the headwaters of the River Wylie which would take them directly to the foot of the processional way at Stonehenge.

Moving the bluestones from Pembrokeshire to Stonehenge could possibly have taken several years, working in the comfort of spring and summer, though Wainwright speculates that it would have been only in the winter months that men would be available to leave their labours to undertake this long journey. There could have been a small team of a few dozen core workers who recruited additional labour to help on specific sections of the journey. Nevertheless it would have taken a degree of logistical planning to feed and shelter this workforce during the course of its journey. For Neolithic men to have transported those bluestones from Preseli to Stonehenge the land must surely have been at peace; neighbouring groups of people were possibly related and had sufficient space with little cause (or desire) to fight each other.

Author Brian John has long challenged what he describes as 'the Bluestone myth' which, he claims, was fashioned after the First World War as part of a patrician campaign to demonstrate that our Neolithic ancestors were even cleverer than the ancients who put up the stones at Carnac. He refers to the Darvill/Wainwright theories as 'fairytales' and in *The Bluestone Enigma* asserts that the bluestones at Stonehenge have come from at least 15 different locations, scattered all over west and south Wales. They are, he says, glacial erratics transported by the Irish Sea Glacier that swept over Preseli during the Ice Age and that these glacial deposits are at least 400,000 years old with traces near Bath and, as far east as Street in Somerset.

This is a debate which promises to continue.

In 1989 a bluestone from Carn Meini was taken to Salisbury Plain to form part of the visitor centre at Stonehenge. Bluestone '89, masterminded by Jim McBrearty as a fundraising event for the Pembrokeshire branch of the Cystic Fibrosis Trust, made no attempt to replicate the original journey of the stones. However, great care was taken by English Heritage in selecting the stone to ensure it came from the same outcrop as those of Neolithic times. To avoid damage to this Site of Special Scientific Interest the RAF loaned a Chinook helicopter to lift the stone to the foot of the mountain, whence it travelled, displayed on a lorry, on a week-long fund-raising journey to Stonehenge. A bus that formed part of the cavalcade was furnished as an information centre and publicised the delights of Pembrokeshire as well as giving details of the work of the Cystic Fibrosis Trust. The whole event was followed by the world's media.

Writing in the *Pembrokeshire Magazine* Jim McBrearty reflected on the original journey commenting that as he stood on the mountain he realised that he was standing on Yr Hen Ffordd (the Old Road), the line of a track which ran along the contour line, and which was the ancient trackway from southern England, through Wales and down to

Whitesands, where travellers used once to set sail for Ireland. It is a part of the most ancient network of tracks in Europe, used by travellers since time immemorial.

As a millennium project, funded by a £100,000 Heritage Lottery grant, another three-ton pillar of spotted dolerite was despatched from the mountain in April 2000, this time with the intention of recreating the original 240 mile journey, and was scheduled to arrive at Stonehenge in time for the autumn equinox. From the outset the project — and particularly its use of lottery money — attracted a storm of local controversy, and because of the many mishaps that beset the event from day one it was constantly referred to in the media as the 'ill-fated bluestone'.

The three-ton rock was dragged 15 miles to the coast at Dale where it was floated but there, at the end of June, it sank to the bottom of the sea. Through the assistance of the Royal Maritime Auxiliary Service the stone was retrieved but later attempts to relaunch the project were hit by bad weather. It was then discovered that one of the two replica curraghs designed to take the stone on the seaward leg of the journey, was holed. The early onset of winter that year prevented any further attempts to move the stone and the project was put in hibernation in the hopes of resuming the journey in the spring, with a revised aim of reaching Stonehenge for the following equinox. In June 2001, however, insurance cover for the seaward journey was refused and the project ended in Pembrokeshire where it had begun.

Representatives of Plaid Cymru, author and historian Dillwyn Miles and many others had called for the project to be abandoned, commenting that it was a waste of money which could better benefit the area, and that the use of modern methods to help the stone on its way had anyway invalidated the project's aims. Undaunted, the then Menter Preseli co-ordinator Phil Bowen said 'One of our aims was to put the Preseli area on the map and there can't be anyone now who does not know that the bluestones at Stonehenge came from north Pembrokeshire. Our project has attracted attention worldwide'.

Early man had also put the future Pembrokeshire 'on the map'. Axes from the early 'factories' in the Preselis have been found in Wexford and Antrim. These factories proliferated in Neolithic times and a report summarised in Clough and Cummins (1988) lists 89 polished stones and flint axes found within Pembrokeshire. About 40% are identified as being from specific manufacturing areas, the majority of them being in the Preselis. George Children and George Nash in *Neolithic Sites of Cardiganshire, Carmarthenshire and Pembrokeshire* state that it is clear that since the early Neolithic, both indigenous and expeditionary groups have used

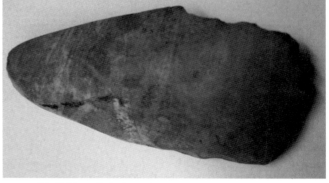

Neolithic polished axe found at The Have, Camrose
by Jim McBrearty

stone from the Preselis as a prestige raw material, with three individual quarries being recognised.

The rest of Pembrokeshire is abundantly scattered with remains from all periods of prehistory, from Old Stone Age to Celtic, so it can safely be said that the shores of Milford Haven would also have been well populated from Neolithic times. The waters would have been busy with men fishing, hunting wildfowl, gathering eggs on the coastal cliffs and marshes, or trading in small boats. At Priory Farm Cave, just downriver from Pembroke Castle, excavations in the early 1900s revealed animal bones — of bears, wolves, reindeer and woolly mammoth — which had been chewed by hyenas, as well as human remains, flints, pottery and Bronze Age tools. This discovery by Dr. Hurrell Style is evidence of occupation through the Ice, Stone and Bronze Ages and later by mediaeval man.

In Burton there is evidence of prehistoric civilisation at the Hanging Stone, together with a dolmen which probably dates back over 4,000 years. In south Pembrokeshire there are three menhirs — the Devil's Quoit at Angle and the King's Quoit at Manorbier, both 4th to early 3rd millennium BC burial chambers, and Harold's Stone at Stackpole, a standing stone from the 2nd millennium BC. Two other standing stones found nearby are known collectively with Harold's Stone as the Devil's Quoit (different from the one at Angle) named from the legend that once a year the stones move to Saxons Ford where they meet and, as the devil sits astride one stone playing the flute, a coven of witches indulge in frenzied dance. There is a year of good fortune ahead for anyone fortunate enough to witness the spectacle.

The Dale peninsula has yielded rich archaeological finds which suggest at least intermittent occupation from the Mesolithic or Middle Stone Age (10-6,000 BC). Flints and stone tools of this period indicate that nomadic groups may have used the area for flint working and flint pebbles still abound on nearby beaches. Stone implements, believed to have been limpet or shellfish scoops, have been found in the region while the fields of local farms have yielded polished axes and other stone tools.

The Devil's Quoit, Angle (George Nash)

Gradually nomadic hunter-gatherers started to cultivate patches of land and domesticate stock, and man turned to agriculture. This saw the commencement of the Neolithic period — the New Stone Age — as tools increased in variety and complexity. This more settled life accounts for the stone tombs of this period, used for the burial of communities, to be found in the regions which they made 'home', tombs which also seem to have helped define each community's territory.

After about 2500 BC round barrows and cairns were built for single burials as individuals gained greater importance and 500 years later new styles of pottery began to appear, whilst stone tools gradually gave way to those of metal. New pottery vessels

Dale finds from Tenby Museum (Gareth Davies)

1. Four spindle whorls (Iron Age) found at Pickleridge, Snailton. These would have been used for spinning as fly wheels to provide momentum on a spindle — probably working with nettle or other vegetable fibre, animal wool or fur. 'String' would be much in use for fishing nets and net bags. It is interesting to note that the holes in the whorls would have to be drilled and it is likely that this was done using quartz sand and a reed rotated rapidly between both hands.

2. Heavy (basalt) stone pounder, date unknown, from Little Sea Meadow, Dale.

3. Conical-shaped red sandstone pounder (Iron Age), height 7.3cm, bottom circumference 23cm. The record is unclear about whether it came from Great Castle Head Camp, Dale or Great Castle Head, Milford Haven.

4. Basalt pebble hollowed out on both sides. (Basalt was a prestigious material.) This artefact is possibly an unfinished ring stone which would have been hafted for use as a hammer, alternatively these countersunk pebbles could conveniently be held between two fingers for use as a small unhafted hammer.

5. Limestone round holed stone — possibly used as a digging stick weight, but it was found in the same area as the spindle whorls and so could be a loom weight.

6. Egg-shaped polished stone — a very attractive item which may well have been designed as grinding powder or paste for artwork or herbal remedies.

known as 'beakers' (which gave their owners the name the 'Beaker People') were found in burials and excavations at Stackpole near Pembroke. The existence of a circular timber house, possibly a Bronze Age domestic house, was also discovered in this area. Indeed, the entire area of Stackpole Warren contains many traces of settlement and agricultural activity from the Bronze Age to the Roman period. The emerging tribes appear to have become quite settled and territorial with both a ruling class and a class of craftsmen who produced tools, weapons and jewellery.

As a legacy of the Bronze Age a bronze ring and a barbed and tanged flint arrowhead were discovered at Short Point, and a shaft which was filled in in the mid-19th century is reputed to have been an ancient copper mine. Excavations at Kilpaison Burrows at Rhoscrowther revealed a Bronze Age barrow which contained primary and secondary interment by cremation and one secondary inhumation burial. Fragments of pottery there had attracted the attention of the Revd. J.P. Gordon Williams and an excavation in 1925 revealed the skeleton of a man aged around 30, a burial in fact dating from the Christian period, but also Bronze Age urns containing the ashes of three women and a boy of 11 or 12 years of age. In the Bronze Age women held positions of social distinction and it is interesting to note that the primary interment — estimated to have taken place about 1500-1000 BC — was that of a young woman, indicating that the barrow was erected in her honour. The secondary burials were in urns dated to between 1000 and 800 BC, all bearing decorative forms and motifs that may well have derived from Ireland.

As population numbers increased there was a need to protect agricultural land and provisions and hillforts were constructed, largely in the Iron Age, though that at Dale dates from earlier than 790BC in the late Bronze Age — earlier than any other hillfort discovered in south-west Wales.

Other Iron Age sites exist at Great Castle Head, a fort with banks and ditches still visible and where excavation revealed pottery and stone

Dale finds on view at Tenby Museum (Gareth Davies).
A collection of nine Mesolithic limpet scoops found near the Iron Age Promontory Fort at Great Castle Head, Dale. These naturally elongated pebbles have artificially flaked and bevelled tips and were probably used for scooping up food products or to detach limpets from the rocks and scoop them from their shells

spindle whorls which would have been used for hand spinning; and at Rosemarket are the banks of an Iron Age fort, now referred to as The Rings but described in the 12th century as the Castle of Ros. Rosemarket also contains a Neolithic burial chamber — the Hanging Stone — indicating continuity of occupation by early man.

Although there was some local opposition to the siting of the National Grid's LNG (Liquefied Natural Gas) pipeline from Milford Haven to Aberdulais the project has enabled a new insight into the history of Wales and great excitement for the archaeologists who were monitoring the work. One of the more significant finds was at St. Botolphs, north of Milford Haven. The area had been identified around 1910 as a Bronze Age burnt mound formed from discarded fire-cracked stones and, consequently, it was one of high archaeological potential. In July 2006 a long wooden Bronze Age object which had been hollowed out was discovered. National Grid Archaeology Project Manager Neil Fairburn said 'it could have been a wooden trough which would be filled with water into which hot stones were placed to heat the water and produce steam — perhaps for cooking, washing or even for saunas or sweat lodges (used all over the world in an age old purification ritual for spiritual healing or healing of the sick). Alternatively it could have been a log boat which had fallen into disuse and was being used as a water trough — something that has been seen previously with other European finds.' During a spell of 14 weeks, archaeological work on the site provided additional evidence of occupation, including structures, pits and ditches, whilst pottery dating from both the Early and the Later Bronze Age was uncovered, so indicating continuity of occupation.

The marshy area where the wooden vessel lay is part of a stream which leads to the Milford estuary, suggesting the vessel may have been used to travel to and from the estuary. This remarkable find is being conserved at Newport, Gwent while tests continue, and a crucial decision has yet to be made on its final resting place as this precious find will need continuous care. The Milford Haven Museum was quick to stake a claim on the grounds that the canoe has rested within the boundary of Milford for more than 3,000 years and also that it would make a good companion for the 20,000 year old mammoth tusk that is already exhibited in the museum.

Further along the route of the pipeline the discovery of a henge monument at Llandowror in Carmarthenshire gives rise to speculation that it was a marker on the 'sacred way' that was used to deliver the Preseli bluestones to Stonehenge. A stream runs close to the site adding to the suggestion that the inland waterways formed part of the route to Stonehenge.

'The construction of the natural gas pipeline between 2006 and 2007 through Pembrokeshire, Carmarthenshire and parts of Glamorgan and Powys has resulted in the biggest archaeological investigation in the history of Wales', says Neil Fairburn. During the construction in 2006 of the first 120km, 129 archaeological sites were identified and recorded, of which 20 developed into major excavations.

While there is no record of a permanent Roman settlement in Pembrokeshire the coast was certainly known to Roman geographers. Ptolemy's *Geography* written in Alexandria in the 2nd century AD includes an outline of Pembrokeshire with what appears to be St. Ann's Head named as *Octapitarum*. A military presence towards the west of the Haven, however, is suggested by coin finds and rectilinear crop marks in the Whitland area with a Roman road, detected in aerial photographs, running west from St. Clears to Llawhaden and thence towards the west coast of Pembrokeshire. It is possible that this may have ended at one of the branches of the river Cleddau, further progress being made by water.

Finds to the north-west of Haverfordwest at Pelcomb Cross, Rosegreen, Newgale, Solva and St. David's indicate a direct line to St. David's Head and the long established crossing to Ireland. The 14th-century monk, Richard of Cirencester, also suggested that St. David's Head was the site of a Roman station called *Menopia* — no evidence of this, however, has ever been found.

Writing in the *Journal of the Pembrokeshire Historical Society* in 1993 John Roche, however, advanced the theory that Pembrokeshire did indeed have a place within the Roman Empire. He points out that the Roman town of *Moridunum* at Carmarthen is accepted to have been the *civitas*, or capital, of the Demetae whose territory incorporated today's Pembrokeshire and most of Carmarthenshire. The amphitheatre at *Moridunum*, which had the potential to house 5,000 spectators, would, suggested Roche, have provided accommodation for a town of the same scale as Roman Cirencester, indicating that *Moridunum* would have been as much a centre for Pembrokeshire as it was for Carmarthenshire.

Roche also refers to a concentration of finds in or near Fishguard, possibly indicating a road following the route of today's A40. Further finds in the south of the county provide evidence of a possible seaborne route running from Laugharne to Pendine, on to Amroth and Tenby, across to Caldey Island and thence to Manorbier, Stackpole, Bosheston and Freshwater East and thence to Angle, and up the Cleddau to Carew. Evidence of a Roman shipping link with the south of the county was discovered in the Roman Legionary fortress at Caerleon where ballast of shattered Pembrokeshire slate was found, used as metalling, behind the quay walls. It is known for certain that in the Dark Ages which followed the Roman occupation, and probably during the occupation years themselves, Tenby was a major site for this slate and it is thought likely that this material was shipped from the Amroth or Saundersfoot area.

What are known as the Dark Ages (broadly between the 5th and 8th centuries AD) correspond in Pembrokeshire with the Age of the Saints when holy men of the Celtic Church roamed far and wide preaching the word of God and living hard and simple lives in caves, cells and other damp abodes amongst the rocks. Their names are all around us, though not along Milford Haven itself, although there is a legend of one holy man who did get to know this waterway all too well.

In the 6th century St. Brynach was returning from a pilgrimage to Rome. He sat, despondent, on a large flat stone on a beach in Brittany waiting, it seemed eternally, for a ship to carry him home to his native Ireland. After three days he called for God's help and immediately the stone on which he was sitting was lifted by a great wave and carried out to sea. Doubtless he gave thanks for this great miracle, but could then have wished he had been more specific in his prayers, for Brynach's stone came ashore in Milford Haven, not the Emerald Isle he longed to see. To add to his troubles he was then accosted by 'some ladies of the place'. Having seen them off in saintly style he was next set on by a group of local lads whose aim in life was to rid the area of Irish settlers.

Brynach wasted no time in getting away from this heathen shore and hastened inland to the north of the present county where he built churches and spent some time communing with the angels atop Carn Ingli (Mountain of the Angels). It is not recorded that he ever returned to Milford Haven.

The recorded history of the area really starts with the arrival of the Norsemen, generally characterised as merciless pirates materialising out of the sea mist to murder and pillage in coastal settlements. Initially this was a true picture. As pressures of population grew in their fiord-side settlements in Scandinavia bands of them set out each spring in what has been described as 'going a-Viking' ('pirating' in their language) with up to 200 men in each of their versatile longships which had ports for 50 oars and which could also carry around 20 tons of cargo. They terrorised all who stood in their path — especially the monks whose churches and holy places were embellished with vessels of gold and precious stones.

The raid on Lindisfarne, off the Northumberland coast, in 793 was to herald a period of trouble that, with varying degrees of mayhem, lasted 300 years. The prayer *A furore Normannorum libera nos, Domine* (From the fury of the northmen deliver us, O Lord) was a part of many a church service as it seemed that all Christian people were destined to perish at the hands of the Vikings.

The French monk Abbo, who witnessed the onslaught from inside a Parisian cathedral in November 885, wrote: 'The wild beasts go through hills and fields, killing babies, children, young men, old men, fathers, sons and mothers. They overthrow, they destroy, they ravage; sinister cohort, fatal phalanx, cruel host.'

In time, though, these wild northmen grew tired of ceaseless wandering and began to settle in some of the places they had come to plunder, notably the Shetlands, Scotland, the Isle of Man, and Ireland. Their towns and trading posts crept ever nearer to south-west Wales until in 887 Hubba overwintered with his fleet of 23 ships of war in Milford Haven. After this the place names tell the story of eventual settlement — Hubber's ton, Herbrand's ton, Freya's thorp, Hoffna's ford and even Melr (sandbank) fiord, Thirston and Dumpledale (regrettably now renamed Ashdale) as well as the islands of Ramsey, Skomer, Skokholm, Grassholm, and Caldey. Dozens of Pembrokeshire names originated with these pirates turned settlers. Indeed a blood type analysis carried out some years ago revealed that the inhabitants of south Pembrokeshire have in their veins a blood group matched only in parts of southern Scandinavia.

Being superb seamen the Vikings became successful traders too, and over time the slim Viking ships that had come to plunder along the Milford Haven were replaced by bulkier cargo carriers, forerunners of the mediaeval 'lymphad' seen on the seal of Haverfordwest, and the waterway was busy with commerce. The small local ports began to see on their quays goods from all over the known world.

Once the Viking raiders chose to settle along the coast of Europe, their townships soon developed into minor kingdoms, some rising to become major powers, most notably that of Normandy. It is also very probable that the Norman traders or explorers probed their way up the Haven making brief contact with the Celts of the embryonic commercial centres of Pembroke or Haverfordwest which was initially a settlement on a ford crossing the river Cleddau.

Before this, however, Wales suffered years of conflict with numerous small independent kingdoms sometimes at war with the Anglo-Saxons and constantly feuding among themselves. From time to time attempts were made at achieving unity as one or other of the Welsh kings brought more of the territories (each often no larger than one of today's counties) under his domain.

Through a number of opportunist marriages Rhodri Mawr, King of Gwynedd, succeeded in uniting most of Wales under his overlordship. It was, however, divided among his three sons (Cadell, Anarawd and Mervyn) at the time of his death in 878 and once more the Welsh were locked in conflict with each other. Cadell, who had received Cardigan and the palace of Dinevwr, dispossessed his brother, Mervyn, of Powys while Anarawd, king of the northern territories, set out to devastate Cardigan, Pembrokeshire and Tivyside — the area bounding the river Tivy or Teifi.

It was not until the kingdom passed into the hands of Cadell's son, Hywel Dda (Hywel the Good) that peace was restored. He secured Dyfed by marriage and created the kingdom of Deheubarth, with Gwynedd and Powys subsequently coming under his 40 year rule. During this time he established the laws under which Wales was governed until Edward I annexed the then principality. He is also remembered as the first Welsh king to issue his own coinage. When he died in 950 the unity of his realm died with him and years of anarchy and bloodshed followed. His son, Owain, had obtained Dyfed but his cousin from north Wales invaded Pembrokeshire submitting its people to two years of atrocities. The conflict between Dyfed and north Wales continued and the *Brut y Tywysogion*, a 13th-century compilation based on earlier documents, records that between the death of Hywel Dda and the Norman Conquest — just over a century — 35 Welsh rulers died by violence, mostly at the hands of their fellow countrymen.

Owain had four sons, Einion, Cadwallon, Meredydd and Lywarch, and when he died in 983 Meredydd assumed the crown; Einion had been killed, Cadwallon was dead and Lywarch was blinded when his eyes were torn out by his north Welsh cousins. Meredydd ruled for 11 years during which time he waged war with the north Welsh, the men of Glamorgan, Einion's sons, the Danes and the Saxons and his death in 994 is recorded in the *Brut* as 'the occasion of better times for peace and government in Wales'.

By wiping out all who had a claim to the various kingdoms Gruffyd ap Llywelyn seized power and established himself ruler of Deheubarth and the whole of Wales — but he, in turn, was overthrown by Earl (later King) Harold in a surprise attack by the English at Rhuddlan. His men deserted him and when he was murdered in 1063 his head was sent to Harold as the price of peace with the English.

Three years later England was conquered by the Normans, and only four more years were to pass before the first Normans were recorded in south Wales. It was just a few years later still that Arnulph de Montgomery stood in the primitive fortress — possibly similar to the earthwork forts or *burhs* which grew up as a part of King Alfred's defences against the Danes — that was to become Pembroke Castle.

Chapter 2

Norman Arrival & Royal Visitors

The death of Edward the Confessor had left no direct claimant to the English throne, leaving the Witan (the council made up of the greater nobles and bishops as advisors to the crown) to choose between Duke William of Normandy, a cousin of the king, and the English Earl Harold. Harold's claim lay through his mother who was descended from the old pirate king of Denmark, Sweyn, the leader of the force which defeated Ethelred in 1003 and who was the father of King Cnut, ruler of England between 1017-1035.

During a visit to England in 1051 William had persuaded Edward to leave him his kingdom in his will, something it was not in his power to bequeath. It was Harold who was chosen to succeed in January 1066, news which rapidly reached William who began to build boats and marshal his forces, promising to give those barons who followed him English lands in proportion to the number of men they brought to his cause. As a result William was able to land at Pevensey with a strong force before going on to win the battle of Hastings. William was crowned king of England on Christmas Day 1066.

William I installed some of his ablest supporters in the earldoms of Chester, Shrewsbury and Hereford along the March, or border, with Wales, giving them almost regal powers within these lordships and freedom to add to them by conquest of lands in Wales. Whilst the *Domesday Book* contains evidence of a pact between William I and Rhys ap Tudor, King of Deheubarth, recognising Rhys's authority in his own kingdom, the Norman lords of the Marches soon established major lordships in Cardigan, Brecon, Pembrokeshire and Glamorgan, decisively defeating Rhys outside Brecon in 1093.

During these campaigns Earl Roger de Montgomery set out to seize Pembroke, which suggests that he was aware of some existing defendable settlement in the area. Some records suggest that he and his forces crossed the Preseli Hills to the Cleddau valley and thence to the shores of the Haven. It is more likely, however, that he sailed his force to the Milford Haven waterway in the double ended sailing ships which were fitted with 'castles' at either end to enable archers and soldiers to shoot down into the waist of the enemy's vessels — the same principle as the earlier boats of King Alfred which had a raised deck so giving his forces the advantage of fighting from a higher level. Once he had seized the area, Earl Roger conferred the site of Pembroke on his son Arnulph.

Map of the Landsker showing the castles built along its 'frontier' and within it

The Norman conquest of south Pembrokeshire largely encompassed the territories already colonised by the Scandinavian races. This subsequently became the Palatine of Pembroke (or *Anglia Transwallia* — Little England Beyond Wales), raised to this status in 1138 by King Stephen by his appointment of Gilbert de Clare to the Earldom of Pembroke, a position which gave him quasi-royal jurisdiction of the area. (The palatinate ceased to exist in 1536 under the Act of Union of England and Wales during the reign of Henry VIII. The county palatine was then combined with other lordships as Wales was divided into 12 counties and the new county of Pembrokeshire came into being. Two county palatines remain in England in the Earldom of Chester and the Duchy of Lancaster.)

The Welsh, although continuing to quarrel among themselves, now had a common enemy in the Normans who had built a series of castles about four miles apart at strategic points on high ground along what became known as the Landsker, a line that soon denoted the ethnological, linguistic and geographical divide between north and south Pembrokeshire. These castles were built to defend the south of the future county, with its increasing English, Norman and, later, Flemish population from the Welsh whom the Normans had dispossessed.

The early Norman castles were very different from those which remain today for it was a century after the Norman Conquest before stone buildings began to be substituted for the original earthworks. These consisted of a raised motte on which a wooden tower would have been built to house the local lord, and possibly around which would have been erected a wooden palisade. A drawbridge would lead across the ditch at the bottom of the mound into a bailey surrounded by a wooden palisade which would have housed buildings for the lord's followers and their equipment.

Strongholds were erected within the Palatine, not only at Pembroke but also at Haverfordwest, Picton, Benton, Upton, Carew, Tenby and Manorbier, all near navigable water on the coast or on the banks of the Haven — a powerful position both for defence and for obtaining stores in time of siege. Norman-style churches were built, townships and villages developed and the feudal system of land tenure was established. In the same way that the king secured the services of the barons for the Norman invasion, a baron, in his turn, obtained the support of various knights by granting them one of his manors. The knight would then grant a certain number of the strips in the manor fields to each villager on condition that he tilled those belonging to the hall or castle as well as his own. There was very little buying or selling. All the services performed today by lawyers, doctors and teachers were carried out by monks and clergymen for no-one else could read or write so these services, too, were 'feudalised'. The system was also responsible for the founding of many 'estate' villages, as at Lawrenny, Upton and Angle.

Initial Norman conquests in Wales were threatened by the end of the 11th century, and the Normans were forced from many of their gains in north Wales, but in the west Pembroke remained in their hands under the lordship of Arnulph de Montgomery. Robert de Belesme, Ralph Mortimer, Philip Braose and Bernard de Neufmarché also acquired territory in Dyfed.

Carew Castle

Llawhaden Castle

Norman control of the Haven only served to increase the existing traffic with Ireland. A find of a Roman 1st-century burial in Stoneyford, County Kilkenny in south-eastern Ireland, an area where there was certainly later trade with Pembrokeshire, indicated that it was the tomb of a Roman merchant, and B.G. Charles, quoting *Historical and Municipal Documents of Ireland* says that three 'Norsemen of Haverford' were listed among those working in Dublin's oasthouses.

From Norman times there was a great demand for war horses and the Irish horse traders did a lively trade. The Normans' Plantagenet successors also imported their garrons (heavy horses) into Britain through Pembrokeshire's ports. Even after horses were no longer used by the military and only by those involved in agriculture, the trade continued. The names of Garron Pill, to the north of Lawrenny and the nearby Garron quarries remain a reminder of these thriving horse trading days.

During one year towards the end of the 16th century, 77 horses arrived in 15 ships, while between 1600 and 1603, 140 arrived in 28 ships, most coming from Wexford which also exported timber on a large scale. In the years between 1560 and 1603 the wholesale price of an average horse was 30s.; a garron fetched between 10s. and 25s.; a hackney or gelding and nags, 40s.; a cow, 6s. 8d. and a heifer, 5s.

The constant traffic across the Irish sea is reflected in the surnames, place names and 'loan' words which are common to both Pembrokeshire and Ireland, as land and estates were accumulated by the same family in each. Examples cited by Edward Laws in his book *Little England Beyond Wales* include Roche or Roch, Meyler, Synnet, Sinnett or Sinnott, Hayes or Hays (the family which gave Hayscastle its name), Stanton (the origin of Steynton near Milford Haven) and the Irish Huskards which was the origin of Hasguard. Kil — a hermit cell, church or burial place — is common in Ireland while Pembrokeshire has its Kilpaison, Kilgetty, Kilwendeg and Kilrue, and among the Irish 'loan' words still found in the Welsh language are *agos* (near), *brat* (pinafore), *cadach* (scarf) and *cnwc* (hill) from the Irish *cnoc*.

George Owen, writing his *Description of Pembrokeshire* in the 16th century, comments that the English portion of his native county was so over-run with Irishmen that, in some parishes, the clergyman was the only person who was not Irish. He also wrote that the Irish made quantities of *aqua vita* (whisky) which they carried about on horseback, selling it so cheaply that in many country houses the spirit replaced wine as the usual drink. Maybe it was as an outcome of this trade that complaints were made to the king, Henry VIII, about the behaviour of 'some 20,000 Irish descendants of the followers of the Norman Conquest' who had flooded Pembrokeshire.

While trade flourished between Britain and Ireland there was also great hostility between the two islands even as far back as the time of the Roman governor, Agricola, the conquest of Ireland was regarded as a necessary factor in the Roman subjugation of Britain. But Agricola was recalled to Italy before he could carry out his plans for Ireland and so it was left to Henry II in 1170 — over 1,000 years later — to make the attempt.

Henry had been given authority over the entire land by Nicholas Breakspeare, the English born Pope Adrian IV, who hated the Irish. During the previous year locally recruited knights and archers had sailed to Ireland from Milford to try their fortune, having been invited by the exiled king of Leinster, Diarmiar mac Murchadha, to help him recover the throne. Their initial success inspired Richard de Clare, Earl of Pembroke, (known as Strongbow) to take a larger force. With Henry's permission he raised a force of volunteers — much as William the Conqueror had done in 1066.

The Irish had never previously seen an armoured knight and Strongbow carried all before him. Henry, anxious to assert his dominion over de Clare in Ireland, assembled a fleet at Milford Haven where he arrived on a blustery September day. However, sailing was delayed by contrary winds and it was mid-October before he finally made the crossing and laid claim to his overlordship. One of his followers, Robert Fitz Bernard, rendered an account of his costs in this expedition: 45s. for carrying 20 knights and five attendants; £4 2s. 3d. to pay seven pilots at Pembroke for 47 days and £15 2s. 4d. for 53 seamen for the same period; wages for five attendants for 30 days amounted to 56s. 3d.

Fourteen years later it was Henry's younger son, John, (named Lord of Ireland by his father) who sailed from Milford seeking the homage of the Irish chieftains. It was not a successful visit. He was recalled in disgrace because of the outrageous and insulting behaviour of his entourage but returned, again sailing from Milford, to redeem his reputation in 1210, establishing a civil government independent of the feudal lords.

In the days of Edward I Pembrokeshire was clearly a place of some maritime importance for the bailiffs of 'Penbrok', 'Kameys' and 'Muleford' were ordered to have 'all ships of these ports of the burden of 40 tuns of wine and upwards before the king at Winchelsea' in readiness for a campaign against the king of France.

A similar order was issued by Edward II in May 1324 and nine years later by Edward III who ordered 'the bailiffs of Penbrok to make such search in ports and places in their bailiwick where ships touch that no silver in money, vessels or bullion be taken without the realm without the king's licence, and to arrest all so taken.'

It was nearly 200 years after the reign of Henry II before the next royal visitor to Ireland departed from Pembrokeshire's shores, when Richard II sought to exercise his authority over the rebellious Irish in 1394. He was entertained before embarking by the vicar of Llanstadwell, Thomas Balymore, and records show that the Exchequer rewarded the cleric with a payment of 40s. for his hospitality.

In 1399 great preparations were made for Richard's second expedition to Ireland, on this occasion to avenge the death of his heir presumptive, the Earl of March, who had been killed in an affray with the Irish. Orders were given that all ships over 25 tons were

English Troops embarking for France
(By permission of The British Library, Roy, 18 E1,f130V)

to rendezvous at either Bristol or Milford and press gangs scoured the country in search of 'volunteers'; the ordinary sailors were nearly all 'pressed'.

As the forces mustered a French chronicler recorded 'Trumpets and the sound of minstrels might be heard day and night. Men at arms arrived from all quarters. Vessels took in their lading of bread, wine, cows, calves, salt, meat and plenty of water. Excellent and beautiful horses were put on board. Everyone made ready his baggage and on the 11th day the King, having taken leave of the ladies, set out gallantly accompanied.'

The great company, which set out on 31 May, was a complicated and technical organisation including the good and the great (bishops and peers of the land) but also a vast army of specialists of all sorts — smiths, armourers, painters, tent-makers, fletchers, bowyers, turners, carpenters, masons, wheelwrights, saddlers, farriers, surgeons, chaplains, trumpeters and pipers as well as pages, grooms, carters and tradesmen, together with an immense number of horses.

The force landed at Waterford the following day and two months later, after little success, returned to Milford. News had reached the king that Henry of Lancaster had returned from exile and claimed the throne as Henry IV. The bedraggled army that Richard brought back deserted in their hundreds and Richard attempted to head towards his loyal palatinate of Cheshire, but was captured, imprisoned at Pontefract Castle and murdered.

During the new king's reign Milford was the scene of another expedition when, under the orders of Charles VI of France, around 3,000 men (including 800 men-at-arms, 600 crossbowmen and 1,200 foot soldiers) landed from a fleet of 120 ships of varying sizes to assist Owain Glyn Dwr in his revolt against the English crown.

Owain was Pembrokeshire born, probably at Trefgarn Owen, but did not have the support of the 'English' Pembrokeshire people. It was with the support of his estates in north-east Wales, the area that was his home, that he initially laid waste castles and the Anglicised towns. Gradually his strength increased due to Welsh discontent at their treatment by the English over the years, and in the face of initially limited English resistance — being a usurper Henry IV had other problems on his hands as well, and his treasury had few resources. In August 1405 a French squadron landed troops in the Haven in Owain's support. In conjunction with Owain the French marched on Haverfordwest, where they sacked the town, damaging the town gates at the bottom of Church Street near St. Martin's Church, and 'slaying all the inhabitants of the town but such as fled', but met with formidable resistance when they laid siege to the castle which, as was the English custom, was held by a strong garrison well able, from their superior height, to harry and destroy Welsh attacking forces. Although the invaders caused considerable damage to the fortress they were forced to abandon the attempt to take it and 'marched away destroying the country round with fire and sword' as they made for Carmarthen. Again they succeeded in destroying the town but before they could progress further an English fleet arrived under Lord Berkeley, Sir Thomas Swinburne and the freebooter, Henry Pay, and succeeded in burning 15 of the French ships. Meanwhile Glyn Dwr's force continued to progress rapidly through south Wales to reach Worcester. Here a stand-off ensued at Abberley when they confronted an English army. Neither side ventured to launch an assault, and after inconclusive skirmishing the Franco-Welsh force, fearing their position could only worsen against increasing English force of arms, retreated into Wales. The leaders of the French contingent then returned to France leaving the soldiers to their fate. The soldiers' first attempt to return resulted in the loss of 14 ships, whilst a second was more successful, even though a further eight ships were lost before the flotilla reached St. Pol de Leon.

Because of its importance as a stronghold Haverfordwest Castle was well defended. Less than 20 years before Owain Glyn Dwr's siege an 'Inventory of Armour' showed that the artillery consisted of two great guns, six iron hand guns, one iron ram for the guns and one iron spike for the guns, an axe, a barrel of gunpowder, 140 stone balls, six crossbows, 400 arrows with heads, 100 quarrell bolts (a quarrell was a small arrow fired by crossbow, a powerful weapon against knights in armour), four belts, two old crossbows, a further 140 old quarrell bolts, six bows and six sheaves of arrows. There were also 18 basinetts (helmets), 18 doublets, 12 pairs of gauntlets of plate, 17 umbiers (used to protect the face), 18 visors and 12 pairs of vambraces — the armour for the forearm.

Eighty years after Owain's French force had arrived, Henry Tudor landed in Pembrokeshire, returning to his homeland after a 14 year exile. He had been born in Pembroke Castle in 1457, the son of Edmund Tudor and Margaret Beaufort, Countess of Richmond, and Pembroke was his home for the first 14 years of his life.

It is said that from the time of his birth it had been his mother's driving ambition to see her son on the throne of England and so it was that in 1485, supported by a ragged army of a mere 2,000 French mercenaries, he landed at Mill Bay near Dale and marched to Haverfordwest. At what proved to be the beginning of this Tudor era the town was clearly a busy and thriving community with a wide range of tradespeople — those recorded at the time are armourer, fletcher, cobbler, tucker, shearman, glover, feltmaker, saddler, tiler, glazier, clergyman, haulier, shipwright, milward, collier, barber/ surgeon, baker, cutler, butcher, brewers, coopers, fishermen, corvisors (makers of baskets and creels), bagman, lime burners, joiner and brazier. When the news of the landing reached them enthusiastic crowds gathered to welcome the young man back to his native country and cheer him on his way as he marched to Bosworth where, just 15 days after his landing in Pembrokeshire, he defeated Richard III and was crowned King Henry VII. It was through his mother that he had laid claim to the throne, a claim he reinforced by marrying Elizabeth of York, daughter of King Edward IV.

Chapter 3

Pembroke

About a mile out of the present town in Cat's Hole Cave on the banks of the Pembroke river, signs of early occupation have been discovered including flints, a skull from the Neolithic period, and a bronze saw and chisels. There is also a suggestion of occupation during the Roman period, evidenced by the finding of a number of Roman coins, including nine discovered in Wogan's Cave below the castle by R.J. Cobb who undertook restoration work there in the 19th century.

Even in the days when the easiest means of travel was by sea, a major land highway existed running from Tenby across a ford near the mouth of the Ritec and along the Ridgeway to Pembroke (a point at which travellers could embark for Ireland — a crossing made often by St. David and St. Patrick on their missionary journeys) and later extending to Pembroke Ferry to form the beginning of the route from Pembroke to Haverfordwest. Ships sailed from the Pembroke quay for centuries; Holyland Road is said to have been named from the crusaders who camped at Kingsbridge Meadows on their way to set sail from here.

From the day Arnulph de Montgomery decided that the high rocky promontory at Pembroke should be the site of his castle, Pembroke was destined to become a place of great strategic importance with a vital military role, the factor which influenced the king, in 1138, to create the Earldom of Pembroke. In choosing Gilbert de Clare to be the first earl, Stephen chose a man who was loyal to the crown and a strong and powerful ruler who could secure control of this area of west Wales.

As he established his own little kingdom, the Palatine of Pembroke, the earl brought in Englishmen to whom he gave high office, appointing a steward, sheriff, coroner, escheator, chamberlain, chancellor and justices, and, up to the time in 1536 when Henry VIII abolished the Palatinate, the Earls of Pembroke were absolute princes, exercising royal jurisdiction and receiving all the rents and profits of the county.

It was this first earl who set up a court for the trial of murder, robbery and other felonies, holding a monthly County Court at which he had not only the power of sentencing but also the authority to grant pardons. His authority over his domain was as great as that of the English Lord Chancellor within England and he used his prerogative

Pembroke Castle, with the keep to the left and the main residential buildings on the right

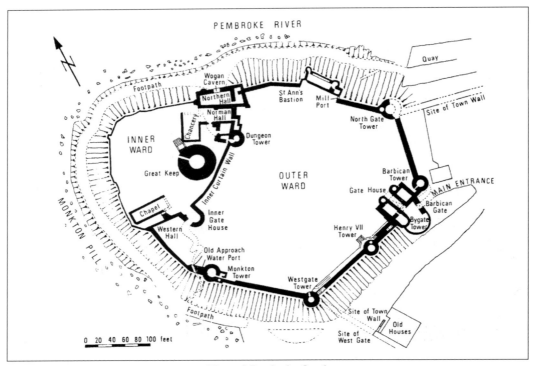

Plan of Pembroke Castle

22

— granted only to earls palatine — to create four baronies: Carew, Dungleddy, Walwyns Castle (which included all the land west of Steynton and Lambton and south of Nolton) and Laugharne. In addition to his own shire town of Pembroke, he incorporated the principal towns of Haverfordwest and Tenby into the Palatine and, as part of his powers, it was also in his command to call on his people to follow him to war.

Writing of the Palatine George Owen says 'Neither had the king of England, as king only, anything to deal or meddle with in the said county, but the Earls were free and absolute princes within themselves' and he described the earldom as 'in dignity and pre-eminence equal to the great and regal earldoms of France, Germany and Italy.'

On the death of Gilbert de Clare's son Richard, William Marshal — through his marriage to Richard's daughter Isabel — succeeded to the earldom and became acclaimed the greatest of the earls of Pembroke. With his wife's considerable inheritance and his own valuable fief of Leinster (which included Kildare, Queen's County, Carlow, Kilkenny, Wexford and part of King's County) William Marshal was an extremely wealthy man. Through his Irish connections the port of Pembroke and the crossing to Ireland — much used not only by Marshal himself but also by his officials — continued to grow in importance. As a result it appears that Marshal completely redesigned the castle and commenced building anew in stone. In an article on Pembroke Castle in *Archaeological Cambrensis* D.J. Cathcart King states that virtually the whole of the defences appear to have been completed by Marshal or his sons, the last of whom died in 1245.

Good use seems to have been made of the vast cave known as Wogan's Cave, a name probably derived from the Welsh *ogof* (cave), which opens onto the river and lies beneath the Great Hall. The floor of the cave is approached by a newel stair at the base of which is a number of openings, one

Pembroke Castle, looking along the curtain wall to the Barbican and Gate House

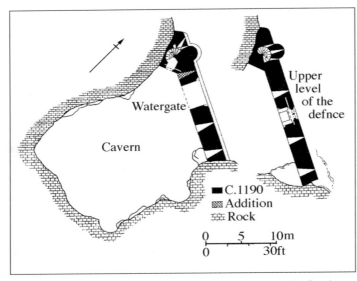

Watergate

Cavern

■ C.1190
▨ Addition
▥ Rock

Upper
level
of the
defnce

0   5   10m
0   30ft

Plan of the defences to Wogan's Cave below Pembroke Castle

of which appears to have been a lamp stand and it is thought that the openings would have been used for night signalling to craft on the river. Cathcart King suggests, too, that the great width of the gateway in the wall onto the waterway indicates that the cavern was used as a boat house with room at its entrance for access by boats up to 70 feet long and with a beam of 11 feet — such as the northern galleys of Viking type.

With the death of the last of the childless Marshal sons the Marshal inheritance passed, through William Marshal's daughter Janet, to William de Valence who made Pembroke his main seat of power and is remembered for founding Tenby Hospital. He was succeeded by his son Aymer who died childless in 1324, his estates being divided between the descendants of his two sisters, one of whom was married to John de Hastings, Lord of Abergavenny, thus taking the earldom into the Hastings family. The title became extinct with the death in 1389 of the last earl at which point the castle passed into the lordship of the Crown.

By this time the structure had deteriorated (the Hastings' time was much occupied with the French wars) although small repairs amounting to £1 15s. 2d. and £2 12s. 8d. (as recounted by Owen in the *Calendar of Public Records relating to Pembrokeshire*) had already been carried out to the roofs of the prison tower, the chapel and the County Court room. The situation, however, was considerably worse when a survey was carried out in 1386 — the castle had suffered extensive damage whilst under the custody of William Beauchamp who appears to have been stripping lead from the roof when it was committed to his care after the death of John de Hastings.

There were concerns as to its capability for defence at the time of the revolt under Owain Glyn Dwr, and when the French sent an expedition to Milford Haven in 1405 additional armaments — 16 crossbows, 3,000 quarrels (arrows), 50 pounds of gun powder, and 50 pounds of saltpetre — were despatched to the castle. It seems, too, that it was garrisoned during the reign of Richard III, evidenced by the victualling ordered in 1483 when the treasurer of Pembroke was ordered to pay £100 for the 'stuffe' of the castle and 20 marks (£13 6s. 8d) for other small items to be purveyed there. The Chamberlain of Carmarthen was ordered to pay one Richard Newton £113 14s. 6d. for his expenses (not detailed) incurred on the castle, and in 1484 firewood for the castle was ordered from the forest of Narberth.

It was not long however, before the military significance of Pembroke's castle diminished further as the use of artillery became more prevalent and even less attention was paid to its upkeep.

From the time of its first charter granted by Henry I in the 12th century, a number of privileges were granted to the townspeople of Pembroke which were designed to improve the economic viability of the town and port. The terms of that first charter were confirmed and extended by subsequent earls and it was during this period that it was decreed that all ships with merchandise on board must tie up at Pembroke bridge to buy and sell goods. Purveyors of cargoes bound for other ports were obliged to pay a toll or customs duty at the cross in the town and all goods bought within the environs of Pembroke had to be shipped out only from Pembroke bridge or from Tenby.

These charters did much to enhance the prosperity of the local merchants and by the time of the reign of Edward I the tradesmen began to assert their importance. In times of enemy attack they were forced to abandon their possessions as they fled to safety inside the castle walls, and as trade developed they began to demand greater security for their property. As a result, town walls were erected and, to provide additional security for their businesses, the burgesses were exempted from any feudal service outside their own immediate neighbourhood.

The attractive terms and privileges of the charters were designed to encourage incomers to the area and burgess-ship was acquired by unchallenged residence for a year and a day, the burgesses then being freed from paying mill tolls and fees for stalls in the markets and fairs. In addition a burgess 'taken' (arrested) by the bailiff was entitled to be released on payment of surety — provided his arrest was not for homicide — and, to provide speedy justice for merchants and other non-residents of the town, a Pied Poudre Court was established. These ancient courts (literally Courts of Dusty Feet) were held in fairs and markets to administer justice in a rough and ready way to all comers, dealing primarily with matters such as debt, trespass, covenants and contracts.

This was the beginning of some prosperous years for the town of Pembroke, but by the early 13th century Haverfordwest had been accorded many of the same privileges. Cargoes could now be discharged there, it was the only Welsh staple port (one nominated for dealing in certain goods) for wool and hides between 1326 and 1353 and in 1383 its merchants were exempted from port dues. Added to the rising importance of Haverfordwest came the scourge of the Black Death which rampaged through Pembroke in 1349, wiping out whole families, and the town suffered a slump from which it did not recover for many years. (In his *Tour Through Wales* between 1538 and 1544 John Leland describes the town as 'well build and the Est suburb hath bene almost as great as the Town, but now is totally in ruine.') At the same time the second Act of Union of 1543 restored Haverfordwest to being a county in its own right — a further blow to the status of Pembroke. Even as late as 1611 John Speede commented in *Theatre of the Empire of Great Britain* that Pembroke had more empty houses than any he had seen the length and breadth of the kingdom, 'more ancient in show than it is in years'.

During this period Tenby became the most important port in the county with a close relationship with Bristol. With 200 households it was twice the size of Pembroke and while he commented on the ruinous condition of part of Pembroke, Leland observed that Tenby was 'very wealthy by merchants'.

Barbara George in *Pembrokeshire Sea Trading before 1900* notes that shipping used Tenby as early as the mid-12th century and that from the early 14th to 16th centuries twice as many cargoes came to Tenby as to Haverfordwest or Pembroke, usually in foreign ships, though some of the local merchants, especially those from Tenby, had their own vessels. Around 70 Pembrokeshire boats were engaged in overseas trade (mostly with France and Ireland) the majority of them small craft of between 6 and 20 tons which would be crewed by three or four men, while just four of the vessels were over 50 tons and carried a crew of around 16.

The establishment of the system of Head Ports in Elizabeth I's reigns to assist in the administration of customs revenue gave Milford Haven jurisdiction over the area from Barmouth to Worm's Head, with customs points at Pembroke and Tenby. As the town of Milford did not then exist, references to cargoes shipped to or from Milford at this period normally refer to the Haven in general, probably meaning Pembroke in particular. One entry in the Port Books for 1565 records a consignment from Bristol of prunes, raisins, hops, honey, pewter, three gross of playing cards, silk buttons and 20 teasel staves (for teasing wool or raising the nap on woollen cloth), and in the following year comes the first reference to the import of fish from Newfoundland with an entry that 19,000 'Newlande fish' arrived on the 50-ton *Perrott of Milford* (owned by Sir John Perrott). It seems that at least part of this cargo was for re-export, for in the same year 5,000 'Newlande fish' were despatched to Bristol from Milford.

Trade with Spain had petered out after the defeat of the Spanish

Henry VII, from a bust in the British Museum. Henry landed at Dale on 7 August 1485 after which his forces took Dale Castle without difficulty, spending the night there before setting out for Haverfordwest and marching through Wales where he met no opposition. He reached Bosworth (probably on 22 August) where his forces defeated Richard III and he was symbolically crowned on the battlefield

Armada in 1588 and the restrictions caused by continuing uneasy relations with France and Spain are reflected in an entry for May 1592 of 147 quarters of wheat* leaving Milford on the 50-ton *Red Lyon* of Bristol to 'Venice or such lands as are in amity with her Majesty', and in November 1600 the *Peeter* of Milford delivered victuals to 'her Majesty's forces in Ireland' — recording a cargo of 12 kilns of butter and the improbable figure of 10,000cwt of cheese.

During the year 1601-2, 27 ships carried 5,548 bushels of malt and 6,860 bushels of corn to the garrison in Ireland, in contrast to the previous year's exports of 2,590 bushels of corn and 584 of malt.

Corn was the most important export from Pembrokeshire's ports during the latter part of the 16th century, but the years between 1594 and 1597 saw a series of particularly bad harvests throughout the kingdom. The crisis for the local people was exacerbated by the policy of the corn merchants who sent prices soaring by buying up the corn in bulk direct from the larger farms for export to Ireland and France.

The export of corn — either along the Severn Estuary's coastline or overseas — at times of local shortage was always a matter of dissent, and in May 1740 a group of colliers broke open the hatches of a vessel moored at Pembroke, removing some of the corn which was destined for Bristol. At the same time they threatened to burn the town and were successful in securing a commitment from the colliery owners to provide them with corn in future. Another failure of the crop in 1799 inspired Lord Cawdor to initiate a subscription at Pembroke by the local gentry to buy in imported corn for the poor, and the following year corn was made available to the poor in Haverfordwest at a reduced rate. In later years a large room above Pembroke town hall was used in times of bad harvest to store grain for the poor.

By the end of the 16th century the sea trade was once more increasing in importance with overseas exports almost double the imports. Exports of coal, largely to Ireland, in Elizabeth's reign, exceeded the coastal traffic along the Bristol Channel and to north Wales. By the 17th century Pembrokeshire anthracite had gained preference over Northumberland coal for salt drying in London and was also used in the Exeter woollen mills. (In 1700 over 6,000 tons, 53% of Exeter's requirement, came from Pembrokeshire.)

There were tanyards alongside the stream on the south side of Pembroke and hides, sheep and lamb skins were also an important export, mainly to Bristol and Barnstaple but with some going to St. Malo, Madeira and Barbados. George Owen in 1603 listed live cattle and sheep among Pembrokeshire's exports but it seems these were driven overland to the English markets for (apart from three mares and four kine sent to Ireland in 1586-7) the Port Books do not record animals exported by sea until 1662 when six shipments were made. By 1680 the number of shipments had increased to 26, mostly going to Somerset and north Devon.

---

* A quarter of wheat would be a quarter of a bushel which, today, is reckoned to be the equivalent capacity of eight gallons. However, early measurements varied from place to l with a Dewisland bushel worth more than double a Winchester bushel.

At the same time, however, there was a growing number of imports of Irish oxen and sheep — 700 sheep, 420 oxen, 50 pigs and some 'cattle' arrived in 1662 and in 1680, 23 cargoes contained about 1,589 sheep, 179 oxen, 110 bullocks, 34 pigs and 7 horses. The trade was still active in the mid-19th century when, in 1857, the *Pembrokeshire Herald* recorded that six cargoes containing 876 cattle, over 750 pigs, sheep, poultry and 1,300 'other animals' were imported from Waterford.

With the increasing acreage under corn at the end of the 17th century there was a corresponding increase in the import of plough horses from Ireland, whilst the coastal trade in lime prospered with the need for more lime to feed the soil.

Oysters abounded in Milford Haven and the cargo of 20,000 which was shipped to Barnstaple in 1592-3 was a typical consignment in a trade which flourished throughout the 17th and 18th centuries, not only around the Severn Estuary, but also with Holland and other places.

The import of salt features in the earliest records (from 1387) and continued through the 18th and 19th centuries, originating on the Continent and transhipped from English ports. Wine also appears in the mediaeval records and by 1600 timber was a major import, growing steadily over the years as shipbuilding and the need for pit props for coalmining increased.

Prior to the Civil War one of the town's large employers of labour and a prosperous merchant trading with Ireland was John Poyer, town mayor in 1641. Poyer, who figured prominently in the defence of Pembroke Castle of which he was governor during the Civil Wars (see Chapter 9), had, for 16 years, commanded one of the local bands of militia and prior to the Civil War was a prime mover in urging the Government to improve the defence of Pembroke. With his knowledge of Ireland, his particular concern was the vulnerability of Pembrokeshire to invasion from that country. Irish immigrants had already settled around Pembrokeshire's main ports, many arriving in small boats at a charge of 3s. each, landing secretly in the small creeks and bays well away from the eyes of officialdom. Poyer viewed with suspicion all ships coming from Ireland. In 1642, acting with the mayor of Haverfordwest, John David, and at the request of M.P. Sir Hugh Owen, he detained vessels, merchants and goods from Ross, Wexford, Kilkenny and elsewhere, along with vessels bound for Ireland. This had been a part of Parliament's plans to foil what they conceived to be a 'Popish plot' but his move landed him in prison following action by an aggrieved party, Zidracke Pope, and he was forced to appeal to the House for his release.

Undeterred and still determined to improve the defences as best he could he later seized some merchant ships in Milford Haven and sold them and their cargoes to pay for a troop of horse soldiers, two troops of dragoons and three companies of foot soldiers.

Little is known of Poyer's early days, but Clarendon in his *History of Rebellion* states that it was through the war that he raised himself from 'low trade'. (In 1617 he was classified as 'gentleman', his son John was a glover in 1633 and in 1643 John Jnr followed in his father's footsteps as mayor of Pembroke). Edward Laws, author of *The History of Little England Beyond Wales* in 1808, records that John Snr was bailiff of Tenby in 1639 and later owned a vessel. A Presbyterian, he presented chalices to the churches of St. Mary and St. Michael in Pembroke but, writes Laws, 'according to Carlyle he was given to brandy and there is reason to suppose he was not particularly straightforward in money matters, he did not hesitate to plunge his native county into all the horrors of a second civil war for the sake of a disputed account; yet for all that Poyer was a great man. He must have expended a considerable sum of money on the fortification of Pembroke which he rendered impregnable to aught but famine. Very probably a considerable amount of this money came actually out of Poyer's own purse. This liberality would give him the leading position he coveted.'

In Pembroke today Poyer is regarded as a local hero, celebrated with a memorial bench in St. Michael's Square with plans, eventually, for a statue to be erected as a part of a Poyer Heritage corner.

Poyer himself was executed after the Civil War and the male line of the Poyer family has died out, but a female descendant married a Nash of Swansea and became the mother of Richard Beau Nash — 'King' of Bath.

Some years before Poyer voiced his concerns for the defence of the Haven several local landowners, including Anthony Rudd, Bishop of St. David's; Sir John Wogan of Wiston; George Owen of Henllys; Francis Meyrick of Fleet and Alban Stepney of Prendergast had expressed their own fears. In a petition in November 1595, addressed to the Lord Treasurer, they pointed out that while the harbour could accommodate 'an infinite number of ships' it was totally unprotected from attack, adding that the castles of Pembroke and Tenby would prove invaluable bases for the enemy while the abundance of corn in the nearby countryside and the wealth of fish along the coast would 'maintain a great army'. The petition continued:

The memorial bench to Pembroke hero John Poyer in St Michael's Square, Pembroke.
The inscription reads: 'A prosperous merchant, Town Mayor and Governor of Pembroke Castle who held off Oliver Cromwell's seven-week siege of the castle and was executed in Covent Garden on 25th April 1649'

the haven also standeth very commodiously to receive victuals from France, Brittany or Spain; all which things may be occasion to move the enemy to affect that place before others; yet also there are in Pembrokeshire eighteen castles; of which though there be but two or three in reparation, yet are the rest places of great strength and easily to be fortified by the enemy, some of which are so seated naturally for strength as they seem impregnable; alsoe there are in that shire to be seen in sundry parts thereoff, divers sconces or forts of earth raised in great height with great rampires and ditches to the number of 26 or 27, which in times past have been places of strength in time of wars: all which castles and forts would yield great advantage to the enemies to strengthen themselves in such sort that it would be an infinite charge to remove them from thence. Again the same is situated within seven hours sailing of Waterford and Wexford in Ireland, so that the enemy having intention to invade Ireland (and by report we have heard he hath) this harborowe in this haven may serve him to great purpose. Further more being lord (as it were) of these seas by possessing the haven what spoil he may make along the Severn, on both sides even to Bristol may be easily conjectured, and if he (which God forbid) should enjoy Brittany withall, our English merchants can have noe trade, which will decrease her highnesses customs and decay the navy — We humbly pray your lordships to consider whether it be not expedient for the withstanding of the enemy that he obtain not this harborowe, to have a sufficient number of ships of warre and fortifications to defend the same, which preparation, if the enemy might perceive, we believe verily it would alter his mind from adventuring his navy upon this coast.
Signed – Anthony Rudd, Lord Bishop of St. Davids; Sir John Wogan
of Wiston Knight; George Owen of Henllys Esq; Francis Meyrick of Fleet Esq;
and Alban Stepneth of Prendergast Esq.

In the same year a report, *Reasons to Prove the Necessitie of Fortyfying Milford Haven,* was compiled and this report was incorporated in a pamphlet issued more than 150 years later (in 1750 as war was once again on the horizon) which read:

The towne having three gates only and the towne walls being strongly defended with six flanking towers in such sort as out of them the whole walles may be [word lost] and defended from approach of enemies. And in some of the same towers are faire springs of cleer sweet runnyng water for the necessary relief of the people. This castle is thought almost impregnable, the weakest part thereof is a small part that adjoineth to the towne, which is only defended with a dry ditch, and which may be made very strong and deepened, the towne walls springeth from the sayde castle and stretching forth and every side of the saide towne. All the castle walls are standing verye strong without any decaye, only the rooffes and leades have been taken down. Within the saide castle is the great cave under ground called the Wogan, able if occasion to receive a great multitude of people, being a place free of all assaults or battery, and in the same is a well of fresh water of great depthe which cannot be taken away, serving for the use of the people within the said castle. [At the time of the second Civil War Cromwell's force did succeed in cutting off the supply from the well.] The gate or entrance of the said castle is made stronge divers waye, as with drawe bridge and portcullis, and other means very defensible. This town and castle thus lying upon the said branch of Milford be unfortified as it now remayneth is thought very perillous if the enemy should fresh possess the same, and would be by them be so fortified and defended as it would be the loss of many lives to them therefrom. Wherefore I have thought fitt to note it here.

The Civil Wars took their toll of trade but with the Restoration of the monarchy sea trade increased. English merchants who had established themselves in Pembroke made use of their links with Bristol and other west country ports and corn mills, warehouses and stores proliferated along the quay. A long established corn grist mill operated by tidal power flourished on the bridge outside the town's north gate and the last of the corn mills — a five-storey building — burned down in a spectacular fire in 1955.

In 1688 the tradesmen of the town included 12 corvisers, seven glovers, two curriers, two saddlers, four butchers (and seven country butchers who rented stalls in the shambles), four weavers, two dyers, three felt makers, nine tailors as well as musicians, pipe makers, a barber, glazier, two blacksmiths and a number of merchants. Pembroke was well on its way to becoming 'the largest richest and, at this time, the most flourishing town of all south Wales' as it was described by Daniel Defoe who also said that between 1724-26 the port owned nearly 200 ships.

With Tenby, the Pembroke markets supplied the needs of the south and south-east of the county but Haverfordwest was the only market town and business centre of the remaining two-thirds. Pembroke's broad streets provided adequate room for market stalls and fairs, the latter in the 1830s being held in April, July, October and November with additional fairs at Westgate in Monkton taking place in May and September. In its earliest days the Michaelmas Fair (now the sole survivor of the town's ancient fairs) was an occasion where local people were able to buy exotic goods such as laces, silks, spices and leather, benefiting too from the cheaper prices of items that could be offered for sale exempt from taxes on buyers and sellers. Soon this became the district's hiring fair drawing in the people of the countryside in search of work. These fairs, where bargains were struck with local farmers for a year's work (but which also became the occasions of 'all the fun of the fair') proliferated around the county and attracted farmers from the Welsh valleys where all the able men worked in the mines, and where farm labourers, shepherds and cowmen were hard to find.

In 1907 the wages offered at Pembroke fair were £26 a year for men, £16-17 for 'team lads' and £12 for girls.

The county also had its 'runaway fairs'. These, such as the one at Little Haven which was a part of the annual pig fair, took place a few weeks after the main hiring fair and provided a second chance for workers who found they had made a terrible mistake in their choice of employer. Farm work normally included living in on the farm and a worker who broke his contract after discovering the conditions of his employment were unendurable would find himself homeless if he was unable to secure other employment.

On the Pembrokeshire farms lime was important in increasing the fertility of the acid soil, and it was also much in demand for limewashing the county's cottage walls. The principal source of limestone was the quarry near Carew, at West Williamston, but there were also quarries just downstream of Pembroke Castle and south of Haverfordwest. These generated a considerable traffic as coastal barges and sloops loaded the stone at the quarries and transported it to the kilns which proliferated all round the creeks and small bays of the waterway, many of them with the lime burner's hut standing alongside the odiferous kiln.

The 40-ton sloop *Ranger* was carrying both limestone and culm in the late 18th and early 19th century. Culm is a mix of anthracite dust, powdered clay and water which was made into wet balls that burnt slowly and were used as fuel on fires to help ensure they stayed 'in' — it was considered unlucky if a fire had to be relit, and if necessary fire would be 'borrowed' from a neighbour and carried back to the hearth. (There are instances of fires which have burned in homes in the county for over 100 years.) The *Ranger*'s logbook records cargoes of limestone from the Pembroke area destined for Dinas Island, Abercastle, Porthgain, Dinas, Fishguard (to be used in 'mortar for the pier') and to 'farmers on the north coast of Pembrokeshire'. In 1839 ten cargoes went to Abercastle from Lawrenny. (This was probably produced by the West Williamston quarry where channels were cut from the river to give barges of 15-20 tons access to the quarries. The barges sometimes carried the limestone up river to Haverfordwest to be burned in the town's many limekilns but generally it was transferred into sea-going boats such as the *Ranger* at Lawrenny.) In the 19th century limestone from West Williamston was also exported to north Devon and Cornwall.

As crushers became available which ground the limestone on site and with alternative fertilizers being produced, the use of the limekilns died out, although according to Peter B.S. Davies' *Pembrokeshire Limekilns* there were still well over 50 limekilns around the shores of Milford Haven at the beginning of the 20th century. Many remain — mostly derelict — but some that are in good condition are still to be seen. One is below the town wall in Pembroke near the old tidal limit at the east end of the common, another is at Landshipping Quay and a restored, well preserved example is to be found at Church Lake, Neyland.

By the end of the 18th century Pembroke had lost most of its maritime trade to Haverfordwest and, increasingly, to the new town of Milford. The larger vessels that were now plying their trade on the waterway could not navigate the shallow Pembroke river, particularly at low tide. Nevertheless in 1818, 28,970 tons of coal were shipped from Pembroke to other ports on the mainland and a further 3,462 tons went to Ireland.

Smuggling, of course, had its place in the area's economy and was said to have continued right into the 20th century, the smugglers often several steps ahead of authority. Barrels dropped overboard under cover of darkness at the right state of the tide would be washed up at Bentlass where the smuggler's confederates waited to collect the booty.

The closure of the Royal Naval Dockyard at Milford and the establishment of the dockyard at Pater — soon to be known as Pembroke Dock — meant that a new town, too, was in the making. As the town developed it began to draw trade from nearby Pembroke and in 1819 a proposal to build a market in the dockyard town drew vigorous protests from the Pembroke Corporation who petitioned Parliament — unsuccessfully — to have the plan withdrawn.

The unease of the inhabitants of Pembroke at the growth of their neighbouring township is reflected in a diary kept in 1812 by John Narberth, a Pembroke carpenter, who wrote: 'On this day the first boatload of men arrived from Milford to mark out the site of the new yard. There will be changes, but whether for the better I know not.'

On New Year's Day 1814 he recorded: 'The whole of the workmen have now been able to come here to commence their shipbuilding with Mr. Roberts as the builder and not so much as one house on the spot, only Paterchurch farm, so poor old Pembroke will be filled with officers and men for a few years.' (Yet, surely this would have been of benefit to Pembroke's early guest house trade?) The carpenter's concern for 'poor old Pembroke' did not, however, prevent him seeking work in the new town and three months later he was writing: 'Mr. Lowless and myself left poor old Pembroke at an early hour to commence the building of its rival. So the first shaving was cut and the first window frames made.'

Yet, say the researchers of *The Pembroke Story*, by the late 18th century a large number of the present houses in Main Street would have been built. Orielton Terrace is composed of Georgian houses displaying an elegance which must have meant prosperity. Pembroke also boasted an Assembly Room. The port was still flourishing, trade was good and Pembroke flourished.

Although the coming of the railway was another nail in the coffin of the Pembroke-shire sea trade, it was a schooner, beached at Tenby's South Beach in September 1862 which provided the transport for the construction materials needed to build more than 11 miles of track between Tenby and Pembroke Dock — the route eventually agreed with the Pembroke and Tenby Railway Company after earlier proposals by Isambard Kingdom Brunel had foundered in arguments with authority and disagreements with farmers who refused access to their land.

The Pembroke and Tenby Railway Act had been passed in 1858 after the company secured the support of one of Wales' best known and most respected railway builders, David Davies of Llandinam, who not only agreed to work on the scheme but also to accept shares as his payment — and so the arrival in Pembroke on 30 July 1863 of David Davies's own locomotive, the *Llandinam*, heralded the opening of the Pembroke and Tenby Railway. On the first day 12 trains made the journey between Tenby and Pembroke taking 30 minutes for each trip but eventually this was reduced to three or four trips daily each way. The line from Tenby also served Black Rock quarry together with other local quarries and lime kilns. By 1900 the line had been taken over by the GWR and today is one of the routes that has survived Beeching's axe.

Travellers to Pembroke, however, still crossed by ferry from Neyland (fare 2d. single and 3d. return) landing at Hobbs Point, named after Nicholas Hobbs who owned land in the Llanion area until it was bought by the Government Ordnance Department in 1758. The jetty had been built for the packet service to southern Ireland but as the number of passengers declined this service was abandoned in 1848 in favour of the route from Holyhead. The jetty was then converted for dockyard use as a fitting out yard, and the giant sheerlegs which dominated the skyline for many years were erected to lift the engines and guns into the warships ready for launch from the dockyard.

Poverty was rife after the end of the Napoleonic War in 1815 and the parishes which, under the 200-year-old Poor Law had the responsibility of looking after their local poor were finding it an impossible burden. By 1834 the Poor Law Amendment Act had been passed which grouped the parishes into unions and Boards of Guardians were elected with responsibility to the Poor Law Commissioners.

The early Pembroke Board included Earl Cawdor of Stackpole, Sir John Owen of Orielton, John Adams of Holyland, Abraham Leach of Corston as well as prosperous farmers, tradesmen and magistrates. Their union served an area from Angle to Tenby, including Caldey Island, Neyland, Llawhaden, Burton and Rosemarket in addition to their own district of Pembroke and Pembroke Dock — parishes which all contributed to the £4,898 cost of building the Workhouse. The 3-acre site was bought for £450.

With accommodation for 180 paupers the building included a bell turret, school-room, chapel, boardroom, hospital, workrooms, dormitories, a 'lunatic yard', kitchens and staff accommodation. The first Master and Matron, a married couple, were paid a joint salary of £70 a year and initially the pauper women were expected to cook, clean and nurse the sick until staff were appointed. Staffing, however, presented its own problems. The first nurse, Mary Lewis, received 2s. (10p) a week plus food, but had to be reprimanded for being drunk, whilst a cook and a porter were reported for alleging that the bread was bad, for insulting the Master and Matron, for threatening to knock down the Matron and calling them 'thieves, rotters and smugglers'.

The inmates were a motley collection of elderly, sick, infirm, unmarried mothers, orphans, tramps and other vagrants, lunatics and the able-bodied unemployed and their families — but while there was accommodation for the families, they were not allowed to live together but were segregated in their own dormitories, yards and workrooms. All who could were put to work. If the women were not engaged on domestic chores they had to spin and knit stockings. The men had the indignity of spending their days picking oakum — a job which was associated with punishment as it was usually carried out by prisoners. Rope, called junk (made of coconut fibres and covered with oakum, a loose film of tar) was bought from the dockyard and it was their task to scrape off the tar so that the rope could be recycled and sold, mostly for use in caulking boats. Whether or not a man had his next meal depended on him picking his quota.

That next meal may not have been particularly appetizing, for it was said that the food was worse than that in the county prison. Breakfast consisted of watery porridge made using skimmed milk, of which one and a half pints was served with seven ounces of gritty black bread per person. Meat was served only on Sunday and tea and sugar were restricted to the over-60s. Differentiating between genuine itinerants and 'idle vagrants', the Guardians fed those they considered idle on mere bread and gruel and left them to sleep on bare boards.

The influx of Irish potato farmers following the famine of 1848 brought problems for the Board who added a separate vagrants' block to accommodate these men who carried typhus (then known as 'jail fever') and, in 1872, when the charge on the parish rates of supporting paupers was becoming too great a burden the Guardians sought to discourage claims by publishing a list of paupers in the local press.

A brave attempt was made to take the children out of absolute poverty by providing the daily schooling that was considered most appropriate in helping them to secure employment — for the boys it was the 'three Rs' (reading, writing and arithmetic) plus religion, while the girls were taught sewing. The youngsters were then offered as domestic servants or apprentices, often accompanied by a cash inducement to the prospective employer.

The 1851 census records the inmates as mostly local people although there were two children from Bristol and one from Ireland, and two women from Cornwall and Kent, whilst 24 people had no known birthplace and five others had been born in the workhouse itself. Ages ranged from three months to 83 years, with 18 adult males and 26 adult females, 26 boys and 23 girls under 15 years of whom 18 boys and 16 girls were described as scholars, while a 65-year-old man, who must have been learning with them, was also described as a scholar.

Between 1837 and 1894 there were 774 deaths in the workhouse, often of babies and small children, but gradually conditions began to improve. A Joint Counties Asylum had been built in Carmarthen in 1865 and the lunatics moved there, then rebuilding of several parts of the old building took place in the early 20th century and the children were moved to their own accommodation at Croft House. The food improved too and at this time the workhouse was using 36,000 gallons of milk and 143 tons of coal annually — whilst the Master and Matron's pay was £60 a year.

When Unions and Workhouses were abolished the premises were handed over to the County Council (in March 1930) but the elderly and passing vagrants were still admitted for a few days. The infirmary, taking the name of Woodbine House Hospital,

The old Workhouse, now 'Riverside', providing accommodation and care for the elderly

The Main Street in Pembroke c. *1910*

remained operational and, at the outbreak of the Second World War, was designated an Emergency Medical Services Hospital and was used for the treatment of hundreds of service personnel. Patients from the Meyrick and Military hospitals in Pembroke Dock were evacuated to Woodbine House and at the time of the oil tank blaze in 1940 many of the injured firemen received treatment under its roof while it also took in many of the civilian casualties of the great air raids of May and June 1941.

In this year, too, a maternity unit and nursery was opened at the hospital, both of which remained for some time after 1949 when the name was changed to 'Riverside', an institution that cared for the elderly. Many radical changes were then made, the entire main structure being demolished with the exception of the entrance to the old south wing, and rebuilding began in 1962 to provide a home for 60 elderly residents in a peaceful atmosphere and setting, far removed from its old workhouse days.

Pembroke power station, built at Pennar Gut in 1968, stopped generating electricity less than 30 years later. It had been one of the largest oil-fired power stations in Europe but in later years the shift away from coal and oil to gas as a means of reducing carbon emissions has seen the closure of many UK power stations.

The power station was totally demolished by 2003 and plans are now underway for the construction, on the site, of a state-of-the-art £800m combined cycle gas turbine power station. There are promises of up to 1,500 construction jobs, up to 100 long-term high quality jobs at the plant, with a long-term benefit to the economy of £10m *per annum*.

Pembroke, which celebrated the 900th anniversary of the first Norman settlers in 1993, is now very dependent on other newcomers to the area — the tourists — and continues to rely on the attractions of the sea. The streets still follow their mediaeval line and although the town's prosperous periods of the 18th and 19th centuries saw many of the houses rebuilt in stone, some of the early houses remain in Westgate Hill. Fortunately in 1977 the town was designated an Outstanding Conservation Area and remains largely unspoiled for the delight of today's visitors.

Sailing ships such as the *Marie Louise, Acacia*, and *Mary Jane* continued to use the quay wall well into the 20th century while the *Kathleen and May* (originally called the *Lizzie May*) which, until 1952, regularly sailed the Irish sea without an auxiliary engine using just wind and sail, was the last vessel to use the old port in 1960. This trading schooner (136 tons gross and nearly 100 feet overall) was launched at Connah's Quay in 1900 and while she traded out of Pembroke called at harbours from London to Oban. She carried on trading, equipped with a Lewis gun and a rifle, during the Second World War and by 1960 was one of only two three-masters still working the ports.

Her working days came to an end in 1967 when she was left to rot at Appledore and it was there that she was discovered by members of the Maritime Trust (now the Cutty Sark Trust) who raised the cash to restore the schooner. After some years on display in Plymouth and later in St. Katherine's Dock in London, funds ran out and in 1996, once more in decay, the *Kathleen and May* was closed to the public.

The Kathleen and May *when at Pembroke, viewed from the walls of the castle*

At that time there were hopes that this historic vessel could be returned to Pembroke to take centre stage in a £3m plan to redevelop the derelict north quay as part of a Maritime Heritage Centre. Although development went ahead amid considerable controversy over what has been described as 'a high density and insensitive modern building complex of luxury flats with heritage not a priority', the *Kathleen and May* has not returned to Pembroke. She had been bought privately in 1998 by Steve Clarke whose dream was that she would become a catalyst for the regeneration of her home port. With the support of a group of dedicated volunteers and after 50,000 hours of work the vessel was once again restored and featured in maritime festivals across Europe. Early in 2008, at the great age of 108, the *Kathleen and May* temporarily became a working vessel once more, carrying her first commercial cargo in 50 years. Under contract to a French shipping company she transported 30,000 bottles of wine from 80 vintage owners in southern France to Dublin — a 'green' alternative for the transport of goods.

At the same time the *Kathleen and May* was up for sale. Its owner could no longer sustain the financial burden of its upkeep — regular maintenance and annual insurance costs of £20,000. Appeals to the Lottery Fund and to the Government to save her for the nation were unsuccessful. The major interest in purchasing the much loved vessel has come mainly from overseas investors and there are fears that the *Kathleen and May*, one of only 60 vessels on the UK's National Register of Historic Vessels, alongside the *Mary Rose* and the *Cutty Sark*, and now the only remaining schooner of her type, may be lost to the nation's heritage for ever.

A new chapter in Pembroke has, however, opened with plans for the redevelopment of the South Quay where only the Royal George Inn and the building housing the Watersports Centre remain to tell the story of the quay as a busy port. With the lesson of the North Quay development much in mind, consultations are underway with active representatives of the community who seek to see the re-creation of what used to be a quayside and public space with attractive and appropriate buildings.

Chapter 4

Haverfordwest

There is no recorded history of Haverford ('west' was not added until 1409 when it became necessary to distinguish the town from Hereford) until Norman times, but from its position on the river the Iron Age Celts would almost certainly have had a settlement at Haefer's Ford (from the Anglo-Saxon *haefer*, a goat).

Anyone wishing to travel across this part of Pembrokeshire would have to cross the river Cleddau and Haefer's Ford, just above where the river met the Cartlett brook, where the steep sided valley opened out into flatter marshland was the ford furthest down the river. A shelf of hard rock gave solid footing, a natural road bed which later became a causeway used by wagons as recently as the 19th century. Such a location would have been ideal for a settlement which could benefit from passing trade. Microliths and traces of fires have been found along the ridge between the racecourse and Priory Mount indicating that bands of Mesolithic hunter-gatherers once camped on the high ground overlooking Merlin's brook, but there is no archaeological evidence of Stone or Bronze Age men by the river itself as such evidence would have been washed away in the tidal waters. However, from the town's location coupled with what is known of other places it can be surmised that the early settlement would have been a fortified encampment on the rocky mound where the castle stands today, overlooking the ford and, by the time of the Iron Age, with a growing cluster of huts, workshops and also stables, for the Celts were famous horsemen. One can imagine smithies for iron and bronze working, carpenters' shops, weavers and potters, leather workers, probably makers of ropes and cords — the whole range of crafts and trades needed to serve a village or small town. It would have been a sea port too, lying as it does at the tidal limit of Milford Haven, and a centre for the passage of goods and people trading along the western coasts of Europe.

The chieftain of the local clan probably lived on the crest of the hill in his hall, where defensive rings of stakes and ditches surrounded the huts and living quarters of him and his close followers. Space would be provided for the common folk to take refuge with their cattle in case of emergency, the entrance contrived so that horsemen could pass through only in single file.

Part of the Bucks' drawing of Haverfordwest in 1748 showing the castle

Domestic arrangements for the vast majority would have been fairly basic — a hut with a central fireplace for heat and cooking, smoke seeping out through the roof, skins and furs scattered about for sitting or sleeping, rushes or bracken on the floor — maybe the furniture just a wooden chest and rough table. The remains of such huts have been found across Wales and one was excavated at Brownslade, near Castlemartin, in 1880.

The town of Haverford would have developed significantly when its first recorded castle was founded about 1110 by Tancred, a Fleming, and great celebrations are planned for the 900th anniversary in 2010. Tancred's son, Richard, was 'lord and governor' of the place when it was visited in 1188 by Giraldus Cambrensis (Gerald the Welshman) who was born, probably in 1147, at Manorbier Castle. After severe flooding in Flanders in 1108 the inhabitants fled their homes to seek refuge in Britain at the invitation of King Henry I who saw in these industrious warriors a means of subduing the unruly Welsh, encouraging them with immunity from some tithes. *The Chronicles of Caradoc of Llancarvan*, a contemporaneous writer, record that 'King Henrie was verie liberel of that which ws not his own' when he gave them land in 'Dyfet or West Wales where Pembroke, Tenby and Haverford are now built.'

The influx of these Flemings had a profound effect on this part of the county and was hated by some, welcomed by others. They are variously described as 'Flemish wolves, the Kingdom sore pestered with them', according to T.R. Dawes in his *Flemings in Pembrokeshire,* and by Giraldus as 'a people brave and robust, ever most hostile to the Welsh; a people, I say, well versed in commerce and woollen manufactures; a people anxious to seek gain by sea and land in defiance of fatigue and hunger; a hardy race equally fitted for the plough or the sword; a people brave and happy if Wales had been dear to its sovereign.' From the *Brut y Tywysogion* comes the comment 'The Flemings occupied the whole of the cantref of Rhos near the estuary of the river called Cleddyf and drove away all the inhabitants of the land.' Edward Laws commented cynically in his *History of Little England Beyond Wales* that the king did not love the race he had invited to his realm as 'he really hoped that the Flemings would first kill a Welshman then get killed in return.'

What is clear is that it was at this period in its history that the area around Haverford and Wiston (the capitals of the Flemish settlements) lost its Welshness and its language with English becoming the dominant language. It is clear too, that with their arrival, the Flemings brought a new prosperity as they established hitherto unknown opportunities for trade and commerce in a place where, until the coming of the railway, the river was a vital link with the outside world.

Haverford became one of the foremost towns in south Wales with flourishing wool, grain and malt centres and a lively sea-going trade. The right, given during the reign of King John, to hold a Sunday market and an annual fair is evidence of the importance of the town and by this time an Augustinian priory had also been established with an endowment of three churches: St. Martin's (within the town walls) and St. Thomas and St. Mary's which are further afield. The priory also received tithes of wool and cheese, rents from the churches and properties around the priory and along the river. The priory had been founded towards the end of the 12th century by Robert de Hwlfordd [Haverford] and was the most valuable religious foundation in the county. Unlike the Cistercians who favoured rural retreats, the Augustinians involved themselves with the community providing succour to the poor and needy.

By the time of Henry VIII's Dissolution of the Monasteries the priory had become very rich. The site was acquired by the Barlow family who exchanged it with Sir John Perrot for land at Slebech. Perrot used much of the stonework to build and repair his home at Haroldston. The buildings also provided room for a blacksmith producing ironwork for the adjacent shipworks and shelter for animals prior to slaughter whose skins were used by the nearby tannery.

In 1982 the site was given, for preservation, into state care by the Haverfordwest Gild of Freemen (see overleaf) and extensive excavation and conservation has since taken place under Cadw (Welsh Historic Monuments) revealing a wealth of the history of this priory. It is now known that because of its position on the floodplain, the ground level was raised — an enormous task involving the cutting of tons of rock and gravel from the slope to the west of the site and depositing it, cart load by cart load, alongside the river. The massive foundations of the church were built as the ground level was raised around them, in which drains were laid. Eventually over 8 feet (2.5m) of dumped material lay between the original marshy surface and the floor level at the east end of the church. Much redevelopment work was carried out in the mid-15th century, a time of prosperity for the priory and fine gardens were formed on the riverside. During the excavation work a mould for lead melted down from the windows during the early dismantling of the priory buildings was discovered as was also a lead ingot, stamped with the rose and crown, which had been buried under the fallen masonry.

The Gild of Freemen

In *Freemen of England*, R. Walker outlines the law surrounding this custom: 'The origin of the system of freemen is not known with any certainty. It is known to have existed in Anglo-Saxon times, but its roots seem to go back into the Ancient British and Roman systems as well. The burgesses (later called freemen) of boroughs were those inhabitants of the towns who were of free status and were permitted and obliged to bear arms for the defence of their towns, being also, in most cases, owners or tenants of dwellings in the town,'

The several charters relating to Haverfordwest granted a number of privileges to the burgesses, one of which granted 'to our beloved and faithful burgesses of Haverford — a merchant guild for the convenience of them and their town'. However the Local Government Bill published in 1971 made no reference to the rights of freemen and it was only after representations had been made by the Freemen of England (later the Freemen of England and Wales) that the Minister to the Department of the Environment agreed to insert clause 248 stating that 'nothing in the Act shall affect any person's status, or the rights of any person to be admitted as a freeman ... [and that] the role of freemen would henceforth be kept by the proper officer of the relevant district council.'

At a special freemen's dinner in November 1971 attended by around 100 freemen together with visiting freemen from London, York, Birmingham and Slough the idea of establishing a Gild of Freemen of Haverfordwest was formulated. The gild was established in November 1973 and it has a badge depicting the lymphad that appears on the town's common seal, the sail bearing the Prince of Wales's plumes with reference to the charter granted in 1479.

In 1974 the Gild decided to appoint burgesses for life from 'persons of repute who have rendered outstanding service to the town'. In 2009 there were 307 Freemen of whom 64 were resident and 243 non-resident (many living abroad), and 36 Burgesses. The affairs of the Gild are managed by a Court of Wardens comprising freemen and burgesses, the members of which wear scarlet gowns bearing the Gild badge.

Through the strength of the Flemings Haverford largely escaped the warfare resulting from a Welsh resurgence in the 1100s, but in 1220 Llywelyn ap Iorwerth, Prince of Wales, unsuccessfully besieged the castle but burned the town to the castle gates.

Prosperity soon returned. Robert, son of Richard Fitz Tancred the castellan of Haverford Castle under the Earl of Clare, had fallen from favour and been expelled from the castle by King John who granted it in 1213 (for the sum of 100 marks) to the Earl of Pembroke, the great William Marshal. The reign of the Marshals dramatically changed the fate of Haverford for they had immense Irish holdings and had already fostered extensive trade links between Pembroke and Ireland. Haverford now joined Pembroke in this traffic and to encourage the growth of the town Marshal gave a charter which created property-owning burgess families by giving them the freedom to sell their property without permission from the Lord, and allowed their heirs to inherit them on payment

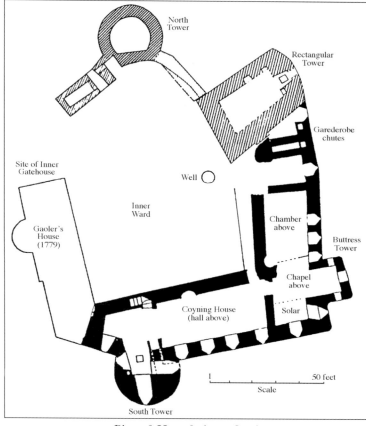

Labels on plan:
North Tower
Rectangular Tower
Garederobe chutes
Site of Inner Gatehouse
Well
Inner Ward
Gaoler's House (1779)
Chamber above
Buttress Tower
Chapel above
Coyning House (hall above)
Solar
50 feet
Scale
South Tower

Plan of Haverfordwest Castle

of a fee of 12d. A second charter gave burgesses a monopoly on trade by excluding merchants other than those from Haverford and Pembroke and, at the same time, Haverford's burgesses became exempt from paying 'tolls, portage and passage'. A later Marshal charter decreed that they should be free of mill tolls and tolls for erecting stalls at markets and fairs.

Large export duties were levied on some articles and an order dated 4 May 1282 directed the sheriff of Hereford to go in person to Haverford to collect 'the king's new custom of woolfells and hides taken out of the realm' at a charge of half a mark for each sack, half a mark for every 300 woolfells and a mark for each last (about a dozen) hides. (A mark was about 13s. 4d.)

There is also evidence of the considerable value of some of the local cargoes in the capture by a pirate ship in the early 14th century of £400 worth of goods from the *La Mariote Ly Yowel*, a vessel which had been loaded at Haverford.

The town was fortified with walls and gates during the Lordship of Humphrey de Bohun III who was granted the title by the king in 1274. The Marshal male line had died out and Humphrey had a claim as a descendant of Eva de Braose, née Marshal. The Red Gate stood at the bottom of Holloway, North Gate was at North Street, West Gate at Dew Street and South Gate at the top of Market Street. Humphrey, though, exchanged the castle with Eleanor of Castile, wife of Edward I, who had fallen in love with it. She did not, however, live to enjoy her castle, dying in 1290, only two years after the exchange.

It was not until 1914 that the first excavation took place in the grounds of the castle when a 17-foot high underground chamber was uncovered, together with the beginnings of other buried passages. More of the castle's secrets were discovered in January 2008 when an archaeological excavation revealed not only pottery dating from 1190 but also a fine mediaeval archway which is assumed to have been part of the main gatehouse — 'the entry to the very heart of the castle' says curator of Haverfordwest Town Museum, Simon Hancock, who has hopes that funding may be available for further exploration of the site.

By the time of Eleanor's death the town had grown considerably, having up to 400 burgages (meaning it was a large town for the 13th century) and the market, which was originally sited around the castle, expanded into the town itself. A 'shambles' developed in St. Mary's churchyard and spread into the adjacent area known as Pillory Street, also the site of the town stocks (which were still in use in the early Victorian era).

With prosperity came responsibilities and frequent orders exist from the reigns of both Edward I and Edward II for the bailiff and men of Haverford to provide ships and provisions for the use of the king in Scotland and elsewhere. One of Edward I's great ambitions was to bring the whole of Britain under his rule, something which resulted in an alliance between France and Scotland and the king's subsequent dispute with the Scottish baron, Robert Bruce.

In 1297 it is recorded in the Close Rolls that the bailiffs of Haverford were ordered 'to have all ships of the port of the burthen of 40 tuns of wine and upwards before the king at Winchelsea on the morrow of midsummer next, ready and well found to set out to such place as the king should then order.'

Not many weeks later the king sailed for war with France and the following year William Hakelute, bailiff of Haverford, was ordered to have the town's ships ready again, this time to set out for Scotland.

The dispute with Scotland continued into the reign of Edward II and a letter from the burgesses to the king exists in the town's records referring to a ship they had provided in aid of the king's service against 'Robert de Brus'. The ship was to be fully armed and provisioned for seven weeks and to be at Olderfleet, County Antrim by Midsummer's Day.

From the time of the first charter made by Henry

A mediaeval lymphad, or cargo ship, illustrated
above on the seal of Haverfordwest Corporation
(from a drawing by Jim McBrearty)

II up until 1479 the affairs of the town were presided over by the 'prepositus' (bailiff). At this time 9-year-old Edward, Prince of Wales and Lord of Haverford (the future Edward V) granted a charter which gave Haverford its first mayor who also bears the title of Admiral of the Port — claimed by his descendants, although no records exist, as being Richard Ffulk. The mayor first mentioned by name was Thomas Browne in 1490. At the same time a sheriff, bailiffs and 'twenty-four of the honestest men of the town' were appointed by the mayor to form a common council. Since that day Haverford has never been without its mayor and Admiral of the Port, the latter appointment made in recognition of the town's maritime importance. The office of sheriff also remains, and as one of only 14 sheriffs that now exist in England and Wales the town has, in recent years, hosted their annual meeting.

It was also an indication of the town's importance that, as in many of the important towns and cities of the country, Haverfordwest had its company of Waits whose duties were to play in the streets, greeting important visitors and accompanying the mayor as he went about his business — often an uncomfortable task in freezing weather. They were elaborately dressed, at the town's expense, in grey frieze (a coarse woollen cloth) faced with green taffeta and embellished with green mockado (an inferior cloth of Flemish origin, probably a type of haircloth) and buttons. The Waits' bands began in the 14th century, developed from the old town watchmen, and they were employed to look out for fire and thieves, to mark the passing of the hours by blowing their horns or trumpets, and to announce the state of the weather. By the 15th century their role had begun to change and their function was more ceremonial although many continued their night watch, starting their rounds in the early hours. (During the Civil War the numbers of towns with Waits decreased as the towns found themselves unable to afford such luxuries which were also no doubt frowned upon by staunch puritans). In 1836 the Municipal Reform Act removed many by then unfashionable officials such as the tipstaff, bellman and, with them, the Waits. Their legacy, however, remains today in the Christmas Carol singers.

By the 1500s Haverford was virtually free of the shackles of feudal lordship and the mayor, a man of considerable influence, was also coroner, escheator (dealing with property matters) clerk of the market and Deputy Lieutenant of the town with power to act on behalf of the Lord President of Wales. He was entitled to the tolls (in kind) on 200 apples out of every cargo arriving at the quay, fowls from the corporation tenants, an allowance of 6s. 8d. towards 'a brawn or diet' at Christmas and the rights to the fishing of the river from the White Stone at Higgons Well to the Priory Mill. On Whit Monday each year the Admiral of the Port inspected these boundaries of the borough, a custom still carried out annually by river boat.

Shortly after Wales was divided into 12 counties by the 1536 Act of Union Haverford was created a county in its own right, separate from the county of Pembroke (a status it retained until 1888), with the right of holding an assize court and empowered to elect its own Member of Parliament. The first representatives were both mercers — Richard Howell, who was also mayor, and Richard Taylor — later, however, it was from the county's 'important' families such as the Perrotts and Stepneys that the parliamentary representatives were chosen.

It was, though, an insignificant young man, William Nichol, who acquired lasting fame in 1558 as one of the three Welsh martyrs of the Marian persecution in the reign of Mary Tudor. Nichol, who had learned to read and write at the priory and was employed by the Chamber Reeve, went out into the streets preaching the anti-Catholic sermons he had prepared at his home near the castle. After the queen's proclamation to 'burn all heritics', he went into hiding but was captured and burned at the stake for his faith. Some today say that he was just a simple minded youth who did not know what he was doing, but his martyrdom is, however, commemorated by a memorial in the town's High Street where members of the Free Church and the Protestant Truth Society still lay wreaths in his memory.

At this same period Sir John Perrot was accused of harbouring heretics at his home at Haroldston, among them Alexander Nowell, later Dean of Lichfield, who composed the catechism that features in the prayer book of 1549. Through Perrot's protection Nowell did not join Nichol and the other two Welsh martyrs, Ferrar, who was burned at the stake in Carmarthen and White, who paid the price in Cardiff.

By the reign of Elizabeth I the town's market was drawing buyers from well outside the town, and is described enthusiastically by George Owen:

> Haverfordwest being seated in the middle of the shire and most convenient for trade is greatlie frequented of the country people, and therefore is the greatest and plentifullest markett of the shire, and is kept once a week on the Saturdaye, wherein me thinketh the towne is very backward in their own proffitte in not sueinge (petitioning) for another markett in the middle of the weeke, which wold turne to the great good both of the towne and countrye; allso they have but one faire in the yeare, whereas if theere were more purchased from Her Majesty it might be beneficiall both for towne and countrye. This markett of Haverfordwest is thought to be one of the greatest and most plentifullest marketts (all things compared) that is within the Marches of Wales; especiallie for the plenty and goodness of the victuell, as namely for beefe, mutton, porke, bacon, veale, goose, capon, kidd, lambe, conye, turkye and all sortes if wild fowl in their season, that it is a marvell to manye, where the victuells, that are there to be seene at noone should be shifted awaye ere night, and for fish it passeth all other in Wales, without anie comparison, both of plenti and varietie.

The lower floor of the Guildhall, the earliest public building for which there is documentary evidence, was used as an extension of the shambles and accounts from the Elizabethan era record payment in 1583 of 5s. for 'planks that mended the great Shambles', in 1599, 3s. 3d. for 'mending of the Shambles, board and a new plank' and in 1600 'for keeping the Shambles clean for a year, 4s.' In the 13th century the building below the church where the South African War memorial now stands (the road between the Guildhall and the church was *Media Strata Juxta Praetorium*) was referred to as a 'gildhus' and was built for the recently established merchants' guilds. Around and near the churchyard clustered a number of inns — the Swan, Blue Boar, Dolphin, Coach and Horses and the Fleece with a further two on Tower Hill: the Six Bells and the Black Bear

— and it was in one of these that the grand jury were accommodated during the Assize and Great Sessions which were held in the cramped upper storey of the Guildhall.

Finds of two wool bale seals dated 1752 and 1740(?) are evidence of the town's role in the wool trade. These seals would have been issued by the Alnager whose responsibility was inspecting and checking the quality of the wool offered for sale. In the early 14th century Haverfordwest was the only staple town — one nominated as a port through which goods, in this case wool and hides, could be traded — in Wales. Between 1318 and 1320, 22 shipments containing 143 sacks of wool left the town, and by Elizabethan times wool had become the most important export from the county after corn and cattle. However, local sheep tended to be small with coarse wool which gave Pembrokeshire friezes a poor reputation — they were said to be thick, rough and drab but were, apparently, good enough to be given to the poor in England on Ash Wednesday. As production methods improved elsewhere, this once important trade which had provided material for winter coats declined, and, with no public revenue, the town had to fund the maintenance of two aqueducts, two bridges — one a main bridge on the river — two quays and two alms-houses.

Despite this period of considerable affluence, in 1616, a time when the population had reached 3,000 inhabitants, the quay had been in such a dilapidated state for the previous 30 years 'that no barque could ride safe there' and some of the burgesses were called to the Great Sessions because of their neglect of this important public utility. Around 300 householders came to the rescue by volunteering to pay for a day's work rebuilding the quay and 48 'of the better sort' also donated the money for a second day. However, eight years later the outstanding debt for the work had still not been paid and the council was once again called to account.

At the same time there was a lack of enthusiasm for the payment of rates. Rates to pay for armour were demanded from 340 people (probably heads of households), and during the Commonwealth after the Civil Wars demands came in thick and fast. Lead was stripped from St. Mary's church to be made into ball shot, the town was called on to pay money 'for Ireland', for the support of wounded soldiers and to provide horses to carry the wounded to Carmarthen (see also p.148).

The protests against this series of levies which began in 1650 were not received favourably and two years later there is evidence of the decline of the town, reduced to less than 200 houses with two-thirds of the inhabitants described as 'very poor'. The townspeople were crippled by additional taxes, the town had been plundered by Royalist troops in the Civil War, the inhabitants seized and ransomed and the Parliamentary army had demanded free quarter in the town. Some of the wealthier inhabitants had also fled and were no longer able to provide employment for the lower orders. The relief of 'poor decayed burgesses who must perish without such relief' was a charge on a town which had, they said, 'no trade by sea or land, nor ability to raise or derive any'.

Despite the town's problems, it was not until 1653 when another was added in the form of plague that the assessments of tax were reduced and the arrears remitted. It is believed that sailors from an infected ship which had berthed at Milford Haven brought the plague to the town when they visited the Saturday market, a theory which

A 1693 map of Haverfordwest, drawn by Phillip Lea

was strengthened by the discovery of a number of bodies of young sailors who had been buried in the mid-17th century on the shoreline at Burton. They were wrapped in their hammocks, and one had in his pocket a coin dated 1650, the time when hanging was the penalty for a captain who ventured within approach of land with any ship carrying plague. It appears that their burial was a hurried and secretive affair.

As the number of victims grew 'Mr. Bateman's stable' in Cokey Street was repaired at a cost of £2 10s. 6d. as a 'cleansing house' for the convalescent, and it was also in Cokey Street, in an area known as the Mayor's Field, that the dead were buried. While the dwindling numbers of better off paid for their care, the majority were dependent on the parish's poor rate for medical care and (with so many of the former breadwinners sick or dead and orphans to be cared for) also for food to ward off starvation. Records show that nearly 1,000 people were 'in want of the necessary food to sustain nature' during the period between 20 May and 2 October alone, and nearly 400 sick and needy outside the pest house, in addition to those inside, were in receipt of relief.

At the same time the restriction on movement brought trade to a standstill. The majority of the stock sold by the mercers, shoemakers, and feltmakers had come from St. Paul's Fair in Bristol — a city where plague still lingered after an outbreak the previous year. Few would risk buying these potentially infected goods and the markets and fairs were either cancelled or moved elsewhere. The town's principal fair, May Fair, was moved to the north side of Fursie Parke, just within the municipal boundary, but only a few people attended. The wool markets were discontinued and transferred to Steynton and Llawhaden as attempts were made to totally isolate the town. Public buildings including the churches and town hall were 'disinfected' with just about anything that was strong smelling, such as lime, pitch, tar, and frankincense, and because the plague was considered to be a divine intervention the people were exorted to repentance and prayer and to avoid sin. But the infection continued to spread, reaching the parish of St. Thomas, Hayscastle, Boulston, Prendergast, Honeyborough, Waterston, Crundale and Hillblock.

Many of the town's inhabitants had already left the area, finally ruined by the taxes imposed on them (some of it a levy for the relief of plague victims in Tenby the previous year). Now, as the infection spread, more of the better off departed, fleeing from a scourge which could kill in just three days. By the time the pestilence had begun to burn itself out the population figures had dropped from around 3,000 to nearer 2,000 and the Commission for the Assessment of Haverfordwest was writing 'There are not any left above 20 that are able to pay anything in the monthly assessment and they but of mean estate'. This presented enormous administrative problems for those trying to govern the town with the majority of the officials and magistrates gone and only 'handicraftmen and day labourers and the poor sort of people' remaining.

In an attempt to restrict the spread of the highly infectious rat-borne disease the sick and their contacts were segregated behind the locked doors of their homes with guards appointed to ensure that this quarantine was faithfully observed. Food was brought in from outside the plague area and anyone who had had contact of any sort with the victims was required to carry a white pole. Two houses in St. Martin's parish, the heart of the outbreak, were rented from alderman William Williams, one as a 'pest house' and the other as a centre for the two 'Tarrcoats' who were employed to attend the sick and bury the dead. These two men, who each received 7s. 6d. a week for this horrendous task, acquired the name from their protective attire — all embracing garments covered in tar to ward off infection, with a beaked hood covering the face in which were powerful herbs to offset the stench of plague and death. The unorthodox theory — which seems to have been successful — was that the disease-spreading fleas would adhere to the sticky pitch, be unable to bite and eventually die. Another desperate measure was adopted by some who had business within the locked and barred town. They killed a pigeon, hacked it in half and strapped a piece to each foot in a bid to attract the rat fleas to the dead bird rather than the vulnerable human being.

The sick were cared for, as best they could, by two barber surgeons, Benjamin Price and James Sonnegon whose ministrations were, unfortunately, marred by some very public professional disagreements. There was also a mystery woman, a stranger, directed to the town, it was said, by divine guidance. 'This woman', as she is referred to in the town accounts, selflessly nursed the victims through their illness and left once the sickness was over. For her dedicated work she was paid 6s. a week from corporation funds.

Another tireless worker and hero of the plague years was the Revd. Stephen Love, the Puritan Rector of St. Thomas who fearlessly visited the sick and organised relief from the outlying areas, riding out day after day seeking gifts of money and food, persuading the country people to give corn, butter, bread, cheese, pork, barley meal and other goods to help to feed the starving of the isolated town. Worn out by his labours, Love died in 1656 and, recognising his outstanding role, the Common Council presented his widow, Deborah Love, with £20, waived the burial fee and also the cost of tolling the bell at St. Mary's church. (A fee of 8s. for ringing all the bells for the death of a burgess or burgess's wife and 16s. for a stranger or foreigner, or 2s. 6d and 5s. respectively for one bell, had been introduced in 1632. The council justified the charge on the grounds that 'the bells of St. Mary's are greatly decayed and in consideration of the ill usage of them in ringing them at the death of everyone whereby no benefit comes to the parish.')

During the Commonwealth years and well into the 18th century the name Bateman (owner of the stable used as a cleansing house during the plague) was a significant one in the town. Richard Bateman was mayor in 1656 and members of the family held office 13 times between 1605 and 1750. William Bateman, however, is remembered not for any part in civic affairs but as the Quaker who embarrassed the authorities by his resolute dedication to his faith.

Under a law passed by Parliament in 1662 Friends Meetings became illegal and two years later the persecution of the Quakers was carried further with the *Law of Meeting Houses* which prohibited gatherings of more than four people over the age of 16, in addition to the family of the house, from worshipping in any building other than the parish church. Fines were imposed for each offence, a third offence carrying a fine of £100 or seven years' exile overseas.

In the early years Pembrokeshire was the focus of many meetings of the Society of Friends, and one in Haverfordwest in the home of 'a merchant of the town' (almost certainly William Bateman) in 1659 was attended by nearly 200 people. The Pembrokeshire County Meetings were held either in Haverfordwest or Redstone and the inspirational founder of the Society, George Fox recorded in his Journal that he attended one 'great meeting' in Haverfordwest, but did not note the location.

Over the years William Bateman and his wife, Janet, refused to be intimidated and were imprisoned for attending 'unlawful meetings, pretence of religious worship and evil principles in great disobedience to His Majesties government'. After being caught at a meeting they refused to promise not to attend any further ones and, with James Jones and Henry and Elizabeth Relief, were imprisoned for a year awaiting trial. The men were then fined 5s. each and the women 5 marks — fines they refused to pay, a stand which resulted in another prison sentence, this time at the Bridewell in London. On this occasion Bateman escaped prison but had his goods distrained to the value of £5.

Four other men, Edmund Williams, David Simmons and John Howell, who were discovered attending a meeting were sent to the House of Correction and Richard Poole who was with them was ordered to remain in prison 'until the wind served to send him to Ireland and then to be whipped and sent thither'.

Even after the passing of the Toleration Act in 1689 the persecution continued, and up to the beginning of the 18th century it is said that no day passed without the presence of a Quaker in the prison at Haverfordwest where they were incarcerated in horrendous conditions. A Puncheston family, Thomas Simmons, his wife Jane and their three sons, together with Ursula Simmons and Lawrence, David and Margaret Edward were confined in this prison for 18 months as they awaited trial. At their trial, after this long and unjust confinement, the evidence against them was judged insufficient, they were acquitted by the jury and released to return to their homes.

The picture painted in the records of all that these gentle Quaker people suffered nationwide is testimony to the strength of their belief. Of those imprisoned in

The Moravian chapel on the quayside at Haverfordwest.
Moravians had strong trading links with northern Canada

Pembrokeshire the Society of Friends *Collection of Sufferings* records 'They were treated very cruelly, forced to share a cell with murderers and felons who took away their food, pikt their pockets and many ways abused them. The hardships they endured in winter for want of fire, having no place to make any in, was very pinching to several of them who were both aged and sickly and had their hands and feet much swelled and their bodies looking black.'

The opportunity for a new life, free of oppression, came in 1682 when William Penn (the founder of Pennsylvania) visited America and returned enthusiastic about establishing a colony for Friends on land he purchased there. He promised a Welsh settlement where the Friends could preserve their own native language and be free to worship as they pleased. The glowing reports encouraged many Quakers to seize the opportunity of securing passages to the colony at a cost of £5 for persons over 12 years of age and £2 10s. for those under 12 — and so the Pennsylvanian town of Haverford was born and later Narberth and St. David's also came into being. With the emigration of so many Quaker families, by 1792 the only listed Meeting House in Pembrokeshire was in Haverfordwest, on the site where the Shire Hall was built in 1835, where the monthly county meeting took place — but this was also the year that Daniel Starbuck and his family, the first American quakers to come to live in Milford, arrived (see p.152). Shortly afterwards Starbuck was appointed clerk of the monthly meeting and within 20 years a Meeting House was built and in regular use in Milford.

Starbuck himself paid the penalty of having his property distrained for refusing to pay church tithes and when his son, Samuel, refused to serve in the Supplementary Militia he was forced to pay £10 to pay for a substitute to serve in his place.

Soon the Haverfordwest meeting was discontinued, Milford took its place and after a period when meetings there also came to an end there are now regular meetings every Sunday in the original Priory Road building. Meetings are also held in Narberth and St. David's and across the county boundary in Cardigan.

Their strength of faith also continues. The distinguished Welsh poet Waldo Williams, who was born in Haverfordwest, became a member of the Milford Meeting. He had registered as a Conscientious Objector during the Second World War but it was the war in Korea in 1950 that determined him to refuse to pay Income Tax in protest against 'the waste and inhumanity of war' until the last conscript was released in 1963. He served six weeks in Swansea gaol in 1960 and a further six weeks in Ashwell Open Prison in Rutland the following year. Some of his household possessions had been distrained to pay his taxes so he was then supported by other quakers who bought back his wardrobe, table and chair (his bed had not been removed) to provide him with some comfort. After his death in 1971 a memorial stone, Carreg Waldo, was erected under the shadow of Carn Meini at Gors Fawr on Mynachlogddu common.

After the depressed years of the Civil War and the visitation by plague the town began to regain its prosperity at the beginning of the 18th century. It was a period that saw the construction of some of the town's most gracious houses, most notably Foley House in Hill Lane, designed in 1794 by John Nash, one of the nation's great architects. The house was built as the town house for the Foley family of Ridgeway, near Colby Moor, where five of its members were killed on the Royalist side in the battle of 1645. It was here that Lord Nelson was entertained by his friend Admiral Sir Thomas Foley, a hero of the Battle of the Nile, on his visit to Haverfordwest in 1802 to receive the freedom of the town. In the mid-20th century Foley House was sold to the County Council.

An early Hill Street property (later the Dragon Hotel and now a drop in centre) was the town house of the Laugharne family of Orlandon and it was here that one of Pembrokeshire's heroes, Sir Thomas Picton, was born in 1758. Remembered now in the naming of the Haverfordwest Comprehensive School, Picton served in the Napoleonic Wars as commander of the Fighting Division and was regarded as the most heroic figure in Wellington's army. His troops at the storming of the castle of Badajoz were said to have been inspired by his battle cry 'If we cannot win the castle let us die upon its walls'. Picton, however, lived to fight another day but after being wounded at Quatre Bras he was killed during the Battle of Waterloo on 18 June 1815.

It was, however, not for many years that the slum areas of Rats Island and Short and Back Row were swept away. John Brown (writing as Christopher Cobweb) in the *History of Haverfordwest* presents a graphic picture of these mean streets: 'miserable thatched hovels with manure heaps in front. A horse bench outside every public house (and these were numerous) and from their doors stream forth an everlasting smell of new drink for the inhabitants are constantly brewing.' He later goes on to describe some of the people living in these squalid conditions — 'people with disfigured countenances, faces ploughed with small pox and eyes terribly bleared, for the dreadful disease spread like a pest, as indeed it was. Moping idiots and madmen gay, too, constantly cross our path.

Troops of neglected children playing about, girls and boys approaching adolescence, with bare feet and legs, for shoes and stockings were a luxury in that day.'

Justice in those days was hard and unforgiving. A Prendergast woman, Dorothy Rees, was convicted at the Quarter Sessions at the Guildhall in 1741 for stealing a flannel petticoat valued at 6d. and was ordered to be transported to the colonies for seven years after being stripped to the waist on a January morning and publicly whipped through the town for a period of two hours 'so effectively that her body be bloody by means of such whipping'. This was a time when a woman working on a farm would have received her working clothes and 30s. a year; when butter cost 4d. per lb, a pair of shoes 2s. 6d. and ¼oz of tobacco 1½d.

Conditions were also hard for the workers. In 1864 two farm hands, John Owen and Thomas Mathias, who worked for Henry Pattison at Castle Pill, Steynton, courageously took their employer to court for not providing them with proper food. Perhaps, unsurprisingly, they did not receive a sympathetic hearing from the magistrates at Haverfordwest Shire Hall, the Revd. Thomas Watts and Mr. O.E. Davies. Mathias, who had been hired at the hiring fair at Little Haven for 12 months at £5 10s., said that in the nine weeks he had been in Pattison's employ he had been served edible meat on only one occasion, the only other time meat was provided it had been 'stinking'. Dinner consisted of porridge made of turnips and about a pound of foreign bacon (not thought of as 'meat') with about five gallons of water. The bread was made of corn burnt on the kiln and the cheese was too 'hot' to eat. When he complained to his employer he was told never to speak to him again or he would 'put a stick about our heads and would put scabs on our backs that we would carry to the grave'. The two men then asked to be released from their employment but had been refused. Samples of food were produced in court by the farmer and when other employees gave evidence that they were content with the food provided, the presiding magistrate dismissed the case saying that the men must return to their service.

While the poor of the town lived in foul conditions and the well-to-do were beginning to establish their town houses, facilities to cater for the entertainment of the better off were also developed. A public library opened in an upper room of the Armoury, a racecourse was laid out in Portfield in 1727, there were balls at the newly built Assembly Rooms, and Hunt Week attracted the aristocracy whose ladies were carried in sedan chairs. When Mrs. Morgan visited the town in 1791 she found it a 'genteel' place occupied by 'a vast number of gentlemen who live at seats upon the banks of the river', as she writes in her *Tour of Wales*. She refers, too, to the delicacy of the whitewashed houses which gave the town 'preference in point of beauty'. It seems that St. Mary's church received the same treatment for in May 1707 alderman William Brown, the previous year's mayor, was ordered to pay 40s. towards whitewashing the church for not taking on the office of sheriff.

Holding office was an expensive business and there was some reluctance among the council members to take on the responsibility. To ease the way when the problem reached crisis point the Common Council agreed that the tolls of the 'dairy and flesh' markets and the common beam for weighing the wool should go to the mayor of the day.

In 1752, the council applied for the removal of the troop of Dragoons (supported at the town's expense) which had been sent to assist the civil magistrates in preventing and suppressing riots, as they said no disturbances had taken place for many years. There was, however, a riot 50 years later when the Hook miners attempted to seize a cargo of butter destined for Bristol (see p.116) but by this time the Pembrokeshire Yeomanry had been established and order was restored by the Fishguard Fencibles.

By the end of the 18th century the council seemed to be prepared to spend money without protest. A new town clock was bought for St. Mary's church tower and in 1798 an annual contribution of 1,000 guineas was voted 'to relieve the public burden during the continuance of the war against us by our inveterate enemy'.

Mediaeval merchant's house discovered in Quay Street, Haverfordwest in 1983, with a conjectural reconstruction of the opposite elevation top right. The plans alongside are of the ground floor (nearest) and first floor. (Photograph and drawings courtesy of National Museum of Wales, St Fagans)

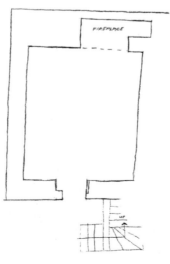 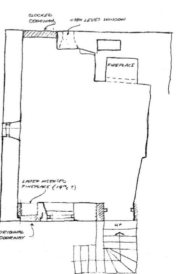

It was in Quay Street, in 1983, that the discovery of a mediaeval house tucked away out of sight behind a business premises, added significantly to knowledge about Haverfordwest's history. The house had recently been used as a store but the new owners were intrigued by the small rectangular building with its high gable ends and steeply pitched slate roof and set about to find out more. The building had a single first storey room approached by an external stone staircase and stood above a vaulted cellar with no internal access between the cellar and first floor. The slight point of the arch is similar to that found in the Bishop's Palace at St. David's which established a date between the 12th and 15th century. The layout was that of a mediaeval hall — this was always on the first floor so that if the inhabitants came under attack they could lock up all they could downstairs, including animals and geese, and take refuge at the top of the narrow staircase. Only one person at a time could mount the stairs making it easier to pick off any attackers.

Because this rather special find, which is just visible in the 1748 Bucks' print of Haverfordwest (left of the bridge, p.40), was inaccessible to the public it was removed, stone by stone, to the National Museum of Wales at St. Fagans to be reassembled there and work began late in 2008 on what is expected to be a two year project. Meanwhile excavations had been carried out on site in the hope of finding mediaeval floors, but the Victorians had got there first and removed all traces. Instead the exciting discovery was made of a mediaeval water and drainage system that was still functioning — a series of drains built into the solid rock which had kept the building completely dry up to the time it was dismantled. The drain was well cut and covered with stone slabs and included a cistern for holding water as it ran from the rocks. Even during the dry period

The part of the Bucks' print showing some of the quays and the priory remains on the left

in which the system was discovered water was still flowing into the cistern indicating that the inhabitants would have had clear fresh water even during periods of drought. Two lavatories, similar to the garderobes of the castle, emptied into the drainage system so that they would be flushed out by the spring water as it flowed from the property. Around 1700 it seems the cistern was backfilled with a large quantity of stones and pottery of the type made in north Devon which confirms the belief that a potter, probably originally from that area, was working in Haverfordwest at this time and which also accounts for the name Potters Lane near the Post Office. The finds, pieced together, yielded up to 40 complete parts of all types of container used in a Haverfordwest house in 1700 as well as glass bottles and pottery from other parts of the country and Europe. There were, however, no trinkets, coins or decorative metal items.

It was not until 1827 that complaints about the fly-infested Shambles prompted the authorities to replace it with a covered building in Market Street. This 19th-century market was 'reconstructed' in 1933 and finally closed and fell into disrepair with the opening (at a cost of £600,000) of the Riverside Market in 1982. It was demolished in June 2001 and has been replaced by a housing complex called Shoemaker's Court to reflect the trade that once thrived in the area.

A filthy lane, Drawbridge Lane (now Victoria Place), led to a rickety bridge across the river and this was replaced by today's stone bridge in 1833. It was built with a £2,000 loan from the architect Mr. William Owen while the Perrot's Trustees (see p.134) contributed £1,200 for the construction of the pavements to and from the bridge. There had been another rough wooden bridge (the site of 12 inns) at the crossing now known as Old Bridge — a bridge which was scarcely passable by pedestrians who preferred to wade across at low water. The stone bridge, erected in 1726, was the gift of 'Good Sir John' — Sir John Philipps, (4th Baronet of Picton Castle and M.P. for Haverfordwest 1718-1722) — and bears a memorial tablet to that year's mayor, Michael Prust, a descendant of the family who entertained Cromwell during his visit to the town. It also records that King George IV passed over it on 13 September 1821 on his return from Ireland. It was at this point, too that Henry Tudor forded the river as he led his supporters to victory at Bosworth.

Further developments followed the 1835 Act for 'Paving, lighting and otherwise Improving the Town of Haverfordwest and the adjoining townships of Prendergast and Uzmaston' with its reference to the town being 'ill paved and cleaned, incommodious to passengers by reason of nuisances, annoyances and obstructions'. It added that 'many disorders and irregularities' were frequently committed at night time because the place was not properly lit and watched. Amongst the changes it heralded, 'Street Keepers' and watchmen were appointed with the powers of constables, scavengers' carts were introduced, and householders had to sweep the pavements in front of their premises before nine each morning. There remained concerns, as evidenced in 1866 when measures were being considered to rid the reservoir of 'newts, leeches, decaying animal and vegetable matter', despite having not only the reservoir but six public pumps and four public wells that the authorities claimed never failed and were supplied with 'no limit of good water for all domestic and general use' by the river Cleddau. A letter in the *Sanitary Engineer* complained about lack of water drainage and general sanitation in the town and protested that despite expenditure of about £12,000 the town was without water for drinking purposes — the Cleddau, after all, is hardly the happiest choice of supply for drinking water.

There had been outbreaks of cholera with a number of deaths in the county during the previous ten years and it was now realised that it was a water-borne infection rather than one caused by the filth of the streets and houses. A request had been made to the Admiralty for a hospital ship in the haven but the response was that there was no money available.

Over the years more gentry houses had been built accommodating many half-pay army and navy officers who had been put on the retired list at the end of the Napoleonic Wars and who had been lured to the county by the low cost of living. So was established Haverfordwest's reputation as 'Little Bath'.

The population had grown to 4,328 in 1833 of which ten families were involved in agriculture, 513 in trade and manufacturing and 286 classified as in other trades. Trade was clearly booming. All life's essentials and luxuries, all the goods required by the town's increased population, came by sea and vessels of up to 200 tons were able to tie up at the Gasworks Quay. Most goods came from Bristol, with others arriving from Liverpool and London, and were traded on village quays and beaches. Vessels brought timber for Lewis's Timber Warehouse — a furniture manufacturer on the banks of the river — and for a nearby shipbuilding yard; limestone blocks and Bridgewater bricks, in consignments of 130,000 at a time, came in on the sailing vessels to be dumped on the river bed from where they were collected at low tide by horse and cart. Salt and wine was imported from France in exchange for coal, wool, hides and ale; iron, sugar and salt were imported from

Haverfordwest in 1837, the year of the completion of the new bridge, with its toll gates. The limekiln in the foreground on the right was one of ten in this area of the town (Roger Worsley)

Spain and Portugal and the Breton onion men (universally known as Johnny Onions) were regular visitors.

Butter and cheese from Haverfordwest went to Liverpool and London. Paper milling was long established in Haverfordwest and paper was exported in large quantity to Bristol. The Haverfordwest Mills (Priory Mill) were manufacturing paper prior to 1815 and the Prendergast Paper Mill by 1842. The latter, originally a corn mill, was rebuilt as a cotton mill in the 18th century, though this proved a short lived enterprise. Sale particulars in January 1805 described it as 'within a mile of the seaport town of Haverfordwest' and record that it contained 1,512 spindles but was capable of working a great many more, and that it was powered by a stream which was never known to fail. The 7-acre site included 'a substantial dwelling, grist mill, other small house, carpenters' and smiths' shops, slaughterhouse, barn and stable'. It had, however, gone over to producing paper by the time Warwickshire mill owner, Benjamin Harvey came to Haverfordwest in 1842. Harvey and his family had been living in Peterhof in Russia where he assisted in establishing a paper mill in the Tsar's new town and once in Haverfordwest this entrepreneur set about creating a thriving business, becoming the main manufacturer in the county producing coarse sugar paper and packing paper made from rags. At its peak the mill employed 150 staff but changes in the paper industry in the late 19th century (when esparto grass was used in the manufacture and the industry became concentrated nearer the major ports) killed the local trade and the mill — now derelict — was used briefly for a variety of purposes, including the manufacture of dog biscuits.

There was a very large trade from the town's corn mills and the ground corn was stored in buildings all along the river at Northgate, Bridge Street, New Quay and Old Quay. During 1831 the total value of exports was about £100,000 with 130 vessels entering this very tidal river with merchandise. Upriver, just below Uzmaston, there was a boathouse and small jetty and it seems loading and unloading regularly took place there, (maps of the 1770s show the field there to be called Shipping Dock), and that it was also a point at which vessels would await the tide so as to reach the port of Haverfordwest.

Change came with the introduction of steam and in 1842 a meeting of the River Committee, formed from amongst ship owners, tradesmen and lime merchants, recommended that the dues on steamers carrying goods up and down the river should be higher than for sailing vessels because of the increased wear and tear on the river banks. They suggested that the sailing boat rate per registered ton for lime and building stone should be 1d., for culm, 2d., for all other goods carried on open boats and sailing vessels, 3d., and steam vessels, 4d. They estimated that the projected revenue would then be:

18,000 tons of stone at 1d.	£ 75
16,000 tons of culm at 2d.	£132
3,471 tons by sailing vessels or open boats at 3d.	£ 43 7s. 9d.
11,360 tons by steam vessels at 4d.	£189 6s. 8d.
	Total £439 14s. 5d.

Many of the Bristol traders used sailing vessels which were vulnerable to bad weather conditions and could be storm bound for up to six weeks at the Mumbles or Penarth, when the town would run out of tobacco, snuff, sugar and rum. However, there were also the 'Bristo'men' or 'bagmen' (commercial travellers) who rode into the town on horseback with their wares in bulging saddle bags. On arrival they hired wicker baskets which, when they had filled them with their goods, were mounted on trolleys to be pushed round the shops until in the evening, as legend says, the police borrowed the trolleys to pick up drunks and remove them to the police station.

Despite the effect of the coming of the railway in 1853 which drastically reduced river traffic, it was well into the 20th century before it ceased completely. A small team of barges operated in the Haven, transhipping cargo from the large sea-going vessels, and a report of an accident in 1906 gives a glimpse of the type of traffic and their cargoes using the river. The 55-ton steamship *Cleddau* with a schooner in tow struck bottom near the timber-built Haverfordwest railway bridge. The schooner's anchor holed the steel hold of the barge which filled with water, ruining the cargo of fruit, Bibby's Cake (a cattle food) and flour from Spillers in Cardiff. The railway bridge, (known in those days as the train road bridge) had to be raised by a type of hand wound windlass to allow these tall masted ships to pass and was protected from passing vessels by a series of horizontal struts attached to the frame.

Until it was sold in 1936 the *Ben Rein*, a two-masted sailing ship with a motor, was one of the most familiar vessels trading on the river and all around the Haven. Its bowler-hatted owner and captain, John George of Glan y Mor, Trefin, was always happy to welcome on board the lads of the town when he tied up to load and unload at the quay. Like the *Thomond* (also owned by Captain George who bought it from a French shipping company for £1,300) it was a fairly large ship of its day and could not have travelled

The Viola *of Chester at Gasworks Quay by the lifting bridge in 1909 (Roger Worsley)*

higher than Haverfordwest Quay, below the New Bridge. Sailing vessels, among them the *Water Lily*, brought lime from the quarry opposite Llangwm to Robert Warlow's kilns at Haverfordwest and another regular visitor was the motorised sailing ship known locally as *Spillers and Bakers* (the name on the sign on the quayside warehouse to which it delivered its cargo of flour).

Culm from Hook colliery was carried by barge to Rowland's coal yard, near Bridgend Square. The most notable of these 'lighters', as these coal barges were called, was *'Appy Folland's Lighter* after its owner, the gigantic Absalom Folland who had a body like a barrel and was known to be the strongest man in Hook. The barge had a broad, flat bottom, about 30 feet long and 12 feet in the beam with a small very low 'cabin' at the front and another at the rear. It was made in the same way as the Llangwm fishing boats — butt built, caulked with oakum and pitched and tarred. Folland's mate was his brother, Thomas, and once the barge had been filled with 30 to 35 tons of culm it would be pulled by rowing boat into the middle of the river where the incoming tide floated it upstream to Haverfordwest, the two brothers taking turns at rowing when necessary to keep the lighter in the middle of the river where the current was strongest.

Writing in the *Pembrokeshire Magazine* in April 1984 Reg Phelps, a native of Hook, recalls that the usual way of travelling to Haverfordwest for shopping on Saturdays during the First World War was by rowing boat:

> Many of the women passengers were a little scared when they saw a large ship on the river ... Sometimes the boat owners, Mr. Bowen and Mr. Thomas, would pull as near to the shore as possible to get away from the wash of these ships. The Saturday

'Appy Folland's Lighter, with the town and castle in the background

shoppers would stay 'in town' as long as possible, but they had to be ready to return when the tide was high enough to float the boat back to Hook Quay with all their shopping. It was a hard climb from the shore at Hook Quay up to the village by way of the Old Anchor path or by the colliery 'dram' incline — and, at the end of the day, after these Saturday outings, cans of drinking water had to carried from Hook 'screw', the village tap, for no water would be carried on Sundays.

Leading to the river, Quay Street, formerly known as Ship Street, was a mixture of warehouses, mills, grand merchants houses, the Custom House, wool market, slums and a plethora of public houses of which now only the Bristol Trader remains. It had been a place of vice (openly frequented by pirates), yet at the same time was the centre of one of the most demanding religions for it was the meeting place for the Society of Friends and later the home of the Moravian movement.

'Appy Folland in his lighter

The picture in the 19th century is one of a bustling quay, a busy town, high life for the gentry, and some hardworking entrepreneurs. One of the town's most prosperous businesses was the Marychurch Iron Foundry and the products of this ironworks still proliferate, notably in the gates and railings of the old City Road Cemetery and of Tabernacle Congregational Church, and in the pre-1844 mile posts (listed by Cadw) erected under the Turnpike Trust, recording the distance between Haverfordwest and Pembroke on the old Pembroke road.

Joseph Marychurch was a descendant of William Marychurch, a mercer who was the town bailiff in 1663. A Parliamentarian, he was commanding officer of a locally recruited company of Militia during the Civil War and the Military Governor of Haverfordwest after the battle of Colby Moor. Joseph, however, blotted his copybook by supporting the turncoats Laugharne, Poyer and Powell and was heavily fined and dismissed from his civic post. From this time on, like so many of the town's burgesses, he was heavily in debt, his business suffered during the plague years when he remained in Haverfordwest while his family took refuge in Llawhaden, and he died, a broken man, in 1670. His son, another William, played a prominent part in the affairs of the town — alderman and sheriff in 1692, mayor in 1694 and, for many years before his death at the age of 90 in 1728, was an early treasurer of the Charity School which was the forerunner of Haverfordwest Grammar School.

He was also an astute businessman and it was he who began to recoup the family's losses. It was, however, his grandson, Solomon, who set up the iron foundry business at the rear of Bridge Street and also a sawmills near the river bank at Jubilee Gardens. The expansion of the family firm continued under his son, Joseph, who extended the enterprise into many other profitable areas. It was said that each time a business transaction was concluded the purchaser was Joseph Marychurch of Haverfordwest. In addition to his father's iron foundry and sawmills (later taken on by MacMaster) the Marychurch empire included general and farm fertilizer merchants, farm implement makers and a house furnishing

The corner of the Grammar School on the left, with the Fishmarket straight ahead. The Fishmarket, also used latterly as a milk depot, was demolished in 1951. The Grammar School moved to Scarrowscant Lane in 1965, its site now being occupied by the County Library (Roger Worsley)

The bill heading of Joseph Marychurch & Son

Looking through the toll gates on the new bridge and into town in 1870

business which employed coopers and carpenters. He also owned several large farms including Dudwell, Cold Blow and Camrose. Today, Marychurch Court, a housing association complex off Albert Street which opened in March 1993, provides sheltered accommodation for people over 55 years of age and keeps alive the name of the business which had ended with the death of his son, yet another Joseph, in 1896.

Despite the falling off in river trade the coming of the railway brought prosperity to businesses whose owners seized on the advantages of this new link with the world outside the county boundaries and within 20 years the Haverfordwest Churnworks was recognised throughout the UK as a leading manufacturer of butter makers, churns and separators. The proprietor of the day, George H. Llewellin, had taken his wares far afield, exhibiting at the Royal and other shows, winning many major prizes and establishing a demand for Haverfordwest made machines quite literally all over the world.

The business began in a small way in 1796 and was carried on by successive generations of the same family until it closed in 1966. At the turn of the century Llewellin's Churn Works employed 30 to 40 staff in the purpose-built, airy and well lit building which occupied an acre of land at the bottom of Perrots Road and, by the outbreak of the First World War, G. Herbert Llewellin was the largest employer in Haverfordwest, expansion restricted only by a shortage of skilled labour. The firm was advertising good wages and steady employment for apprentices and in one month exported 150 churns and a similar number of butter makers to various parts of the world. They were producing a weekly average of one hundred churns — an output again curtailed only by labour shortage.

Beechwood and sycamore was bought locally from Sir Owen Scourfield's estate at Williamston but the Llewellins had to go to the tropics for hardwood, to Russia for crown oak and America for canary wood. The hardwoods were used for the larger churns, the blenders and rollers and for the staves of the barrel type churns, while the soft canary wood was used for constructing the churn stands.

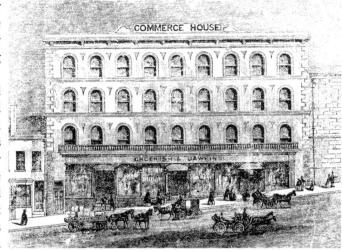

During the Second World War the workshops were used for the manufacture of farm carts and trailers as well as portable buildings for the Army and Observer Corps. After the war the building was leased to agricultural merchants, but sustained thousands of pounds worth of damage when a bottled gas cylinder exploded. The old churnworks, so long a feature of the town, remained

The sign of increasing prosperity in the Victorian era: Commerce House, home to Greenish & Dawkins

empty for some years and was bought by the District Council prior to its demolition in 1987 to make way for a by-pass and road scheme.

Another man to make a major impact on the town, giving it its 'noble thoroughfare', was the architect William Owen. He was appointed County Surveyor in 1832 after the previous incumbent died when he fell from his horse on his way to work from his home in Narberth. Owen's work included the removal of Short Row, where his own business was located. The Market Hall, the new Shire Hall (with Marychurch ironwork) and

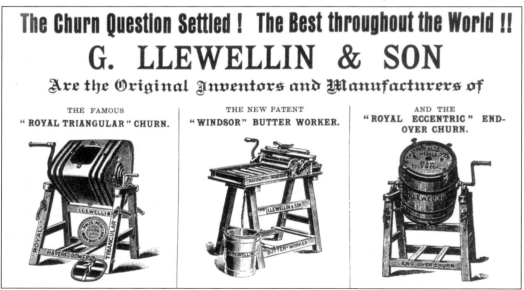

Part of an advertisement for G. Llewellin & Son's churns and butter workers

the Corn Market were all to his design. He financed the building of the New Bridge, lending the council £2,000 on the agreement that he would receive the toll for 21 years and did so well from this deal that eventually the council bought him out for £1,000; they were already paying him large sums of interest on money he had lent to them over the years.

His plans for the town swept away the slum areas and there was considerable controversy over the compulsory purchase of many properties that stood in his way. He is also credited with bringing the railway to Haverfordwest. Originally the line was destined to end at Swansea and, as a shareholder in the GWR, he attended a meeting in London where he met Brunel and set out to convince him of the advantages of continuing the line. No doubt he and his wife were among the 800 ladies and gentlemen attending the banquet 'on the most extensive scale, ranking amongst the most elegant entertainments ever witnessed in Wales' which celebrated the arrival of the first train into Haverfordwest station.

A Liberal and a Nonconformist (though, according to his obituary, 'never troublesome') he was four times mayor of Haverfordwest, High Sheriff of Pembrokeshire and a director of the Milford Docks Company but, when he died in 1879, he had failed to realise his great ambition of being selected as a Pembrokeshire Parliamentary candidate.

While much is written of William Owen less has been recorded of his wife who, when she died in November 1886, was said to have 'led a life of true philanthropy' — certainly she had wide interests with a great concern for the poor and for their education, an area sadly lacking at this time. It was her influence that resulted in the opening of an infants school, the first in the district, in August 1833. The school was held first in the disused Friends Meeting House on the Shire Hall site in High Street and was run by a committee of ladies, of whom she was secretary, and later moved into the small stone built schoolroom which still remains in Dew Street. It was through Mrs. Owen's efforts, too, that the first British Boys School (funded by the British Foreign School Society) opened in a chapel in Old Bridge Street (a school that functioned until the introduction of state aided schools). After taking care of the children her thoughts turned to their mothers — 'indigent women' — through the establishment of a Mothers' Friendly Society which raised subscriptions for their welfare and also ran Ladies Sewing Meetings to make clothes for the needy. The Temperance Movement which was introduced around 1836 also secured the support of the Owens, both by hosting meetings in their home and through their financial support.

Priory Mount Workhouse (another Owen design) was built in 1836, as a result of the Poor Law Amendment Act of 1834, in the year that Charles Dickens' *Oliver Twist* so graphically exposed the social inhumanities of his day. The workhouse (often called the Union) provided accommodation for destitutes and male and female itinerants who would be required to carry out tasks such as breaking stones for road making in return for their keep. Families were separated and discipline was harsh, and in 1883 there was a public outcry at conditions which were described as 'shocking', 'worse than a prison' and 'gloomy and depressing'.

The opening of the South-Wales Railway: The Narberth Road Station, Haverfordwest
'Success to the Railway' proclaim the banners in both Welsh and English, as Brunel's railway
arrives in Pembrokeshire (Roger Worsley)

After 1948, when the National Health Service took over responsibility for the care of the sick and the Workhouse became redundant under the National Assistance Act, the old building was used variously to house the chronic sick, as a geriatric hospital, as Fernlea Children's Home and as St. Thomas's Hospital where many of the town's babies were born, until in 1984 the listed building was converted into council flats.

With so many improvements planned in the 19th century this was a good time to be an architect and those working in Pembrokeshire seem to have been highly acclaimed. Even Haverfordwest's slaughterhouse at the Horse Fair was declared 'the best in Great Britain'. It all began in 1883. There had been a public enquiry into the need for a public abattoir when the inspector visited the existing slaughterhouses dotted all over the place, more or less in the farmyards themselves. He returned saying 'I want to see no more — it is enough for me what I have seen — very disgusting'. With the need established, Lord Kensington gave the abattoir site to the town, and with an alacrity all too familiar in local government the Borough Council held a special meeting more than a year later, on 23 January 1885. The architect appointed was Thomas Powis Reynolds who was also surveyor to Milford Urban District Council and the designer of a number of schools including Rosemarket School, Prendergast Board School and the old Taskers Girls School on Tower Hill.

The town's papermills in the 19th century when producing paper that was shipped to Bristol

The slaughterhouse was completed by January 1886 at a total cost of £2,600, money which had, once again, been borrowed to fund the project, and which they then had to set out to recoup. Mr. Dawkins' tender of £3 was accepted for the nine-month contract to remove the slaughterhouse manure, whilst the tanner, Mr. Richard Williams of Dew Street, was given permission to erect, at his own expense, a shed on the slaughterhouse grounds for storing hides at a rent of £1 10s. for a similar period. The fee for killing pigs under six score was set at 1s. for the first pig, then 6d. each for other pigs belonging to the same owner. Later it was agreed that the building should be lit by gas and, to improve ventilation, two iron-barred windows were fixed on one side. This may have improved conditions inside but nearby residents were soon complaining of offensive smells and David Edward Thomas, inspector of nuisances, was directed to immediately see to the removal of 'manure and excrement'. The slaughterhouse continued to operate until the 1960s after which it was used for a short time as a works depot by the District Council, but then fell into disuse and inevitable decay before it was converted to public housing.

The slaughterhouse had been built within easy reach of the cattle fair which took place on St. Thomas Green — a big event, even a social occasion, which extended up past Grove Place into Merlins Hill and so to the Horse Fair area. Much of the town's cattle, sheep and horse dealing was carried out at this fair and it is possible that the name Shipman's Lane, the lane linking Hill Street to St. Thomas Green, is derived from Sheepman's Lane, being the place where the collector of the dues on the sheep on their way to market was sited. Later, in the 1930s, the Haverfordwest Cattle Market moved to the bottom of the town to cater for the Irish trade.

The Cleddau as seen from the New Bridge at the beginning of the 20th century

Also prominent in the town in the late 19th century was Joseph Thomas who, when he was only 30, took over Richards' ironmongery in Quay Street and settled at Wilton House where he operated a corn and manure merchants' business. Known as 'Joe Flint' he left estate valued at £52,000 when he died, aged 88, in October 1910. He had been a Justice of the Peace, High Sheriff, a member of the council, mayor and was one of the first members of the County Council. He is, however, best remembered for his stand as an advocate of total abstinence. He opened the Temperance Tea Rooms with adjacent stables in Broad Haven and also built a school room in the village for non-denominational instruction and use as a Baptist Sunday School.

It seems that it was often the prosperous tradespeople who were the town's main benefactors. At the beginning of the 20th century 'a band of gentlemen who passionately loved Haverfordwest' set up an Improvements Committee which was notably responsible for providing their beloved town with the once beautiful walk at Scotchwells, since desecrated in the name of progress and the motor car to provide a car park. One member of the committee was the chemist T. Maddocks Phillips who donated the fine ornamental gates which led to the walk and to him fell the honour, on a brilliantly sunny day in June 1908, of performing the opening ceremony with a silver key which was then presented to him 'to be preserved by his descendants as a memorial to his lavish generosity and our undying gratitude'. Five hundred flags had been hired from Swansea to add colour to a splendid occasion and a pair of royal swans, the gift of King Edward VII, floated regally on the waters of the leet. Everyone who was anyone — and the general public too — was there, enjoying a public tea with seating for 200 people as they listened to the band of the Wiltshire Regiment.

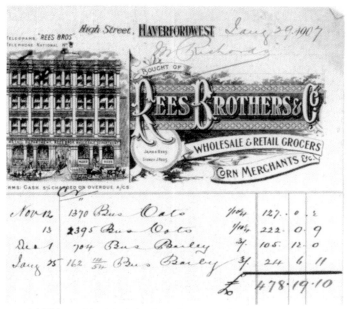

High Street, HAVERFORDWEST

TELEGRAMS 'REES BROS'
TELEPHONE NATIONAL N°

BOUGHT OF

REES BROTHERS & C°

WHOLESALE & RETAIL GROCERS

CORN MERCHANTS &c.

TERMS: CASH 5% CHARGED ON OVERDUE A/CS

Nov 12	1370 Bus Oats	1/10¼	127.	0	2
13	2395 Bus Oats	1/10¼	222.	0	9
Dec 1	704 Bus Barley	3/	105.	12	0
Jan 25	162 ⁴⁄₅₆ Bus Barley	3/	24.	6	11
		£	478.	19.	10

A bill issued in 1907 by Rees Bros and Co, one of the town's major businesses, who employed a commercial traveller, James Oliver, to tour the farms and village shops by horse and trap seeking orders for the wholesale business. Their errand boy, Sid Bowler, later took over the grocery business which remained 'Bowlers' until after the Second World War. The greater part of the facade of this fine building remains unchanged

The scheme was to have cost £300, and a public appeal brought in £236 10s. 1d. together with £78 worth of gifts. A further appeal eventually raised the extra £64 and a guaranteed £50 *per annum* to pay a man £1 a week to look after the walks which were on land leased from Sir Charles and Lady Philipps of Picton Castle at a nominal rent of 5s. a year.

Secretary of the committee was grocer Sidney Rees who, in 1923, first offered to buy the Bridge Meadow for £1,000 which he would then convey to Haverfordwest Borough Council to enable them to create a public recreation park. Terms were finally agreed in June 1938 and, determined that there should be no misunderstandings, either then or in the future, he would not sign the conveyance until it was entirely to his liking. Some crystal-ball foresight made him ask his solicitors 'You will not forget to insert in the deeds that the Corporation cannot sell or allow the field to be built on, on any consideration. You never know what future Corporations are going to be like in 40-50 years hence, when we are under the daisies.'

Forty-six years later a storm of controversy and protest greeted Welsh Office road proposals which included compulsory purchase of a part of the Bridge Meadow (the town's football ground and site of the Community Centre), but today the much loved Bridge Meadow is lost to the town, for the road scheme went ahead and the ground which was once valuable open space has been developed as a shopping complex. The building of one new road, Thomas Parry Way, did, however, lead to the discovery of a forgotten part of the town's history. Finds of 22 mediaeval and post-mediaeval coins on the site of the road suggest that this area of Haverford may have been a mediaeval market place, something of which there had been no previous knowledge. The finds included coins covering eight reigns, a period of over 400 years, and a lead seal bearing the name Alice. Some of the coins had been cut into halves or quarters, a means of creating halfpennies and farthings at a time when smaller value coins were either rare or not minted at all. This problem was also overcome by citizens and traders issuing their own small denomination tokens. One of the latter, a Haverfordwest copper token farthing issued by T.B. Boulton, 'Gentleman of Haverfordwest', was found on a local beach.

Older residents of Haverfordwest complain that much of what was good and of historic value has been lost. In 1992, Bill Richards, a man with 50 years experience as a Pembrokeshire newspaper reporter wrote in *Changing Face of Haverfordwest*:

> Looked at from any angle, what has happened in Haverfordwest in less than twenty years is breathtaking. Layouts which had existed for hundreds of years have gone; many buildings familiar to succeeding generations of townspeople have fallen before the bulldozer, sports areas have been changed; and replacing all this are the so-called modern amenities such as huge roundabouts; new shops in new locations; under-passes and an overhead pedestrian crossing; a multi-deck car park built in stone (it has been described as Colditz!) which blots out the view of Haverfordwest's majestic Norman castle from Cartlett Road; a pedestrian area at Old Bridge now renamed 'Riverside Quay', 'Old Bridge Square'; and not forgetting an avalanche of pebbles which descended upon the town to act as a sort of decoration of the central reservation in Cartlett Road and at other places. ... All this has drastically changed the face of Haverfordwest for ever. Only history will decide whether it was right or wrong.

Haverfordwest does, however, remain the county town and administrative centre of Pembrokeshire; shopping developments along the river keep up with the times, local produce is on sale in the fortnightly Farmers' Market as well as in privately owned local shops and its long history is recorded in the Town Museum which functions alongside the ruins of the castle. Haverfordwest is still beloved by its people.

Chapter 5

Pembroke Dock

Because of the problem of piracy in the early 14th century much pressure was put on the Privy Council to fortify Milford Haven, and it was around this time that the tower house at Angle (known locally as The Old Rectory but also as The Pele Tower) was erected as part of the home of a well-to-do family with property to protect, for Angle, nestling in its secluded inlet, was particularly vulnerable to attack from pirates.

It was possibly the residence of the Sherbourne family who had been granted various lands in the vicinity in 1278. They were Lords of Angle in the 14th century and it may be that this fortified home was partially a status symbol advertising their wealth and importance, for it was more than a lookout tower or emergency refuge, being a substantial mediaeval home with accommodation on three floors, a fireplace in each room, an undercroft and a garderobe. The only entrance was the doorway on the first floor, reached across a drawbridge. An overhanging parapet was supported by stone corbels round the top of the tower. North of the tower there are traces of a walled enclosure with a moat, covering the area where Castle Farm is today. Of the original building only the one tower and a nearby mediaeval dovecote

Tower House, Angle, in 1999
(Martin Cavaney Photography)

71

remain, both restored in 2000 by the Pembrokeshire Coast National Park Authority with grant aid from the Heritage Lottery Fund and Cadw (Welsh Historic Monuments) and it is now open to the public with access by permission of the owners, Mr. and Mrs. Rees of Castle Farm. The tower, now a Grade 1 listed monument, is Wales's only surviving example of a true tower house although they are to be found in abundance across the water in Ireland and there are others in the border counties of northern England and Scotland — as well as in southern Greece.

Because of the military importance of the Haven fortification plans were constantly under consideration, particularly at times of national crisis when fear of invasion caused panic in high places. All too often, though, the danger had passed before work even began and the plans

Inside the Tower House, Angle (RCAHMW)

were shelved. On other occasions work started and was abandoned, on others the type of defence was overtaken by advances in the style of warfare and the fortifications became obsolete because of the increasing range and effectiveness of artillery.

Thomas Cromwell has been credited with being the first to order the surveying of the harbour with a view to its possible fortification. The result was the construction, in 1580, of the two blockhouses — West Blockhouse at Dale and East Blockhouse at Angle — on opposite sides of the entrance to the Haven as part of an overall scheme for coastal defences which did not progress further, despite a national fear of invasion in 1595.

The historian and author George Owen, who was Deputy Lord Lieutenant and Deputy Vice-Admiral of Pembrokeshire, had prepared a plan in 1595 based on the triangle of Thorn Island, Dale Point and Stack Rock, but it was very many years before the basic concept of siting the forts to cover one another with crossfire was implemented.

It was not until the Civil War that the next fort, an armed encampment and gun enplacement at Pill, was constructed by the Royalists for the defence of this inlet anchorage. It remained an earthwork until the 1990s when it was removed to make way for building on the site. Talking and discussions continued and even went as far as to produce a report in 1689 that stressed the need for fortification of the harbour. Sixty years later there were suggestions (but again no action) for small forts at Stack Rock and Great Castle Head.

Overlooking Dale, from a postcard of the 1930s

A visit by William Pitt the Elder dashed hopes of any major development of the area when he declared the Haven too broad to be defended by shore based guns and it took the outbreak of war in 1756 to concentrate Privy Council minds (Pitt was by this time Secretary of State with management of war) into panic proposals for six forts or batteries to be built around the Haven, together with a floating battery anchored 500 yards north of Chapel Bay. This scheme was not only too expensive but was also impractical as cannon range was then only around 500 yards which rendered the defence potential ineffectual. However, the authorities forged ahead with part of the plan and land was purchased at Paterchurch (Pembroke Dock), Llanion and Neyland to accommodate three forts. Work was actually begun on the Paterchurch fort when, in 1759, the threat of invasion passed, and it was not completed.

The first vessels were built in the dockyard at Milford Haven in the closing years of the 18th century, yet even for the first three years of the 19th century it was left to a battery of guns on either side of what is now the town of Milford Haven to provide protection for the new venture. There had been some alarm following the French invasion of Fishguard in 1797, even though the invaders were rapidly repelled (see pp.136-8) and when the Royal Naval Dockyard moved to Pembroke Dock in 1813 the strategic importance of the waterway increased. More talks on defence were initiated in 1817, and again in 1828, yet again in 1829 and finally, in 1830, the partly built Paterchurch fort was completed and garrisoned, only to be dismantled six years later.

Further fears of the motives of the French with the rise of Napoleon III eventually resulted in the fort being renovated to the plans of a young lieutenant of the Royal Engineers who was resident in Pembroke Dock for a short time before embarking for the Crimean War. He later found fame as General Gordon of Khartoum.

After years of procrastination, an intensive period of fortification began with 11 of the 14 haven forts being built during a 20-year period. In the mid-1850s a three-gun

tower was built at Stack Rock, a tower that still remains but is enveloped by casemated work that was added ten years later. The tower had a basement for stores and the magazine, and, at ground-floor level, the main gun battery. The first floor provided accommodation for a garrison of an officer and 30 men. The additions to the fort were completed in 1871 at a total cost of £96,840. At this time the ground floor had the entrance and the casemated battery covering the Haven where 16 10-inch Rifled Muzzle Loader (RML) guns were mounted behind armoured shields. In the back entrance of the gorge (the rear face of the fort) were three 9-inch RML guns with magazines and stores underneath the casemated battery. Casemated barracks for five officers and 175 men faced inwards above the gun casemates at first-floor level and in the gorge was a casemated battery for four 9-inch RMLs. Plans for three turrets mounting two 25-ton guns in each never came to fruition.

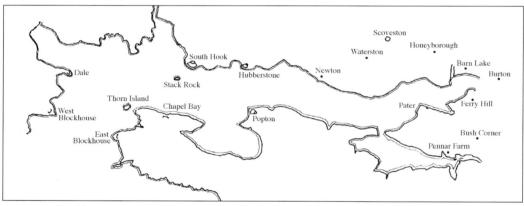

Map showing the location of the various suggested defensive works, not all of them built. One of the reasons advanced by the Admiralty for siting the dockyard at Pembroke Dock had been the ease with which it could be defended, for its Martello towers, ten forts, the Pater battery of 23 guns and the Defensible Barracks on the hill overlooking the yards made it one of the best defended bases in the UK. By the time of the 1858 report on the Sea Defence of Milford Haven and Pembroke Dock the existing defences were: West Blockhouse Point: six guns; Dale Point Battery: nine guns; Thorn Island Battery: nine guns; Stack Rock Tower: three guns; Pater Battery: 23 guns; Two towers: one and three guns; Defensible Barracks

Stack Rock Fort around 1865 as casemated work was under way enveloping the original tower

The gateway to the Defensible Barracks in 2001

This era of fort building culminated with Scoveston Fort. The moated defensible barracks on the hill above the town (developed at a cost of £80,000) initially provided accommodation for the Royal Marines of the Portsmouth Division who had previously been stationed in the cramped quarters of the old wooden battleship, the *Dragon*. Two of the 14 forts were Martello towers, one erected off the Hard at Front Street and the other on the western approaches to the dockyard, the former armed with a 32-pounder brass gun and four 12-pounder brass howitzers, and the latter with three guns. The towers were occupied by sergeants of the artillery with their families and gun crews, but were obsolete by 1905 when they were used merely for storage.

The contract for building the towers in 1849 went to Joseph and Charles Rigby of London who brought their workforce with them. Many of these men married and settled in the town where their skills and those of their descendants contributed to the growth of this dockyard town.

One of these craftsmen, William Noakes, born in Sussex early in the 19th century, was a carpenter by trade and rose to become under-foreman with the London firm. He was the father of a daughter and five sons, one of whom, David, lived to the great age of 102 when he was believed to be the oldest man in Wales. During his long life he married twice and sired 21 children, leaving 50 grandchildren at the time of his death.

In an interview on his hundredth birthday David Noakes recalled the move to

The Defensible Barracks in 2001. The building was sold in the mid-1980s for £20,000 to property developers who had plans to convert it into an hotel run on military lines.
The plan never materialised and the building now houses the South Pembrokeshire Golf Club and a number of flats

The Martello tower by Front Street in 1861 with the Great Eastern *in the distance*

The Martello tower on the western approach to the dockyard

Pembroke Dock in 1849. The family travelled by sea to Tenby where a horse and cart waited to take them on to Pembroke Dock. Most of the houses then, he said, were small two-roomed cottages. He had left school at the age of 12 to learn the butchery trade (in the 1881 census he was living at New Slaughterhouse, in Pembroke Dock) with John Eastlake, who had secured the government contract to supply all the meat required by the regiments garrisoned in Pembroke Dock. 'When the wooden warships, sailing and steam, used to put in to Pembroke Dock I would kill 30 animals a day to supply them', he said. 'I did the killing for 35 years'.

Direct descendants of William and David Noakes still live in Pembroke Dock and other branches of the family are to be found throughout Pembrokeshire. Many worked in the

The Martello tower off Front Street, now used as a Tourist Information Centre. Notice the cart being used to unload the ketch on the right

dockyard and one son, John, was bailiff and mace bearer to Pembroke's mayor and corporation, an office also held for some years by his son Frederick.

The naval dockyard had initially been established in Milford Haven where seven vessels were built between 1806 and 1814. Under the direction of French trained Louis Barrallier, the *Nautilus* and *Lavinia* had been built and launched there as well as the 74-gun *Milford* and it was hoped that these successes would secure the Milford Dockyard, but shortly after the launch of the 74-gun *Rochefort* in April 1814 the Admiralty decided to transfer their lease on the Milford Haven Dockyard to Pater. It is said that their decision was due to a dispute with the developers of the new town of Milford, when Robert Fulke Greville refused to agree the Admiralty's valuation of £4,455, a sum which had been agreed by his brother Charles who died before the deal had been completed. This was a devastating blow to the town where William Hamilton's plans (see chapter 10) were already facing delays and bankruptcies.

This was a time when the art and science of shipbuilding was more advanced on the continent and French and Spanish warships were better that those built in Britain. Only too well aware of this situation the Admiralty opened the Royal Navy's first School of Naval Architecture in Portsmouth in 1810 and possibly aimed to establish a brand new model dockyard in the Haven, free of what has been described as the 'hidebound traditions, stultifying conservatism and legendary corruption of the Royal Dockyards'.

Initially all the fitting and building at Pater was done in the open air, with just one slipway on the sheltered deep water close inshore, and administered from an office sited in the old frigate *Lapwing* which had been run ashore for the purpose. Gradually more slipways and dry docks were added. In 1816 a small crowd watched the launch of the 28-gun *Valorous* and her sister-ship the *Ariadne*, the latter remembered as the vessel commanded by Captain Frederick Marryat, who, after an adventurous career during which he won the Royal Humane Society's Gold Medal for Bravery, resigned to concentrate on writing. He drew on his experiences to write *Mr. Midshipman Easy* and children's books such as *Masterman Ready*.

By 1816 it was the only dockyard in the country that was expanding and shipwrights from Portsmouth and Plymouth who had been laid off by these south coast yards began to flood into the area. At its height the dockyard employed over 2,000 men and, with its 13 building slips, it came to be described as 'the first shipbuilding yard in the world'. The town grew as accommodation was desperately needed for the wives and families coming into the area. To meet this need the workers started building their own homes in Bush Street, which became known locally as 'Pig's Parade' because of the squalid nature of the hastily thrown up shacks. Four houses had already been built on what is now Front Street for the Foreman of Shipwrights, the Foreman of Blacksmiths, the Issuer of Stores and a publican — this latter house now believed to be the *Shipwright Inn*, formerly the *King's Arms*. The dates tally. In *The Pubs of Pembroke, Tenby and South Pembrokeshire* Keith Johnson notes that the first reference to the pub was in the *Carmarthen Journal* in 1824.

The influx of workers also brought a demand for provisions for their families and around 1826 the Admiralty, not entirely out of the goodness of their hearts, agreed, at

Buildings dating from the hey-day of the naval dockyard

considerable expense, to build the stone Market Hall, a structure which did not then find favour with the townspeople but which is still standing and still a feature of the town. (A proposal in 1953 to convert the building into a light engineering factory never materialised.) By ancient charter the right to trade within the Borough of Pembroke, which included the dockyard, was reserved for the Freemen of the Borough. In addition to the building costs the Admiralty had to pay the Freemen £3,000 to breach their monopoly. There had been a deal that the Admiralty would build the market in return for being allowed to construct the huge dockyard wall.

By the time the Duke of Clarence (later King William IV) visited the yard for the launch of the *Clarence* in 1827, a total of 32 vessels had been built there by the workers drawn from across the country.

In accordance with the rules for a naval establishment the dockyard had to provide a means for public worship. The old *Lapwing* which had been in use for offices and storage was later used for Sunday services, and when the old vessel was broken up in 1828 services took place for three years in a wooden shed until it was replaced by the 1,000-seater Garrison Chapel. This fine building, designed by naval architect George Ledwell Taylor had a gallery on either side and

The Garrison Chapel prior to restoration

on the west end, a nave, two side aisles, a chancel, choir stalls and sanctuary. The Dockyard Choir sang before the Duke of Clarence during his visit and in the 1870s on Sunday mornings the Pembroke Dock Garrison worshipped at the chapel, and the regiments at the Defensible Barracks and at the Hut Encampment near Hobbs Point marched to and from the chapel, headed by the band.

The last service was at Christmas 1879 after which the congregation joined the service at St. Johns Church and from then on the old building had a chequered career. It came back into use with the arrival of the flying boats, was an RAF Garrison Theatre during the Second World War, was neglected again after the departure of the RAF and for a short time was revived as a

The Garrison Chapel after restoration. (Photograph by Acanthus Holden Architects, award winners for best reuse of a Georgian building, 2008)

Motor Museum. In recent years it became derelict and the victim of vandalism with its rare domed roof stripped of lead, and the building — believed to be the only surviving Georgian classical church in south Wales — was gutted. Today, as part of the Pembroke Dock Townscape Heritage Initiative, the Garrison Chapel, a focal point of the old Royal Dockyard, along with other fine stone Georgian structures including the Market Hall and the dock wall, has been restored to its former splendour.

In 1860, there began a revolution in both shipbuilding and in defence with the launch from a commercial Thames shipyard of the *Warrior*, the first iron-built battleship in the world, which brought about the final days of the old wooden battleships and a major change in the long history of marine warfare. The vessel was ordered because of the French war scare of the 1850s, and was considered so vital to the future of the Navy that the Thames ironworks received a subsidy of £50,000 to prevent the business going bankrupt during its construction. The *Warrior* was the biggest, fastest and best armed ship on the seas and her 4½-inch armour plating backed by 18 inches of seasoned teak made her invulnerable to any cannon afloat. All the lifeboat and capstan handling was by manpower, with 90 of the 700 crew needed on the bars to the upper deck capstan, stamping in unison as they heaved to music.

The advent of such vessels meant that the Haven's forts had to be remodelled to accommodate 7-inch muzzle loaders in the hope that they would prove the most effective weapons for countering the 'ironclads'. Fortunately these outmoded fortresses, several on ground where there is evidence of fortresses going back to the Bronze Age, were never put to the test. Indeed they saw little use until the First World War when they

Admiral Sir G. Tryon's ships (the A Squadron) anchoring in the Haven,
from a drawing published in 1889

were garrisoned for coastal and, eventually, air defence, while the Second World War saw many of them serve as anti-aircraft batteries. Today most are derelict, although Dale Fort has long been established as a Field Study Centre and West Blockhouse has been restored as holiday accommodation managed by the Landmark Trust.

Work is also under way to restore Chapel Bay, a scheduled ancient monument which was completed in 1891 as a coastal defence battery at a cost of £11,779. The first in the UK to be built principally from mass concrete it had at that time provision

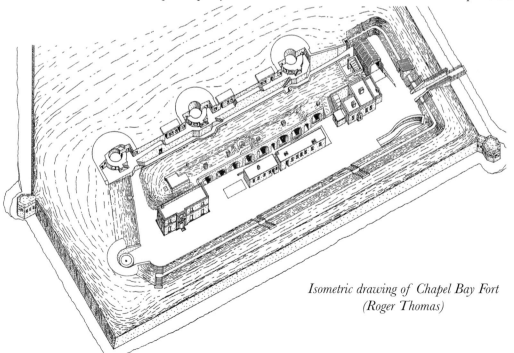

Isometric drawing of Chapel Bay Fort
(Roger Thomas)

to accommodate seven officers and 84 men in time of war. During the First World War the fort was the examination battery for Milford Haven, ensuring that no ships entered or left the port without authority. It was disarmed in 1920. Standing high over the Haven this extensive fort with a 35-foot deep dry moat and a maze of underground tunnels was acquired in 1994 by military historian Major George Geear as the beginning of a £1.6m restoration project which is administered by the registered charity Chapel Bay Fort and Museum. Among the collection of weaponry that will be on display once the museum is completed, is one of the fort's original three 10-inch, 18-ton, rifled muzzle loading guns, the largest of its kind in Wales, which

Chapel Bay Fort.
Top: One of the three original 10-inch guns
(Adam Robinson)
Middle: 6-inch gun emplacement (Roger Thomas)
Bottom: 4-5inch gun (Roger Thomas)
Right: The south-east caponier and drawbridge
(Roger Thomas)

was recovered from the sea below the fort. Also to be included is a Depression Range Finder designed to train the fort's guns on the enemy, the only remaining complete and original one to have carried out service in a fort. While it never sustained damage through enemy action this 19th-century fort had long been the victim not only of natural decay but also of mindless vandalism. Working under the auspices of a project called Military Aid to the Civic Community, the 170 (infrastructure Support) Engineer Group of the Royal Engineers has removed 1,200 tons of rubbish from a section of the moat while a small team of volunteers continue to work steadily on the buildings which already have the feel of the privations of the life of the men who were stationed at Chapel Bay.

Nearby is the now privately owned Rocket Cart House with its coastguard lookout tower. The rocket gear used by the Pembrokeshire Life Saving Apparatus Company to propel a line out to rig a breeches buoy onto a wrecked vessel and so haul survivors to safety was housed in the building, and carried by horse and cart to the site of the disaster. The rocket was developed by Henry Trengrouse after he witnessed the drowning of the crew of *HMS Anson* in a storm off the Cornish coast in 1807, and one of the 44 main guns on board the *Anson* is now in Major Geear's collection. Rocket Cart House remained in use for its original purpose until the 1930s and then was used as a look-out post in the Second World War.

The *Warrior* that was the herald of change in the Milford Haven waterway spent the last years of her long service in the Haven where she was put to use as a floating pontoon for the Admiralty oil tanks at Llanion. She later lay in the waters of the estuary for many years, a rotting hulk, before being restored to her former glory in 1980 and going on permanent display near Nelson's *Victory* at Portsmouth.

There had been considerable fears that the advent of the ironclads would sound the death knell of the Pembroke Dockyard, where the skills lay in building wooden ships. The Pembrokeshire yard, distant from major ironworks and 'at the end of the line' — a problem encountered over and over again in today's rapidly changing economy — seemed an all too probable choice for closure. Just a few years before the *Warrior* came

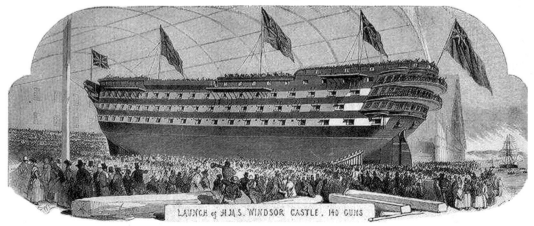

The launch of HMS Windsor Castle *in 1852. The vessel was re-named* HMS Duke of Wellington *following Wellington's death at the time of the launch (Pembrokeshire Life Photograph)*

off the stocks in London the *Windsor Castle* was launched at Pembroke Dock — on the day in 1852 when the Duke of Wellington died. When the news reached the Admiralty it was decided, in tribute to the great general, to change the name of this 140-gun three-decker screw vessel to *Duke of Wellington*. For a brief period this woodenwall battleship was the most powerful warship in the world.

In *The Book of Pembroke Dock* Phil Carradice records that this huge vessel was remarkable for the fact that mid-way through completion it was decided to extend her length to provide extra displacement for engines and boilers. The hull was cut into two separate sections, the rear portion launched into the Haven and positioned 23 feet away from the front half. A new middle section was then built. Although she was fitted with a screw propeller, the first really large vessel to be so equipped, she retained her masts and sails and remained very much a wooden sailing ship.

Alongside the dockyard, the town of Pembroke Dock had grown into the largest township in the county. The original settlement known as Pater (or Patrick) Church, consisted of just a few cottages, some barren land 'not worth 5s. an acre', and a small church built by the Knights Hospitaller which was later used for seamen's missions.

At this time, however, Pembroke Dock was not a naval base. Hulls were launched and despatched to Plymouth for fitting out and completion including the installation of machinery, and rarely returned to the Haven. Concerned for future employment the public directed petitions at the Admiralty requesting that the dockyard should be equipped to fit out the vessels completely. The also asked for a receiving ship (an old warship or hulk used to accommodate recruits until they were drafted to sea-going vessels) to be stationed at Pembroke.

The dockyard had developed despite the transport problems which meant that some consignments would take three weeks to arrive from London, but the distance from engineering centres made the fitting out of vessels uneconomic and it was felt there were insufficient potential recruits to justify a receiving ship. Fortunately the town acquired its railway link in 1864, the year in which the government decided to concentrate

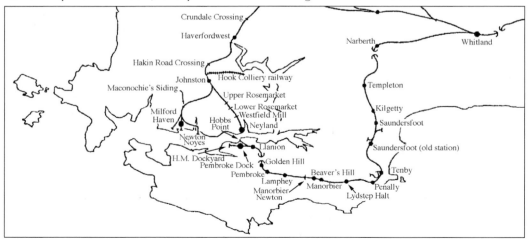

Map showing the full extent of the railway lines that eventually reached the Haven

its shipbuilding in fewer centres. The rail link secured Pembroke Dock's position as an important dockyard, and the axe fell on the yards at Deptford and Woolwich. It was a stay of execution for the yard which had employed around 1,000 men in 1855 when the Royal Dockyard was one of the biggest employers in the county. Work began energetically to re-equip the yards and retrain the workforce to specialise in building composite gunboats such as the *Bullfrog* and the *Cockchafer*, both launched in February 1881, in which wooden planking was laid across their iron frames.

The very size of the workforce and the nature of the work meant that the Admiralty had responsibility for providing medical care at a dockyard surgery for the treatment of industrial injuries and until 1895, when facilities were provided on shore, the more serious cases were sent to the dockyard hospital ship, the ageing *HMS Nankin*. The vessel was replaced by a naval hospital ashore which was later used as a wartime military hospital and is now modernised as the South Pembrokeshire District Hospital.

In 1874 Edward J. Reed (later Sir Edward) former Chief Constructor of the Royal Navy stood as Conservative candidate for Pembroke Boro, promising that, if he was elected, he would build a private dockyard in Pennar. He was returned with a 29 majority and kept his promise by setting up Milford Haven Ship Building and Engineering Company in Jacob's Pill (named after a Jacob Jenkins who used to live in the vicinity of the creek).

With Pembrokeshire's economy in great need of inward investment today there is always hope of attracting Japanese money, possibly repeating the events of 1877 when the Japanese Ambassador, representing the Mikado, visited Pembroke Dock for the launch of the armoured corvette *Hi Yeti* which had been built at the new Pennar yard. The vessel had been ordered by a Japanese shogun but by the time it was completed the power of the warrior lords had waned, feudalism had been replaced by imperial power and the *Hi Yeti* was appropriated to become a part of the new Imperial Japanese Navy.

Four royal yachts were built at the shipyard during Victoria's reign. The second of them, a luxurious vessel designed to combine lightness and strength, was constructed mainly of mahogany and East India teak, the decks laid with Canada fir planks with felt between the beams and the deck to deaden sound. It was launched prematurely on a cold January day in 1855, uncompleted because in the days of the Crimean War the slip was needed for laying down the *Alma*, one of a new line of battleships, its name commemorating the Anglo-French land victory the previous year. (Although when the keel was laid down the battleship was described as the *Alma* there is no record of the launch of a vessel of that name. However three battleships, the *Sutle, Brunswick* and *Repulse* were launched in April, June and September 1855).

With war still uppermost in government minds six gunboats came off the slips in Pembroke Dock during the months of February and March 1856, by which time, however, Sevastopol had fallen and the Treaty of Paris had been signed.

There had been moves nationally in 1848 to raise brigades and battalions for the defence of the ports where Royal Dockyards were sited and so the Pembroke Dock Brigade of the Royal Dockyard Corps came into being. Its officers and other ranks were drawn from men of various grades working in the dockyard, the 'private men'

HMS Defence, *launched at Pembroke Dock on 27 April 1907. An armoured cruiser, she served as the flagship of the 1st cruiser squadron under Rear Admiral Sir Robert Arbuthnot which also comprised the vessels* HMS Warrior, HMS Duke of Edinburgh *(both also built at Pembroke Dock) and* HMS Black Prince. *She was hit by two salvos in the battle of Jutland and disappeared in a cloud of smoke. Admiral Arbuthnot and 900 officers and men were lost with the shop.* HMS Warrior *and* HMS Black Prince *were also sunk*

receiving one shilling per drill or exercise period attended. Retired senior Royal Marine NCOs acted as adjutants and instructors to the Government- funded brigade's Infantry, Artillery, Engineer and Boat sections. Although the sections trained individually they appeared together from time to time accompanied by the Brigade band. The Royal Dockyard Corps formed an important part of the district's defence during the Crimean War (1854-1856) but seems not to have survived beyond 1857.

Over the years the dockyard was the scene of a number of royal visits. In May 1899 Princess Mary (later Queen Mary) launched the yacht *Victoria and Albert*, the last of the four royal yachts to be built at the yard. In August 1902 the royal visitors were King Edward VII and Queen Alexandra. This was a momentous occasion for one 13-

Fitting out a 'County' class cruiser at Hobbs Point in 1912

The fire at Pembroke Dockyard on 24 June 1922

year-old dockyard employee, J. Rossiter, who had to run from the dockyard to the Head Post Office with a telegram announcing that the king had arrived safely at the main landing stage. This lad was one of 17 children and his wages were vital to help support his brothers and sisters.

Unfortunately for Pembroke Dock and the whole of the surrounding area the boom years did not last, the yard closing in 1926. Over a period of 106 years more than 260 ships were built in the yard from the time of the first two in February 1816 to the Admiralty oiler *Oleander* in 1922, a vessel which sank in Harstead Bay, Norway in 1944 after being damaged by German dive bombers.

At its peak the whole establishment covered around 90 acres and in 1890 the workforce of 2,092 included joiners, millwrights, blacksmiths, plumbers, coppersmiths, wheelwrights, painters, patternmakers and men whose skills lay in the armour-plating shops. About 200 workers were employed in the blacksmith's shop alone. But in a recession in 1906, 700 men lost their jobs and a serious fire in the summer of 1922 brought the end of the viable days of the dockyard even closer. Valuable records stored in the Moor Loft were lost as well as a precious collection of warship figureheads from Victorian times and earlier.

The status of the establishment was reduced to 'Care and Maintenance' and four years later it closed altogether. Many of the skilled workers left the area and much of the yard fell into disrepair. There was no work anywhere for these specialist skills. The closure led to many bankruptcies in all sections of the community. The baker and grocer Hugh Edward Hall of Main Street, Pembroke, blamed bad trade caused by the closure of the dockyard, heavy bank charges and the high running cost of his motor vehicles for his £4,000 bankruptcy. In Milford, Daniel Victor Hughes, a marine store dealer on the docks, attributed his losses to depression in trade, the coal strike and losses on the purchase of a trawler.

Llangwm born Jim John, a shipwright rigger whose father William had been a rigger at the dockyard, found work as a ganger at Hook Colliery. With his fellow miners

Cargo ships laid up in Pennar Gut, 1923

he survived a water break-in at the pit but his working days underground ended when an accident with a tram left him permanently disabled. Jim John, however, found other work and went on to become a highly respected Alderman, County Councillor and Rural District Councillor in addition to being regarded locally as the 'uncrowned king of Llangwm'.

In the early 1930s the establishment of a flying boat base brought some help, while at peak periods some 200 men were employed by shipbreakers Thomas W. Ward who leased part of the yard from the Admiralty in 1932. But many skilled workers, if they could find any work at all, were forced to take labouring jobs as Wards demolished the giant sheer legs and the granite block dockyard buildings which were later replaced by brick-built barracks for RAF personnel. The ship-breaking work and what employment it brought extended to Ward's Castle Works at Pill, Milford Haven, where the larger vessels of 12,000 tons and over were towed for further breaking once the initial work had been carried out at Pembroke Dock's Carr Jetty. The work at this time was all destruction as opposed to the construction of the previous 100 years. The town where so many fine vessels had been built became their graveyard and there was drama and near disaster when the last Admiralty vessel to be scrapped there turned turtle in the dock with workmen on board.

This vessel, the submarine *XI*, had never been commissioned but was one of the largest built up to that time. One of those on board was an apprentice, Laverick Breeze, who in his retirement in 1982 described some of the work of Wards Yard in an article which appeared in the *West Wales Guardian*. 'The last liner and cargo ship to be broken', he recalled, 'was the *Waxahatchi* in 1938. Her holds were full of scrap metal from

America. Ironically most of the scrap went to Germany, probably later to be dropped on Pembroke Dock in the form of a mine or a bomb!'

He described the gallery of the former Gunnery Shop with its wooden block floor. Here joiners, cabinet makers, carpenters and shipwrights — all ex-Dockyard men — made use of the teak, mahogany and pitch pine to turn out household and garden furniture, fruit bowls and garden gates. Much of the furniture bore a brass plate recording the vessel from which the wood had been recycled and sold well to the people who had sailed on those ships. Wards generated their own electricity supply using the old Test House as the generating station and after the whole of the electrical ventilation system had been dismantled the parts were sold to Hong Kong, while electric motors, control gear and other machinery was sold after being reconditioned. When liners came in for breaking the luxury furnishings were sold by Bowlings of Pembroke Dock. During the war the firm also supplied BOC with oxygen.

As a 14-year-old apprentice, whose father was a crane driver at the yard, Laverick received 10s. a week (with 2d. deducted for the nurses' home) while labourers were paid £2 and craftsmen £3 7s. 6d. To get to work he left his home in Port Lion at 5.30am and cycled to Neyland where he joined 13 other employees who rowed over in a boat they rented from Wards, each paying 1s. a week which was deducted from their wages. The young lad was not allowed to row, the big oars would have taken him overboard, and his chore was baling — something which kept him busy throughout the trip. When eventually the antiquated boat sank they had to resort to using the ferry!

However even this modest contribution to the local economy did not last. The deep recession in the steel industry in 1935 drastically reduced the amount of work coming into the yard. In order to retain their workforce Wards introduced a policy of one week on and one week off — a gesture which was appreciated by the workforce who had feared total unemployment for very many of their number.

While it is the Sunderland flying boat that is best remembered at Pembroke Dock's RAF base, maritime aircraft had used the waterway during the First World War and as early as 1927 there was speculation that there was to be an RAF base at the old dockyard.

The yard had closed in 1926 and was transferred to the Air Ministry in 1930 to establish the RAF base which, over the following years, was to be an important element in the Boro's (as it is still known locally) recovery. The establishment began in a small way with two Southampton flying boats, but by the outbreak of war in 1939 it was fully operational and during the mid-war years P.D. (as it rapidly became known to the services) became the largest operational flying boat base in the world. Manned not only by the RAF but also by airmen of the Canadian and Australian air forces, Sunderlands went out on patrol, helping to combat the attacks of the German U-boats on merchant ships, protecting the convoys and helping to keep open the western sea lanes.

John Evans in *Pembrokeshire County History (Vol IV)* writes that on one occasion 99 flying boats were on the water or in servicing areas around Pembroke Dock and Neyland on the opposite shore, where part of the railway yard was converted for the purpose and a slipway had been specially built.

In November 1940 a Rochester built Mark 1 Sunderland T9044 sank at its moorings during an 80mph gale just a few weeks after joining 210 Squadron. At the time no trace was found of the aircraft, but in 2001 Celtic Divers reported that they had discovered a Sunderland wreck in the Haven after which a Bristol Pegasus radial engine, complete with three-bladed propeller was recovered and, following many hours of conservation work, these are now on display in the Gun Tower Museum. An estimated two-thirds of the fuselage — turrets, two engines and at least one float — remain buried in the sea bed. These are protected under by-laws of the Milford Haven Port Authority with a 100m exclusion zone placed around the site, preventing divers and fishermen operating in this area. The Sunderland has been listed under the 'Adopt a Wreck' scheme and the *Pembroke Dock Sunderland Trust* was formed with plans to raise what is now the only Mark 1 Sunderland left in the world and the aim of setting up a permanent centre in Pembroke Dock for a Battle of the Atlantic exhibition with the aircraft as the main exhibit. This is a massive and costly enterprise but the expertise is available. A Heritage Lottery Fund grant enabled a full technical survey in 2007 and there are hopes of European money to help pay for completion of the project.

War not only brought the Sunderlands and the armed forces to Pembroke Dock, it also brought the Luftwaffe. Pembroke Dock was an early casualty of the attentions of the German air force with its first raid coming in July 1940, a minor event in comparison with what was to follow. There were no casualties, apart from scores of fish, because one bomb fell into the water between Neyland and Pembroke Dock while others fell harmlessly round the 17 oil tanks at Llanreath.

Further raids followed and while, at this stage, no-one was killed or injured, property was damaged, fear set in and a number of the townspeople began to leave the town to sleep. Controversy raged, even through the medium of the local press, between those who left and those who were unable to do so. But as the number of raids escalated the town became almost deserted at night time.

It was on 19 August 1940 that the German planes were successful in their attempts on the oil tanks, causing a fire which blazed for 18 days with clouds of dense black smoke filling the sky. Fire bombs had destroyed 11 tanks, each with a capacity of 12,000 tons of oil, with an explosion that could be heard in Haverfordwest while the flames and smoke were visible as far away as the Devonshire coast.

During the inferno five firemen died and hundreds of the 600 men from the 22 brigades in attendance were injured. Leading the Pembroke Dock Fire Brigade was their Chief Officer, Arthur Morris, who with his men was first on the scene and who remained on duty throughout the conflagration — a hero to the people of the town. Once again there was much local controversy when it was learned that neither he nor his brigade were among those awarded bravery medals.

During later raids more property was destroyed but, miraculously, without loss of life until a direct hit killed an elderly couple in their grocery business in Bush Street. Bill Richards, formerly chief reporter of the *West Wales Guardian* who was living in the town at the time of the raids, wrote afterwards:

As the hordes came over the big guns down the harbour would start firing and between the scores of searchlights, ack-ack bursts like splashes of gold dust would add colour to the beautiful lattice pattern in the sky. Sometimes, but not very often, an aircraft would get caught in a search light beam, and small and glistening thousands of feet above the earth and looking so pretty and harmless, it would turn and twist while all the guns for miles around opened up. For hours the all pervading drone of the 'planes with the intermittent crack of the guns and the zip of falling shrapnel would go on until the last final flight had passed on its mission of death to the north. A lapse of perhaps half-an-hour and the performance would start all over again as the bombers hooked it for home, obviously in less orderly flight and some of them making ominous noises which spoke of rough handling by our ground defences and night fighters. The next morning the news bulletin would tell which town had received the bombardment. Liverpool and Merseyside were attacked time and again. Swansea had its merciless three-nights blitz — All these nights Pembrokeshire watched, listened and waited. There was an inescapable feeling that one night it would be Pembroke Dock's turn and, sure enough, it came on May 12th [1941], when the town was almost reduced to a shambles under the terrific bombardment.

In that bombardment — a night of terror — high explosives, incendiary bombs and land mines rained down on the town and during the night 30 civilians and two servicemen lost their lives, four people were missing and a large number injured while parts of three bodies could not be identified. Nearly 2,000 houses were damaged as was the ordnance factory — extensively so, the gas works received a direct hit and the Three Crowns and Prince Albert public houses were destroyed. Ferry boat sailings were cancelled because of the danger of mines in the harbour and for some days afterwards a minesweeper swept the path of the ferry before it crossed to and from Neyland.

Because the Luftwaffe tended to raid the same town on two or three successive nights the nightly exodus was resumed and this time the hundreds of servicemen billeted in the area were given the order to get out of town, sleep where they could and keep away until morning. In a first hand account Bill Richards described the scene:

As dusk gathered military trucks went round the streets and men, women and children piled into them to be carried away from the danger area. Refugees fleeing along the roads of France a year before could hardly have presented a more pathetic picture than the people of Pembroke Dock as they poured out of the town that bright spring evening. An unforgettable scene was witnessed at Mill Bridge, Pembroke. Down over the hill from Pembroke Dock they came in an endless stream, in cars, lorries and overloaded buses on motor cycles, bicycles and horsedrawn carts and wagons. Hundreds came on foot, weary mothers with infants in arms, and little boys and girls hardly of school age running behind, wonderment written plain on their pale faces; old men on sticks, young men with grim expressions, subdued boys and frightened girls. Nearly every person clutched tightly some valued possession. Many of the vehicles were piled high with articles of furniture and household ware. Dogs, cats, caged birds and parrots accompanied their owners. Many of the older folk obviously found it difficult to get along. Women bit their lips and some failed to stem the tears that filled their eyes. Children's noise and chatter was nowhere to be found. There was no spark of gaiety no sign of happiness in that motley, unending procession. Dusk fell and still they came, and long after the stars had studded the sky there were stragglers hurrying from a devastated town.

Some with nowhere to go slept in the open in Bush Woods or in fields and under hedges but hundreds stayed in Pembroke where homes, schools and vestries were opened to them, others found their way to other parts of the county where friends — and strangers — made them welcome. As expected the raiders returned in the early hours of 13 May but the target that night was Milton aerodrome, yet it was many nights before these refugees began to return to their shattered homes. The last big raid, an incendiary attack, was on Pembroke Dock in June 1941. In this raid two young Air Raid Precaution messengers, a boy of 13 and a youth of 18, were killed when a stick of explosives fell beside them as they were extinguishing incendiaries, a man died as he was helping children out into the safety of the fields and an RAF man lost his life in saving his wife.

After the war came the reckoning — homes to be built or repaired, industry to be re-established on new industrial estates. Initially rebuilding provided some work for an area which, over the post-war years lost its military presence, its small ship repair yards and the naval refuelling facilities. Gradually, however, this dockyard town which, in its hey day had seen the building of 260 ships of all kinds from the frigates *Valorous* and *Ariadne* in 1816, cutters, the 100 gun *Royal William*, royal yachts, to cruisers, submarines and tankers, began to see a resurgence — and most particularly in the area in which lay local skills.

When the Sunderlands left Pembroke Dock in 1957 there was great sadness for these splendid machines were held in much affection, not only by the men who flew in them but also by the people of the area — and their presence, too, had provided a relatively small but not insignificant boost to the town's economy. A memorial plaque in St. John's Church commemorates Pembroke Dock's flying boat links.

It was, however, in the 1950s that rumours began circulating that the Haven was the most likely choice for large new oil refineries, and various small local firms were established — though not all survived — to meet the potential new requirements of the port. With this opportunity in view the small firm of R.J. Hayes was formed and by the time the first refinery, Esso, was on stream in 1960 this firm's rope running service was in operation; during the berthing of large tankers its 26 foot rope running vessels were used to pull the very heavy mooring lines to shore moorings. Later R.J. Hayes became Milford Marine Services and when the company was bought by the Milford Haven Port Authority in 1977, began operating as Marine and Port Services, now Williams Marine and Port Services following a 2004 partnership with Williams Shipping of Southampton. In the early 1990s the company constructed a slipway at Pembroke Dock of over 900 tons capacity — the largest in Wales.

However, in 1978 the area had suffered a severe shock with the news that the apparently thriving Hancock Shipbuilding Co was in receivership with debts of £1¾ million and the jobs of a workforce numbering more than 300 were in jeopardy. The firm had been in business in the waterway since 1890 and in 1923 was the only firm actively involved in shipbuilding in Wales. During the war years, then trading as Peter Hancock and Sons, the firm had a workforce of up to 500 repairing convoy ships and damaged warships including the battleship *Rodney* and cruiser *Wessex*. The 1970s saw them diverting into general engineering work for the oil refineries and for Pembroke

The Fastnet Rock *on the stocks at Hancocks' Yard at Pembroke Dock — and launched*
(Photographs by Gordon Pilot)

93

The Fastnet Rock *team, from left to right: John Howard, Peter Trainer, Mike Osborne (representative of Lloyds of London who issued the sea worthy certificate), Eddy Stephens, Gordon Norris, Gordon Pilot and a representative of Dublin Coal Distributors*

Power Station, while in the five or six years prior to its collapse Hancocks had turned out 50 ships and barges, mostly for foreign customers.

The Coal Distributors of Dublin's *Tuskar Rock* had been launched in 1977 and its sister ship the 1,600-ton coal carrier *Fastnet Rock* was already on the Hancock stocks when the blow fell. Work came to a standstill and with their livelihood at stake the employees set out to establish a co-operative to complete this and other outstanding orders. Their bid failed when they were unable to secure the necessary grant (a fraction, it was said, of the sum going to the refineries), but Coal Distributors saved the day through an agreement with the receivers and the unions for the completion of their vessel. Seventy men were retained, among them the foreman Gordon Pilot who had joined Hancocks ten years earlier and ran the squad working on the *Fastnet Rock*. Once the vessel was on its way to Dublin to take up coal carrying from the UK to continental ports, Gordon was offered a post with the Milford Haven Port Authority where he remained in a managerial position until his retirement, delighted that he was able to remain in the dockyard, retaining his involvement in shipbuilding.

It was also decision time for Engineering Manager Peter James who had joined Hancocks as an apprentice straight from school — and the decision was, with his wife, to invest in engineering equipment, use his many contacts and set up his own business, Kingswood Engineering. After two years the small firm needed to expand into new workshops and the couple were joined by their son Clark who now runs the busy business in Criterion Way, carrying out steel work — and still some shipping — for clients throughout Wales. His father remains a director and his mother Company Secretary.

94

Increased levels of economic activity across Pembrokeshire in the last few years — particularly through the advent of LNG — has given a particular boost to the area of the Milford Haven Waterway.

Ledwood Engineering which had its roots in Pembroke Lifting Services was relaunched in 1999 with investment from the Port Authority. Its core skills lie in the delivery of challenging projects in mechanical construction, fabrication and maritime work, and after a difficult few years it became a major sub-contractor to the LNG project. With a national and international client base it employed a workforce of over 350 in late 2008.

Low wages and a relatively narrow industrial base have long caused graduates and skilled workers to leave the county. There are now hopes that the opening in 2007 of the £10m Technium Centre at Pembroke Dock may reverse the trend and at the same time boost the economy. The Centre, which is a joint venture by Pembrokeshire County Council, the Welsh Assembly, and the University of Wales Swansea, is a centre of excellence in environmental research and modelling. The laboratory and workshop facilities of the Research and Development department are managed by Swansea University while, with the proximity of the oil refineries, the LNG terminals and the proposed new power station, there are opportunities for businesses to expand or new businesses to locate in the 'growth units'. A Swansea University team is researching climate change via the Blue Ice supercomputer provided by IBM. The computer, recognised as the most energy-efficient in Wales, allows its users to perform calculations in a fraction of the time needed by a regular computer.

Undoubtedly the Port Authority's investment in the oil industry is still an important part of their business, but they are anxious to stress that the Milford Haven Waterway is much more than an oil port. Diversification over the years has seen the construction of the ferry terminal in the 1970s, the acquisition of Milford Docks ten years later, Pembroke Port bought from the receivers in 1998 and most recently the purchase of the Ministry of Defence Royal Maritime Auxiliary Service (RMAS) depot adjacent to Pembroke Port.

The lowering for the last time of the RMAS flag at its Pembroke Dock depot ended a 200 year history and cut, for ever, the auxiliary services' link with the Admiralty. The RMAS was a British government agency which ran a range of civilian manned support vessels for the Royal Navy. It was paid for by the Admiralty to avoid lengthy negotiations and tendering processes with private companies. Local riggers, ships' chandlers and ship builders had long worked alongside the Navy and since 1997 the RMAS used Pembroke Dock as its headquarters from where it organised moorings throughout the UK, including the eastern Solent, the Thames area and the Wash. It maintained and deployed moorings and navigation marks for military ranges including Aberporth, Castlemartin, Manorbier and Pendine ranges, a total of 240 navigation marks and up to 500 moorings.

The Port Authority's acquisition of the Depot has given them access to the 100-metre Carr jetty and the opportunity for further regeneration of the site — a continuation of the Port Authority's overall expansion programme.

The Authority built the Ro-Ro terminal in the old dockyard in 1979 and 20 years later expanded the terminal to meet the requirements of Irish Ferries, the Authority's biggest clients, who now operate from the port. The purchase from the receivers of the Port of Pembroke for its potential for general cargo handling and warehousing brought with it the need for investment in the inadequate structure which had been underused, they say, prior to receivership.

In the past five years the port has seen a 50 per cent increase in freight with 96,000 freight units (lorry loads) leaving the terminal over a 12-month period — an average of one unit every five minutes.

The two former Grade II Listed Sunderland hangers have been restored and are in use for boatbuilding, large scale manufacturing and as storage for pending cargo. Redundant Gulf Refinery machinery has been stored here for shipment to Pakistan where it is being rebuilt. Pembroke Port can now provide chilled storage for potatoes and Pembrokeshire cheese and space for conversion of cooking oil into bio-diesel. The uses are wide and varied.

While the Port Authority has invested in the leisure industry in Milford Haven it has also looked at leisure and tourism in Pembroke Dock. The once derelict former Guardhouse and Sunderland House, occupying prominent positions greeting ferry visitors to the port, have been restored to their Georgian graciousness and now provide high quality office accommodation. The Captain Superintendant's building, latterly the disused Commodore Hotel which was ravaged by fire in 2006, was subsequently acquired by PEM Developments, an Irish owned consortium, to give them a base in the county. The property has planning consent for a restaurant and apartments with some additional town houses in the rear stable block.

The Pembroke Dock Townscape Heritage Initiative is aiding the town's transformation, which also includes the reconstruction of the Grade II listed dockyard walls, the Front Street dock and sea wall across the front of the town's former private dockyards, as well as the Market building, another Grade II listed building within the Conservation area. It was for many years the focus of life in the town and in the dockyard's hey day was used for entertainments such as the visiting Buffalo Bill Wild West Show.

As more visitors are drawn to the area as a result of the Irish Ferries terminal and cruise ships visiting the port, the town has developed its tourist potential. The Gun Tower on Front Street has been developed into a Tourist Information Centre with a difference. There is an original working cannon on the roof and down below, in the depths of its magazine, one may see where nearly 20,000lbs of gunpowder were stored. In between, the officers' and men's quarters show that life was decidedly cramped for these soldiers, waiting for the French invasion that never came. Full sized models of soldiers and many authentic relics provide an exciting picture of Pembrokeshire Military heritage. The Gun Tower also houses information on the dockyard itself and there are displays on the flying boat squadrons which were once so much a part of the town.

Through its past Pembroke Dock is looking to its future.

Chapter 6

Neyland

Like the town of Milford, Neyland itself has little ancient history and because in 1856 Isambard Kingdom Brunel chose this little fishing village with its scattering of small boat building yards as the terminus for his railway, he is now regarded as the founder of Neyland town. The arrival of the railway certainly brought major changes to the whole area, initially creating a need for additional housing for the workforce. With a train service into the town there was also a need for an hotel to accommodate the travellers and the South Wales Hotel opened in 1858. A ferry steamer service between Neyland and Waterford then became a viable proposition, in turn adding to the numbers using the rail service. This included servicemen making the crossing to and from Ireland, among them Irish volunteers on their way to fight for the Pope in the wars leading to the unification of Italy. Edward, Prince of Wales, later King Edward VII, also arrived by train before embarking for Cork on the royal yacht that had been built at Pembroke Dock.

At the same time shipbuilding continued. Even after the opening of the dockyard at Pembroke Dock in 1814 shipbuilding in the small yards had remained an important means of livelihood locally.

Cheap labour in this remote part of Wales and the proximity of less expensive iron and timber had been a factor in bringing this industry to the creeks along the coast from an early date, and the growth of the coastal trade in the latter part of the 16th century increased the demand for vessels. To meet the demands of these small shipbuilding yards, timber was imported from Ireland. Launching the small vessels did not call for deep water and their production was not sophisticated, requiring (according to Roy Mason in a talk on the maritime traditions of Llanstadwell Parish) 'little capital and resources — a steam box, saw pits, shipwrights tools, wood in abundance and, possibly, 15 to 20 men under a master shipwright.'

The creek at Westfield Pill was much in use in the 17th century and there had been a small settlement at Neyland at least from the early years of the century. The inlet in the Pill — known as 'Shipping Gut', later cut off by the building of the railway — provided a berth for trading vessels, while a mill in the area continued to grind corn until the beginning of the First World War.

A survey of the Haven in 1758 recommended Westfield Pill as a suitable site for building ships for the navy due to its very adequate depth of water, and plans for a dockyard were considered. This never materialised, on the grounds that it would be too difficult to defend from invasion, but the warships lost during the Seven Years War had to be replaced and private enterprise came to the rescue. Two warships, the frigate *Milford Haven* and the 74-gun *Prince of Wales* were built in Neyland (by the Milford Haven firm Bird and Fisher) in 1759 and 1765 when the launch attracted hundreds of spectators, with naval ships, sloops and private vessels joining in the celebrations. In 1778 the *Prince of Wales* was the flagship of Rear Admiral Samuel Barrington in the West Indies and she saw active service against the French in December of that year.

Small sailing vessels under 100 tons were built at Scurlock's Yard on Westfield Pill, an enterprise which lasted for more than 50 years, while, during the 19th century, Warlow's Yard was thriving at Hazelbeach (near Llanstadwell church) where the pier provided access at all states of the tide. The remains of a stone quay are still there and this little port, now the home of Neyland Yacht Club, was particularly busy throughout the 17th, 18th and 19th centuries as small ships transferred their cargoes to horse and cart for local delivery. The cargo would include grain, coal, limestone and culm.

Along with timber, sugar was also imported from Ireland. By law sugar manufactured in Ireland had to be weighed and passed by Customs on the British mainland. The Customs House where this took place was initially at Pembroke but was removed to Neyland during the 1870s. By this time the GWR was running the Neyland–Waterford ferry, Neyland was the headquarters of their Marine Department, was the port of registration for all GWR vessels and was the port of call for many types of shipping, not just those vessels engaged in trade with Ireland. The new wooden building at the bottom of the gardens of the South Wales Hotel was shared between the Custom House and the Marine Department offices, the latter closing in 1906. The decline in shipping by the 1940s saw the closure of the Custom House, and along with much of the railway installation it was demolished in the late 1960s.

The Customs House at Neyland

It was only after a series of setbacks that Brunel eventually chose Neyland as the terminus for his railway. He had planned a route joining the Great Western near Gloucester through to Carmarthen, then west through Treffgarne Gorge to Fishguard to link, via the Brunel steamship, with Ireland and a further network of railways. The potato famine in Ireland, when more than a million people died and the Irish economy collapsed, rendered the project unviable. Work on this line came to what was expected to be a temporary halt, but just as it seemed worthwhile to resume construction the Minister for War intervened, declaring the port of Fishguard was to be kept available for naval use in case of war.

No longer able to use Fishguard, Brunel set about diverting the line to Abermawr, a small bay about 4 miles to the north. Jetties were built, plans were drawn up for a steep incline with two high embankments, a breakwater and a ledge to hold the station. But this proved to be an over ambitious scheme and in 1851 this too was abandoned, leaving traces of the workings still to be found in the woods around this isolated bay. Ten years later the submarine communications cable from Wexford came ashore at the bay. Messages from Ireland were retransmitted over lines from the small Abermawr cable hut to the London offices of the cable company to continue their journey to the recipient.

The latest change in Brunel's plans meant that the line was turned south at Clarbeston Road to continue to Haverfordwest and reached the terminus at Neyland in 1856. The line remained in use until Beeching's axe closed the Neyland section of the link in 1964.

The people of Milford had not been happy at the choice of Neyland for the rail terminus which dashed their hopes that the line would continue to Milford and aid its own development. By 1864 Milford, Pembroke and Pembroke Dock were served by their own railway and the Admiralty obstructed any large scale marine development at Neyland to avoid congestion of the deep water channel between Neyland and Pembroke Dock.

While the railway itself brought many benefits, the years of its construction proved a considerable disruption in the county — not least from the 'invasion' of navigators or navvies. Writing in the *Pembrokeshire Magazine* Roger Worsley described the navvy of the 1840s as 'a man of phenomenal strength and an equally pronounced appetite for food, drink and for female company, making his name a feared byword, a man from whom no lady was safe, a man whose fights were legendary — and who was someone to be ignored, or perhaps converted to Christian morality if a parson of brave enough demeanour could be found and sent into the navvies' camp. A man wasn't considered to be a proper navvy unless he could shift 10 tons of earth.' They also shocked the local vicar, Worsley said, with their notion of marriage, the couple being considered to be wed once the bride and groom had leapt, hand in hand, over the navvy's shovel.

Jetties and cattle sheds had been completed in Neyland as part of the railway company's plans and even before work on the station had finished the owners of the cargo ship *Transit* sought permission for the vessel to dock in Neyland. In January 1886, with the line completed, the ship put in to load 900 tons of coal and ore which had been

Artist's impression of the opening of Neyland Railway Station in April 1856, from the Illustrated London News *(courtesy of Simon Hancock)*

brought by rail from Port Talbot and was destined for Australia. The exercise was seen as a considerable boost for the new facilities and the crossing was made in a commendable three months — but it was not repeated.

With the opening of the railway in 1856 came the establishment of a connecting ferry service to Waterford, the enterprise of Captain Thomas Jackson and Captain Robert Ford. Their company, the Milford Haven and Waterford Steam Shipping Company, began operating in August, at first with a twice weekly paddle steamer service in each direction. After a train journey from Paddington of around eight or nine hours the on-going passengers faced a similar period at sea as they made the 118 mile crossing to Waterford. By May of the following year, the two captains extended the service to Cork, a less successful exercise which they later discontinued, but the Waterford crossings remained. However by 1872, with an ageing fleet in constant need of repair, the company was struggling financially and happy to sell to the GWR, with Captain Jackson remaining as manager for a further year. New ships joined the fleet, which was increased to seven, and the facilities improved.

Neyland looked set for a long period of prosperity as trade soared. Large numbers of cattle, sheep, pigs and horses were imported, while a profitable ten-week mackerel season added to the work of the busy port. A slaughterhouse was built near the station, butchers were employed and locally slaughtered bacon was added to the rail cargo.

In 1859, three years after the coming of the railway, the Anglo-Luzo-Brazilian Steam Ship Company began using Neyland as its British port of call for what was planned as a long term monthly service to Lisbon and Rio de Janeiro.

The 2,000 tons *Milford Haven* carried a widely varied cargo on her return from her initial voyage from the port. It included a parcel of diamonds, 144 elephants' teeth, 608 bags of nuts, 25 bags of ginger, 425 cases of oranges, 257 bags of orchilla weed, and 801 bags of coffee. However, local hopes of great benefits from the trade plummeted when, less than a year later, the line transferred its operation to Liverpool.

Attention then focused on plans to compete with the existing south Wales coaling ports by creating docks in Neyland. This proved to be another scheme which never got off the ground. After 12 months only £4,000 of the share capital of £220,000, offered in £10 shares in 1863, had been subscribed. A number of subscribers who were concerned at the bitter rivalry between Milford and Neyland withdrew their support and when the death occurred of Sir John Philipps, the principal promoter of the project, the plans were quietly dropped.

However, local shipbuilding continued to prosper. James Gaddarn was a large employer and his yard at Limpin Hill with its work force of around 200 men was one of the more important ones. In 1864 Gaddarns was building clippers, among the fastest sailing ships of the 19th century, used to carry wool and wheat from Australia and New Zealand and tea from China. By the 1870s they had progressed to building steamers and it was only in the early part of the 20th century that the last vessel emerged from this yard. Joshua Mills's boatyard, which stretched the length of Eastern Terrace, continued to produce vessels up to the First World War.

Employment created in the Neyland/Llanstadwell area was not confined to shipbuilding. Ropes were hand-made from jute, hemp, manilla and grass fibres and a ropewalk, where the rigging for the ships was made, extended from the top of St. Clements Road down to the shore, with another sited at Newton Weir at Llanstadwell. Hemp, usually perceived as a product of Asia, was grown in Britain for centuries. Indeed, in Elizabethan times it was mandatory for every farmer to grow an acreage to make rope and sails for the navy, as well as making clothing for farmworkers.

George Owen, writing in 1594, referred to 'a hedge of herring all round Pembrokeshire' and to local people 'much taken to trade, to sea, as seamen and mariners'. This trade obviously continued over many years for, around the mid-18th century, more than 100,000 herrings were landed annually in this part of the waterway. A report on British Fisheries in 1785 shows Neyland to be one of the biggest herring ports in Wales, while in one month in the spring of 1887 over 96 trains laden with mackerel left Neyland station for markets in the Welsh valleys and further afield.

In pre-refrigeration days, when supplies of salt were of immense importance for the preservation of food, Neyland had its own salt factory which opened in 1797 and (according to Fenton who is not, however, always noted for accuracy) supplied the whole country.

Many of Neyland's houses stem from the prosperous years that followed the advent of the railway. They were the homes of managers, shipwrights and senior employees of the growing number of businesses, and were built along with cottages originally designed to provide accommodation for the labourers engaged in building the railway and various installations within the port.

The GWR passenger ferry Roebuck *which caught fire while wintering at Neyland on 26 January 1905. She was repaired and commandeered for Admiralty work during the First World War and was sunk in collision with* HMS Imperieuse *in Scapa Flow on 13 January 1915*

In 1869 the Bath House was built in Picton Road. This fine building, the gift of philanthropist Francis Trewent, a local draper, was constructed to allow the tide to flood the basement where the fishermen could bathe as they came ashore and before they ventured into the town. It was also open for use by the general public. The unique building later became a gentleman's residence and had a number of owners over the years before falling into disrepair. It was demolished without consent in 2005 but has since been rebuilt following a planning direction.

Despite achieving the status of becoming the rail terminus, Neyland's prosperous days were not to last and the area was blighted in 1906 when the GWR moved the Irish ferry to Fishguard.

Deciding that wringing their hands solved nothing and that the situation could only be resolved by positive action, a group of socially conscious — and astute — businessmen set about forming the Neyland Trawling Company, establishing a fish market at Westfield Pill. At its opening, the company chairman, Sir Charles Philipps of Picton Castle, commented that the 'new town' of Neyland was in a deplorable state and expressed the hope that the newly established fishing industry would help to remove the depression from the town. With much of the land in the ownership of the Picton estate he may well have had more than a charitable interest in its success.

The *Hero* was the first vessel to land a catch and soon trains, destined for the London markets and the industrial areas of the south Wales coal industry, were rolling out of the town loaded with herring and hake. Employment for between eight and ten men was secured when, in November 1908, Lady Philipps opened the ice factory at Barnlake which was designed to serve the new fish market. It had been built by Messrs. Davies and Griffiths at a cost of £3,297 and was designed by E. Glover Thomas of Tenby. The steam trawlers reached the Pill at high water when their holds were filled with the ice that came cascading down the shute. A serious ice shortage in Milford Haven three

General view of the fishmarket at Neyland on the opening day, 16 November 1908

years later when their two usual suppliers — the Cardiff Pure Ice Company and the South Western Company — were unable to meet the demand, provided a boost for the Neyland factory. But shortly after the outbreak of war in 1914 the fishing industry decreased sharply when many of the trawlers were requisitioned, and by the 1920s trawling was less viable.

The ice factory and market in winter

Inside the fishmarket at Neyland on 16 November 1908

Increasing competition came from foreign fishing vessels working in pairs using bull nets, a type of seine net (one which hangs vertically in the water with floats at the top and weights at the bottom edge, and in which the ends can be drawn together to enclose the fish) that is dragged between the two vessels. In addition, the distance of Pembrokeshire from the main markets (still an economic problem for the county), together with the general depression took their toll. Despite being repaired and enlarged

Hazelbeach, Neyland, c.1932. Hazelbeach was used by the Rouse family as an operations base for their salvage fleet during the 1930s. The fleet consisted of the tug Taliesin, *the barge* Tiger, *the* Lion *and the tender ship the* Eden, *which is believed to be the vessel in the photograph*

Workmen using lime to clear seaweed off the ferryboat slip in Neyland.
In the foreground is Billy Lloyd's yawl Fair Maid, *used to ferry passengers*
across the Haven right up to the last war

in 1932, the Barnlake factory fell into disuse when a new factory was built in Milford Haven in 1939 and it was eventually demolished in 1975.

Its strategic position on the waterway inevitably involved Neyland in wartime defence, particularly during the Second World War, but even in the late 18th century, during the American War of Independence, a battery was built at Bath House Quay to defend the naval dockyard at Pembroke Dock. Its gun platform still projects onto the shore although other traces were lost during recent building work. Scovaston Fort, built in the 1860s as one of a chain of forts for the protection of the dockyard and the reserve fleet anchorage, was used during the First World War as a military camp. It became an unofficial air raid shelter for Neyland people during the early years of the Second World War and was later used as a munitions store in preparation for D Day. At the same time embarkation hards were built on the foreshore with capacity for two tank landing vessels. The foundation blocks are visible at low tide and the rectangular hards (known as biscuits) remain below Picton Road and the Neyland Yacht Club.

Use of the South Wales Hotel had declined and during the Second World War it was used as a billet for servicemen as well as providing accommodation for personalities such as Vera Lynn who were on their way to entertain the troops. These entertainers were often carried in Sunderlands to the Middle East, India and later the Far East. Take off was at last light, a roundabout route then being taken via Gibraltar to avoid German aircraft patrolling the French coast. It is also suggested that Winston Churchill spent a night at the hotel when he visited the county during the war.

In later years the building was used as County Council offices, and in the 1950s became a hostel for workmen employed building the Esso Oil Refinery. It was the end of an era for Neyland when, in May 1970, the once grand Victorian building, sadly deteriorated and dangerous, was demolished. The adjacent station master's house, a listed building, remains, as does the Victorian post box which was originally on the station precinct.

Today Neyland is thriving once more, not only with many marine based activities but with a range of other businesses attracted by the vibrant atmosphere of

The former station master's house, now a listed building

the two business parks which employ more than 300 people. A 400 berth marina opened in 1985 and the once tiny village is now very much a part of the 21st century. Design and graphics companies, along with those supporting computer systems and allied software

The first roadside letterboxes in the British Isles resulted from a recommendation by Anthony Trollope, then a surveyor's clerk for the Post Office, in 1852. The hexagonal design of Neyland's box became standard between 1866 and 1879

rub shoulders with shipbuilders, chandlery and dive charter companies and meat and fish processing operations.

An interpretation panel showing the *Great Eastern* off Neyland is displayed at Neyland Yacht Club at a spot which faces that on which the great vessel was berthed. The panel describes how Brunel's first ship, the *Great Western*, arrived at Pembroke Dock in 1838 for refitting, almost 20 years before the arrival of the railway.

And, prominent on the quay, there stands a bronze statue of Brunel, the only one in Wales, a reminder of this famous engineer, the founder of Neyland.

Brunel Statue

106

Chapter 7

The Villages

During the Middle Ages the Welsh ports and creeks were grouped into three 'head' or legal ports to assist in the administration of re-organised Customs revenue arrangements. Milford Haven became one of the three administrative ports and held jurisdiction over the area from Barmouth to Worm's Head. Customs houses were established at Pembroke and Carmarthen and, at the same time, the Port Books came into use to record commerce through the ports. Unfortunately many of these books have been lost or damaged although some Customs accounts for the period between the 13th and 16th centuries survive.

It was not until the charter of 1326 which granted it port status that Haverfordwest was given a similar status with the already thriving town of Pembroke which had benefited from charters in 1154 and 1189 requiring all vessels entering the Haven to buy and sell their cargoes only at Pembroke Bridge — by this time there was trade enough for both ports.

In Norman times, before Haverfordwest and Pembroke achieved prominence, it was the small village of Rosemarket (Ros Marché) on Westfield Pill that was the commercial centre of the cantref of Rhos. This is the area between the Haven and the Landsker, the Englishry established south of a line stretching from Amroth to Newgale, fortified by a line of Norman castles at Roch, Wiston, Llawhaden, Narberth and Amroth, a secure area in which trade could prosper. Rosemarket's market was controlled by the Knights of St. John of Jerusalem whose commandery was at Slebech and in his history of the village Geoffrey Nicolle quotes the local saying: 'Rosemarket used to buy and sell when Ha'fordwest was a furzy dell'. One of the village houses near the church is built on mediaeval foundations and its cellar is the place in which the merchants of old would have displayed and sold their wares.

There are records of a corn mill at Rosemarket in 1230 and a fulling mill in 1338 (it is believed that it was the Flemish settlers in this region who introduced the cloth and flannel trade to the district) and the manor of Rosemarket, in the lordship of Haverfordwest, remained in Hospitaller hands from the 12th century until the Reformation.

After it had lost its status as the main settlement Rosemarket became just another village. When the railway reached Neyland in 1856 it further harmed the prospects of Rosemarket, together with those all along the Haven. These small villages, hamlets and clusters of cottages had long played an important role in the coastal trade, but this now declined rapidly and the people for whom the waterway had been their livelihood and their means of communication found themselves more isolated than they had been for 200 years. The opening of the dockyard at Pembroke Dock saw many families moving to Neyland from Rosemarket, Burton and other parts of the county to become part of the busy daily traffic of workers and dockyard men making the crossing to Pembroke Dock.

John Brown's *History of Haverfordwest* described Rosemarket in 1882 as 'a mean and miserable' village. Burton had fared slightly better in the meantime, as a road from Haverfordwest terminated at Burton Ferry (the horse ferry crossing to Pembroke Ferry) on the route between the castles of Haverfordwest and Pembroke. The 13th-century fortified tower of Burton church, which was used as a look out and possibly a beacon, and the nearby stronghold of Benton Castle, thought to have been built by Bishop Beck who was elected Bishop of St. David's in 1280, highlight the significance of this route.

From mediaeval times, a network of ferries crossed the Haven and its estuary carrying pilgrims, itinerant merchants and other travellers. The oldest recorded ferry crossing was from Minwear, at the Sisters House (see opposite), across to Slebech. Further up river, at Lammas Ford, it was possible to walk or wade to the opposite bank at low tide.

The tower of Burton church

A grist mill of very early origin existed at Blackpool — there is a reference, pre-1555, to a grist mill at 'Canyston Mylne together with the Wayre and le Blake Pool' and a deed of 1573 mentions two grist mills and two fulling mills in the area. Its position just below the tidal limit made it possible to receive and export cargoes of fair size and because of this access by water and the abundant supply of timber and anthracite, the area developed into a minor industrial centre supporting an iron forge and lime kilns. The iron forge was established at the beginning of the 16th century, possibly earlier, and in the late 1700s the then owner of the

There are no records to establish the history of the Sisters House at Minwear. Because of its proximity to the commandery at Slebech with the important mediaeval ferry linking it to the Hospitallers, it has been suggested that it was a hospice for female pilgrims, or even a nunnery in the Middle Ages. There is, however, nothing of certain mediaeval date and it is considered likely that it was built as a 16th-century house by Roger Barlow on land acquired from the Crown after the Dissolution. Records in 1546 show it as Systerne House and, in 1613, that John Barlow owned 'the manor of Mynwere containing one capital messuage called Sistern House'. The Barlows ceased to use the property after 1700 and it was ruinous by the early 19th century and is now almost inaccessible. Thirteen buildings have been identified within an enclosure, including a former mansion (built over an undercroft), a large barn, a walled garden and water feature

land, Nathaniel Phillips, a plantation and slave owner, received 10s. for every sloop and 5s. for every lighter loading and discharging at Blackpool.

In 1813 the iron forge at Blackpool was replaced by the corn mill which was still in use in 1954 when electricity was installed and the tenant, a Mr. Williams, used the mill for grinding and storing corn. The building was restored in 1968 as a visitor attraction. At one time extensive prospecting for coal and silver was carried out at nearby Minwear but did not reveal sufficiently worthwhile seams.

At Slebech, about a mile down the opposite bank of the river, the Knights of St. John of Jerusalem established their commandery between the years 1161 and 1176 with a recorded household which included a cook, baker and his assistant, dispenser, the bailiff of the manor, reaper, oxherd, swineherd and his boy as well as a number of officials such as the Esquire to the Brethren and the Chamberlain who was responsible to the Preceptor for the general management of the estates.

The house was renowned for its hospitality, offering a welcome to any stranger at the gate who sought food and lodging. At the same time the commandery was distributing large quantities of barley, beans and peas to the poor and needy and this generosity was

The one time mill at Blackpool

a considerable strain on the resources of the Order. William Rees's *History of the Order of St. John of Jerusalem* records that the Order considered its Welsh houses were especially exposed to abuse of their hospitality — because of the many strangers from Wales 'who come and go in great numbers from day to day and are great wasters [devastatores]'.

The Order farmed 53 acres of arable land at Slebech, and had a further 360 acres over the water at Minwear which extended almost to Canaston. Even so the entire crop scarcely met the annual needs of the poor and for 80 quarters of wheat for bread-making, 80 quarters of barley malt and 120 quarters of oat malt to brew the ale for the household, with a further 80 quarters of oats required to feed the horses owned by the Preceptor and his guests. Working the land and transporting produce from Minwear created a vital need for communication across the estuary — a need which was met by the Minwear-Slebech ferry's regular and frequent crossings of the treacherous tidal waters. In the early 15th century it was recorded that 'the arm of the sea at time greatly swells so that the parishioners and inhabitants and others who have to cross it cannot do so without danger of drowning, a fate which has overtaken many in times past', and moves were initiated for the building of a causeway to be built across the estuary. The Pope gave permission (in 1419) for alms to be collected for this purpose and for the following ten years everyone 'enjoined to penance' was exempted if they contributed to the fund — there is no indication, however, that a start was ever made on this costly project.

With the suppression of the Order at the time of the Reformation in 1540 and the steady rise in coal workings further down the river, the Landshipping-Picton ferry became the main crossing as the ferries became increasingly a means of travel to work. (By the later 1200s an Anglo-Flemish settlement was in existence at Picton, where the church of Boleston [Boulston] and chapel of Piketon had been granted or confirmed to the Order by Philip, son of Wizo the Fleming.) There was employment to be found at

110

Landshipping, for coalmining in this area dates back to the 17th century. Landshipping House, built in the 1750s but destroyed by fire a hundred years later, was probably the coal agent's house which had been altered, not many years before its destruction, to become a gentleman's residence with fine views over the Cleddau. The manor house, though, was Landshipping Old House, (shown on Colby's map of 1831), also known as Great House, Big House and Green House, one of the finest 17th-century mansions in Pembrokeshire, owned by the Owens of Orielton up to the time it was demolished around 1840. At the time of the Hearth Tax assessment in the latter part of the 17th century it was shown as possessing 20 hearths making the property one of the largest Pembrokeshire residences. It also had two fine walled gardens which were probably created by Sir Arthur Owen around this time, and a water folly is recorded in 1697. Aerial photographs reveal well preserved remains of formal garden terraces and courts, three formal ponds, and two other ponds to the south with an L-shaped adjacent depression which is likely to have been the site of the house. The Landshipping gardens are regarded by Cadw as the most remarkable 17th-century example surviving as structures and earthworks.

Everything suggests that this had been a place of considerable affluence and by the mid-19th century anthracite from the district's many pits was being transported to Landshipping Quay to be shipped out on barges to the deeper water off Lawrenny where it was transhipped to sea-going vessels for transportation to Ireland and other parts of the world. Landshipping Quay was rebuilt in 1801 and it was at Landshipping that the first steam engine in the county was installed, to pump water out of one of the levels of the pit.

The quay and an extended causeway served the coalfield, with a tramway leading to them which, with adjacent weighbridge, extended into the river to allow access at all states of the tide. Little remains of the causeway but the quay's substantial stone and timber revetted dock and wharf frontage survives and has considerable 21st-century usage by leisure craft. Other, possibly ancillary, industries existed in the area — the

Landshipping Quay

Brickyard Hotel shown on the first Ordnance Survey map indicates the presence of brickworks, (though the hotel itself did not survive to the second edition) and there were also quarries and lime kilns in the neighbourhood.

Single metal tallies issued to the Landshipping miners and which would have been handed in by the men as they went underground so that the number of men in the mine could be established in the event of an accident, have been found in three different locations. Two of the copper discs show a rampant lion, the Owen family crest, on the obverse and Landshipping colliery on the reverse. The other is stamped with the name of the colliery and a worker's number: 80.

In 1842 the colliery owner, Sir John Owen, M.P., was the largest mining employer in the county with a workforce of 132 males and 31 females. Two years later came the Garden Pit disaster when 40 people, including 15 boys, drowned after water from the river Cleddau broke into the workings. Working continued at the other Landshipping pits but a general decline in the industry towards the end of the 19th century led many miners and officials to move away from the area.

Legend has it that after the Garden Pit disaster miners arriving for work in another pit two miles away discovered, attached to a wall, a mysterious paper bearing writing in a language they couldn't decipher. The parson was consulted and translated what proved to be a message in Latin which predicted that the coalmining industry in the area would never again prosper while that generation remained in Landshipping. In fact, the industry never did regain its former prosperity. More and more pits were abandoned and well before the beginning of the Second World War the mining industry had finally left Landshipping, the cottages that had once housed miners, surface workers and officials, the shops and public houses began to fall into ruin, leaving as reminders of former times the empty quays and the disfiguring scars of the coal industry. The village, once linked to Haverfordwest by water traffic and by a road leading to the Landshipping Ferry crossing and, for a short time in the early years of the 20th century, by a Friday steamer service taking passengers from Landshipping Quay to Pembroke Dock became a quiet neglected backwater. On the Picton side of the water a bus service had run to Haverfordwest. This too came to an end and Landshipping was left a deserted village.

As late as 1950 a Pembrokeshire County Council survey described the plight of the village. Most of the foodstuffs and many minor household items were brought to the village by travelling salesmen but in bad weather it was quite possible that the baker, butcher and grocer might not appear. In all weathers children walked two miles to school in Martletwy, where there was also the nearest shop. However, walking was no novelty to the people of the village. Pigs were walked to Templeton railway station to be trucked and sent away to provide food in the cities, and around the time of the First World War cattle were driven ten miles to the cattle market at Narberth.

The 1950 survey also showed that the village had no church, chapel or village hall, no railway, no bus service and no water supply apart from what were described as 'a few doubtful wells'. Although a water scheme had been sanctioned it had not materialised and while an electricity cable ran through the village no-one had a supply connected. Eventually mains water came to Landshipping, but, during the bad winter of 1963 when all the pipes froze, the locals were happy to return to their 'doubtful wells'. Yet even in its isolation Landshipping was described as a happy, self-sufficient village. 'Those who can not surmount the difficulties leave', said one respondent to the survey, 'Those who are left find pleasure in helping one another out'. He added that it was significant that 'wireless entertainment counts for little — probably because of the lack of electricity and the high cost of batteries.'

It was the Hook colliery that was the last survivor of Pembrokeshire's coalmining industry, continuing to produce coal from its pits up to and after nationalisation when the Coal Board, despite promises that the pits would remain open, decided the colliery was no longer economically viable.

A recent publication, *Where the river bends*, refers to the 13th-century legend that Spaniards who had been bound for the Cornish tin mines were blown off course and found themselves in the Milford Haven estuary where they sailed up to Hook and saw coal burning. Deciding that this fuel would be an improvement on charcoal for smelting tin they took home a sample, returning at a later date to barter daffodil bulbs in exchange for coal — and so one export trade was born.

In 1563 the Bishop's Census recorded a mere 15 households totalling 60 to 70 people in the combined areas of Llangwm and Hook while Freystrop had even fewer in just 12 households. A hundred years later with the expanding coalmining industry in the area the Freystrop population had doubled and the 1670 Hearth Tax revealed 72

Boys and girls were employed to pick stone out of the coal as it came from the screens;
it was often their first job on coming to the Hook colliery (Roger Worsley)

householders in Llangwm, making it the third largest village in Pembrokeshire after Steynton and Camrose. Of these 72 householders, 30 were liable for tax, the other 42 (58%) being classed as paupers. As the parish vestry had responsibility for the poor, the Llangwm churchwardens were charged with establishing a poor house in the village.

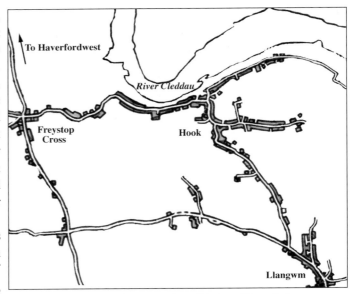

Map showing the routes from Hook to Haverfordwest

The Hook colliery was clearly a prosperous concern by 1785 when 5,728 tons of culm and coal were shipped, much of it going to north Wales and London, where, it is said, it went to supply the breweries. Caesar Mathias Junior, who had been exporting coal from the Freystrop colliery from the quay near Little Milford House since 1756, built Hook Quay in 1791 'to promote his mining interests'. The greater part of the land

Colliers' wives making the 'New Road' to Hook just after the First World War. At that time women were still employed at the mine to collect 'boughs' for the miners to use to prop up the roofs of the shafts in which they worked. The women were paid 9d. a hundredweight for gathering the wood and taking it anything up to 9 miles to the pit-head (Roger Worsley)

here was owned by the Owens of Orielton who leased the colliery to J. Harcourt Powell, and shortly after the building of the quay their agent Thomas George reported to the owners that it was said 'on account of its bad formation to have sunk by about seven feet and cost some hundreds of pounds'.

In this remote corner of Wales mining procedure had not moved on from Tudor times. W.G. Thomas in his book *Llangwm through the Ages* records that coal was still hoisted to the surface in barrels by a windlass, a horizontal drum supported on vertical posts and turned by a crank known as the 'druke and beam'. (To this day the word 'druke' remains in Pembrokeshire dialect to express any winding procedure.) The coal was then carried from the pithead on carts drawn by bullocks.

For most of its history the only direct link between Hook and the commercial centre of Haverfordwest was by boat — it was not until 1922 that the 400 inhabitants of the village secured the road for which they had been agitating for 50 years. Previously the only road link was via a lengthy detour, first travelling south through Llangwm before returning north to join the Haverford road at Freystop. To reach this road was 'a disgrace to civilisation, people going through a sea of mud that was sometimes knee deep, and doing their best to cross along the shores of the inlet of the sea and endeavouring to exit onto the road respectfully attired'.

Public subscriptions of £1,200 towards the costs, the result of 200 community meetings over a period of five years, eventually encouraged the County Council to replace the quagmire. There was great celebration in the village on the February day when the road was officially opened, an occasion when the chief constable commented 'Hook is now out of the wilderness and into the promised land'. Another dignitary declared 'Ireland has got her Free State and Hook has her new road'.

By 1934 the mine saw a peak of production of over 40,000 tons, but closed in 1948, a year after nationalisation, with the loss of 100 jobs. Josiah James who lived at Kirkland, Llangwm Hill, Hook was born in 1912 and was probably the last of the colliers to have worked in Hook colliery from 1929. His grandfather before him, as a boy in the 19th century, had to earn a wage working down the pits pulling the skips. In articles featured in the *Pembrokeshire Magazine* Joe James recalled his conversations with his grandfather and going one day, as a lad of 12, to show him his new boots and being warned to look after them and not to kick stones.

The old man then said 'When I was a young lad like you, I was working down

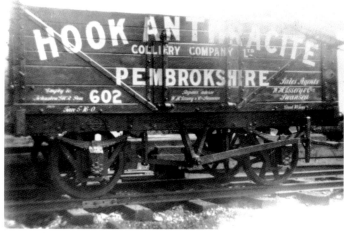

A railway wagon for Hook anthracite (Roger Worsley)

the Commons Pit and I never had any shoes to wear at all. I used to put on my feet 'brattish', like a sacking type of thing it was. Sometimes it was bitter cold, and one day when I was going to the pit I went under the stile and it was hard frost and my feet was sticking to the ground, it was that cold, and to get them free I peed on them. It was all I could do, and I went on to work and carried on from there. But when I went home that night I told my mother and she bought me a pair of clogs, I don't know how she managed it. But, do you know I was ashamed to wear them because my mates was wearing brattish, same as I'd had myself, for that was what we was all wearing, pulling the skips underground.'

Joe James also described what was known as the 'country trade' — the point near the colliery where the washings from the coal were dumped for collection by the farmers of the district and miners who received a quarterly allowance of a ton of this culm (see p.32). In Hook the culm was mixed with clay in the traditional way to form the balls which were a staple fuel, but in Llangwm as there was no clay it was mixed with what they called 'slime' from the edge of the tide.

At the end of the 18th century the local coalmines were the main employers of labour with a work force of between 65 and 90 of whom around a third were women who were paid even less than their male counterparts. Families struggled to exist on a wage of between 6d. and 9d. per day, with a total income of between £9 and £10 a year, from which they had to pay an annual rent of £5 or £6 for their cottages.

Compared to the workers the owner of the land, Sir Hugh Owen of Landshipping, received over £9,000 from his mining interests and the rentals on his Welsh estates and Sir John Philipps, a member of the family which had bought the rich Kilgetty coal deposits in the 17th century, made an annual expedition to London from his home at Picton Castle, a journey that cost the equivalent of around four times one of his worker's annual wage. In June 1758 the journey took nine days and cost £38 14s. 3d. — a sum which included the cost of inns, provided a £3 4s. allowance for drinks for his servants, and tips along the way. His entourage consisted of his family with eight servants travelling in a coach and post chase with seven coach horses and six saddle horses.

In the year that Caesar Mathias was building his quay at Hook Mrs. Morgan was writing her book *A Tour of Milford Haven* in which she recorded her visit to stay with her Uncle Caesar at West Hook Farmhouse. Her experience and her world was far removed from that of the miners. 'The fish here is extremely good', she wrote. 'Salmon, lobsters, oysters and several other kinds generally appear at table twice a day, besides Welsh mutton, Welsh ale and excellent wine.'

With high food prices and such pitifully low wages existence was almost impossible for the Hook miners and their families. In sheer desperation in August 1795 a mob of them, many accompanied by their wives, armed themselves with sticks and marched to Haverfordwest. They had planned to seize a sloop and its cargo of butter but when fighting broke out in the town's High Street the Pembrokeshire Militia was called in and the Riot Act was read in Castle Square. Faced with organised, well armed opposition the miners retreated to make their weary, dejected way home.

This episode so alarmed the magistrates and the mayor, William Ayleway, that they called on Colonel Knox (this was two years before he played his part in repelling an intended French invasion) for help, and 100 men of the Fishguard Fencibles, under the command of the Duke of Portland, remained on duty in the town for a week.

The mine owners had little regard for even basic health and safety, not just for the men but also for the wider surroundings. Mrs. Morgan records of her friends: 'As the family were one day sitting at dinner they saw the stones of the floor rise up one by one, then two or three together, jumping about. While they were planning to leave the house the mine was worked out and the fissure in the wall began to close and the pavement was replaced.'

Mrs. Morgan also comments that the houses were hemmed in on all sides by coal pits, many of them worked out which made them even more dangerous as their entrances were left open to become hidden beneath an overgrowth of weeds and brambles.

Hook Quay, constructed in 1790, fell into disrepair with the closure of the local pits, but has recently been restored by working parties of The Friends of Pembrokeshire National Park. It is now a worthy landmark of an all but forgotten county industry which once employed many hundreds of people.

Another wealthy coal owning family were the Philipps of Picton Castle, one of the aristocratic Pembrokeshire families with strong links with Ireland. Until the early

Picton Castle in 1810

117

1400s the Wogan family owned Picton Castle, one of the strongholds erected within the Palatine of Haverfordwest, and they also had estates in Ireland. When John Wogan died his Pembrokeshire estates passed to his daughter, wife of Sir Thomas Philipps of Kilsant, and the castle at Picton has since been occupied continuously by members of the Philipps family. At the end of the 17th century the family invested in coal, buying the prolific Kilgetty mines, and they also had interests in the south Wales herring fisheries.

During the Civil War the Philipps supported the Parliamentarians with the result that the Royalists stormed the castle capturing not only money and other valuables but also, it is said, one of the Philipps children. Eventually Parliamentary victory restored the fortunes of family and castle. By 1752 the Philipps were said to have Jacobite leanings (supporting James II after his abdication). Sir John was president of the élitist — and possibly Jacobite — Society of Sea Serjeants which was restricted to a membership of only 25 'gentlemen', all of them drawn from the local aristocracy in the counties of Pembrokeshire, Carmarthen, Cardigan and Glamorgan.

Details of the Society exist for the years between 1726 and 1763 but its origins are believed to lie in the period of feuding between the houses of York and Lancaster and to have only been revived in 1726. Fenton suggests that the members formed a kind of freemasonry (they certainly had rules to which they swore allegiance and a vow of secrecy, although they proclaimed their membership with a badge in the form of a silver star with the figure of a dolphin in the centre) which became an active bond 'at the time of any great jarring of national interest, such as the time of the reformation, civil wars or the revolution'.

In 1754, when Sir John Philipps was a parliamentary candidate for Bristol, the accusations that he had a Jacobite allegiance were rife among his opponents. In reply he said 'I acknowledge that I am of that ancient society which is composed of gentlemen of first rank and fortune in Wales who are as good and as well affected subjects as any in his Majesty's whole domain ... the intent of the annual meeting is to spend a week together in innocent mirth and recreation as other gentlemen in England do at a horse race and for no disloyal purpose whatsoever that I know of.'

This annual meeting took place at a sea port (at this time Haverfordwest came into that category) and culminated in a ball at which a lady patroness was elected for the coming year. In 1745 the meeting took place in Carmarthen and the accounts for one day's meals show an expenditure of £9 6s. 8d., comprising:

> Breakfast of tea, coffee and three packs of cards - 10s.
> Dinner for 31 gentlemen, including 12 bottles red port, 2 bottles white wine,
> 6 pints Rheniser, 42 quarts ale, 25 quarts cyder, punch and tobacco
> - £6 18s. 10d.
> Supper for 17 gentlemen (were many unable to stay the course after that
> dinner?) - 20 quarts ale, 6 quarts cyder, punch, tobacco, ale to the boatmen
> and ale to music at the bumper - £1 12s. 6d.
> Added to this was four men's dinner 2s., ale 1s. 4d. and coffee in the evening 2s.

For centuries the most important ferry was 'The Passage' — the Pembroke Ferry to Burton horseferry which connected with the main turnpike road linking Haverfordwest and Pembroke. In 1832 the charges were ½d. for a foot passenger, 1d. for a man and horse and 1s. per wheel for carts and carriages. The extensive use of the route had encouraged the landowners to apply to set up a Turnpike Trust and this came into being in 1788, covering an eight mile area. Three toll gate cottages were built by Lord Cawdor and the proceeds of the tolls were scheduled to provide for the maintenance of the highway, but the Trust seems to have been pretty casually administered. The Hays Corner gate and that at Burton, opposite the present Stable Inn, were destroyed in 1843 by the Rebecca Rioters, but only the former was replaced the following year. All traces of the Hays Corner gate have since disappeared, but that at Merlins Bridge opposite Haylett Grange still remains, though now a derelict ruin.

Mile Post near the site of the Pembroke Ferry at Burton

Among the casualties of the Rebecca Riots in the late 18th century were the flood gates of the grist mill at Blackpool on the banks of the Eastern Cleddau. Like a number of toll gates they were destroyed by the Daughters of Rebecca in their protest against road tolls, tithes payable to the Church of England and the general social economic conditions of the day.

In an area where 79 per cent of the people were nonconformist chapel-goers, the resentment at being called upon to support the upkeep of the churches was enormous. Poverty was rife and the 1836 Tithes Commutation Act decreed that the tithes could no longer be paid in produce but had to be in cash, something which was considerably more difficult to find in the depressed economy which followed the Napoleonic wars. At the same time the multiplication of toll gates on the roads that were the means of getting to markets and fairs, but which despite the tolls were badly maintained, added fuel to the flame of unrest. Feeling that they had no remedy but to take the law into their own hands, groups of men with

The now derelict Toll House at Merlins Bridge

119

blackened faces and dressed as women set out to destroy the gates, led, it is believed, by Thomas Rees of Twm Carnabwth (Stone Cottage) from Mynachlog-ddu. It was this leader who locally acquired the name Rebecca, believed to be a reference to the quotation from Genesis 24 v.60: 'And they blessed Rebecca and said unto her, Thou art our sister, be thou the mother of thousands of millions and let thy seed possess the gates of those which hate them.'

In 1791 a turnpike road was built by Charles Greville (one of the founders of Milford) from St. Clears to Milford which, after passing through Haverfordwest, ran through the village of Hubberston which was the post town — a central collecting point — for the area for a hundred years from 1700. By 1817 the road had deteriorated to such an extent that Henry Leach, Collector of Customs and Controller of the Post Office packet at Milford, was informed that it would be impossible to continue the mail services to Ireland unless the road was improved. Leach blamed the lack of repairs on misappropriation of funds by the trustees of the turnpike. In 1826, Telford was asked to survey the possibility of an alternative road terminating at Hobbs Point (north of Pembroke) and seven years later the road was under construction. But Turnpike Trust funds were low and to make up the deficit the Surcharge Act of 1836 was passed imposing a surcharge of one halfpenny on letters carried from Ireland to Hobbs Point. The daily Waterford packet had continued running to Milford until about 1832 but was then transferred to Hobbs Point, possibly because of the poor condition of the Milford road.

Up to 1837 the ferries were powered by oar or sail and when William Griffiths (widely known to all as 'Billie Darkie') died in 1938 he was the last of the ferrymen who rowed from Neyland to Barnlake — the link which carried workers from their homes in Neyland across Barnlake Pill from where they travelled on, probably on foot, to the Trinity House depot. There was employment to be had at the depot for a 65-year period after the completion of the Smalls lighthouse in 1861 until the service station was moved to Swansea (in 1926), for it was from the small village of Burton that the lighthouses, lightships and buoys were serviced. Work was also carried out on the fleet tenders on the large timber jetty which remains as a reminder of those bustling days.

The Roose ferry for which there is an early reference in 1762, landed at Lawrenny on the confluence of the river Cleddau and the twin arms of the river Carew (once an important oyster fishery) and Cresswell. Shipbuilding businesses existed here between the 1780s and 1850s during which period more than 60 vessels were completed on Lawrenny beach. At the same time ship repairing was being carried out and large numbers of vessels found safe moorings in these waters.

The occupations of the local residents — shipwrights, fishermen, carpenters, blacksmiths, ferrymen and many farmworkers — reflect the industry of the area. Employment was also provided by the local oyster fisheries whose wares were despatched to the London markets on vessels from Rochester and Chatham, so explaining the presence on the 1851 census of two Rochester-born oyster merchants.

The original castle at Lawrenny was destroyed by Cromwell and was replaced in 1856 at a cost of £70,000. Carmarthenshire Antiquities Society records show that the carpenter and stonemason working on the building were paid 15s. per week and the foreman mason and foreman carpenter 18s. The 'castle' undertook to provide a boat in good repair for the ferryman who had rent free accommodation for himself and his family but whose only pay came from his fares — 2d. to Cosheston Ferry, 3d. to Roose Ferry but, because the ferry was government run, free to policemen, postmen and soldiers.

During the Second World War a marine Fleet Air Arm base was established at Lawrenny Quay for 764 Squadron's fleet of rear-engined Walruses and Kingfishers which were moored on the river between Lawrenny and Coedcanlas. The officers were billeted in the 40-room castle which was blown up in 1952 by its owners, the Lort Phillips family, who had found it cold, damp, uneconomic to run — and unsaleable. (It was their ancestors Roger, Sam and John Lort who were among the signatories of the document demanding the demolition of Haverfordwest Castle in 1648).

Today Lawrenny, with a population of less than 100 and a great community spirit, takes pride in having been acclaimed 2007's Best Village in Wales, a title which brought with it prizes totalling £3,000 towards community projects. A focal point of the village is the Community Shop which was born out of the planned closure of the village Post Office and shop in November 2006. A vociferous campaign by the rapidly formed Lawrenny Village Shop Association prevented the removal of the Post Office equipment and enabled part of the post office service to be maintained. Fundraising, gifts and grants secured equipment for the shop and Mrs. Marijke McBean was given the franchise to run the business, which now includes a craft shop. Unfortunately the latest round of Post Office closures resurrected the plans to remove the Post Office equipment, but the shop continues. It has proved that it can stand alone, well supported not only by the local residents but also by the tourist trade during the summer months.

At the same time there are major developments planned for Lawrenny which could double in size if the multi-million pound eco village built from local materials and powered by methane from a nearby dairy and biomass plant go ahead.

Looking towards Mount Pleasant from near the boatyard on Lawrenny Quay

Even more into the 21st century is the Lawrenny-based HMS Beagle Trust which is planning to build a replica of the original *Beagle* which will follow Darwin's route and, equipped with laboratories and contemporary equipment, will carry out original research in conjunction with the NASA International Space Station.

Another ferry crossed from Lawrenny to Cosheston where there were yet more shipbuilders, providing custom-built vessels using local oaks. It is said locally that sea captains from Liverpool would stay in the village during the final stages of the construction of their ships to supervise the completion of the work.

The advent of the 'ironclads' brought an end to the demand for Cosheston's wooden boats and in the mid- and late 19th century the shipbuilders moved on to a new venture — the production of naphtha which they sold to a Neath firm for use in explosives, working in a purpose-built building which became known as 'the Chemicals'.

Cresswell (originally Church's Well) Quay, at the head of the Cresswell river is listed in the 1566 *Report of the Commission to Suppress Piracy* as a port, even though it had less than five houses. It was once the outlet for coal from mines owned by the Allens of Cresselly House, which the antiquarian Richard Fenton visited in 1806. He described the busy quay with barges setting off at every tide to take stone, coal and culm to Lawrenny for transfer to larger sea going vessels. When the local coal seams ran out, the 'trade' reversed. Coal was brought in from Hook colliery until the mid-20th century in the *Lady Jane* (owned by William Davies of Williamston), whilst a ferry carried miners from Llangwm to Coedcanlas (where recent aerial photography has recorded the site of Newhouse, a mediaeval house) to enable them to walk the rest of the way to the colliery at Landshipping. Animal feed stuffs were brought from Pembroke by boat and lorry to the co-operative depot on the quay and were collected in carts by farmers from miles around.

During the First World War Cresswell played its part in the war effort, providing timber from the nearby wood to shore up the trenches at the front. It was stockpiled on

A reminder of earlier days on the Cresswell river

Cresswell Quay

the beach near the river before being rafted together and floated down to Lawrenny Ferry for transhipment to France.

Today, like so many of the coastal settlements Cresswell is no longer an industrial centre and has developed into a popular pleasure harbour.

Other ferries which feature on the 1920 Ordnance Survey map are those between East Pennar and Bentlass, Herbrandston and Sandy Haven, and Neyland and Hobbs Point. The opening of the Royal Dockyard at Pembroke Dock in 1814 had created a demand for a new passenger service and the ferry trade boomed. James Huzzy of the Ferry House at Hazelbeach paid the landowners, the Owens of Orielton, an annual fee of £200 for the rights of the service from Hazelbeach to Pembroke Ferry and when the Hobbs Point pier was completed in 1832 to serve the Irish Mail this made an appropriate terminal for the Neyland ferry. There were further developments when an Act of 1837 enabled a steam ferry to be established at or near Pembroke Ferry, shortly followed by the arrival in Neyland of Brunel's railway. The Neyland pontoon was built and the steam boat ferry service to Hobbs Point opened, supplemented, until the early 20th century, by the small boats whose owners were ever-ready to take over when the weather was too rough for the steamer to sail. One of these boatmen, Billy Lloyd, in his gaff-rigged yawl, *Fair Maid*, was still operating up to the beginning of the Second World War.

The early boats, the *Amy* and the *Pioneer* were privately run, but in 1848 when there were problems with the service the County Council took over the 55-year-old *Lady Magdaline* (a steamship later converted to carry four cars), the paddle boat *Alumchine* which was 28 years old and could in later years accommodate up to six vehicles, and a water launch, the *Mary*. The purchase of the vessels, the yard and equipment cost the council £12,695, and it was also soon incurring an annual loss of £1,830. An appeal to the Ministry of Transport for a grant towards capital expenditure and annual maintenance would be considered only if a free ferry was established. Both ferries were later superseded by the *Cleddau Queen*, built at Hancocks Yard at Pembroke Dock, and the *Cleddau King* which remained in service until the opening of the Cleddau Bridge in March 1975.

An article in *Pembrokeshire Life* in August 1991 records the story of Ivor Evans who was, for 20 years, ticket collector on the ferries and one of the crew on the *King*'s last crossing. With the skipper, Kevin Rowlands and Peter Walters, another crew member, he was afterwards employed in the ticket booth of the newly built toll bridge. He had many recollections of what was often a rough crossing, among them the unofficial 'sound location' method employed by the crew on days when Hobbs Point had disappeared in fog. 'A fitter called Billy John', Ivor said, 'lived at Hobbs Point and he used to beat a drum and we would follow the sound. One day we followed the drum beat and when the fog cleared we found ourselves further down the Haven off the Marine and Port Services jetty. A chap there was mending something and the sound was just the same!'

The opening of the bridge (and its controversial tolls) should have been the final chapter in the story of the Neyland to Hobbs Point ferry, but in October 1999 the ferry returned to ease the crisis of the temporary closure of the structurally hazardous Westfield Pill Bridge which cut off access to the Cleddau bridge. A local boat owner, Dave Anderson, who operates pleasure and angling trips during the summer months, provided a half-hourly ferry between Hobbs Point and Neyland Marina fishermen's pontoon. The ex-Royal Navy launch, *Penguin*, (a 57ft. steel-hulled vessel built to carry 60 naval personnel and originally used to carry submariners to and from their vessels at Gosport) ran daily between 7am and 6pm for £1 a trip — a service which was particularly appreciated by Pembroke Dock Texaco staff and other workers who lived in the Neyland area.

After making the decision not to build their dockyard at Neyland, the government transferred their thoughts to Milford where a naval dockyard was active by 1802. However, like so many projects in the history of Milford this was to prove a short-lived boost to the area.

While the majority of the settlements on the waterway were interdependent, the village of Llangwm tended to stand alone and even has its own patois. Writing over 100 years ago, Timmins, in his book on the county, said 'A curious place is Llangwm and a singular race are the people that dwell therein'. Those words could still have been written during the Second World War when the Llangwm fisherwomen could still be recognised by the style of dress that had remained unchanged over the centuries. It is suggested that Llangwm people are 'different' as they represent the Norse remnants left in the midst of surrounding Flemings. Certainly this was a community of great loyalty to its own people and one in which strangers were said to be unwelcome, a caution which possibly stemmed from the cholera outbreak of 1854 in which 62 people died. The source of the outbreak was eventually discovered to be the brook which provided the village water supply, but local talk was that it had been brought into the village by a stranger from 'outside'. Watch was kept to prevent any further possibility of a carrier coming into their midst and unwary visitors found themselves greeted by a barrage of stones aimed by the inhabitants. Well into the 20th century the legend persisted that strangers visiting Llangwm could expect to be stoned.

Although the major source of oyster fishing in Pembrokeshire in its earliest days was at Pennar Mouth it was later taken over by the Llangwm fisherpeople, and according to George Owen the industry was well established in Llangwm by the 10th century. The dredging, he said, was carried out with 'a kind of iron made with bars, having a piece of horse or bullock skin sewn to it like a bag ... fastened to a rope's end and cast into the bottom of Milford at eight or ten fathoms deep and dragged at a boat's end by two rowers which row up and down the channel.' The catch was then thrown overboard to settle into the beds at Black Tar where the movement of the tide kept them alive and fresh to await the arrival of the coasters which sailed up on the tide as far as Llangwm Ferry. Loaded with shellfish they then returned on the next tide to the English ports.

The Haven was famous for its oysters and one eyewitness reported seeing as many as 50 coastal vessels beached at Guildford to collect barrels of oysters which were shipped to Holland and other parts of the world. The oysters were also sold locally and in the early 1800s Fenton recorded that they were taken to Haverfordwest every day by the Llangwm fisherwomen and sold at between 6d. and 8d. per hundred. The industry must have continued in Llangwm into the 19th century for the village was described at that time as 'a busy fishing village although not of pleasing appearance with its huge mounds of oyster shells'. In later years when a trench for the main sewer (it reached Llangwm in the mid-1950s) was excavated, a 3-foot seam of oyster shells was discovered 2½ inches below the road surface, while cottages 400-500 years old were found to have foundations made of oyster shells.

Eventually, however, oyster farming died out as it did in other parts of Pembrokeshire and after the Second World War a South Wales Sea Fisheries scheme to restore the Llangwm oyster beds was abandoned, due it was said, to lack of local support and the danger of contamination from partially treated sewage from the Llangwm sewage works.

Through the years the Llangwm women worked side by side with their menfolk, fishing with them from their small fishing boats and, the following day, setting out in the early hours to walk to the towns to hawk their wares from door to door. These included a selection not only of oysters but also fish, cockles, shrimps and prawns. A good 3-mile walk took them to Burton Ferry to catch a boat across the Haven and from there they would walk on to Pembroke, Tenby or Stackpole. The journey to Haverfordwest was also made on foot and if they were to sell in Narberth or Carmarthen they first rowed themselves to Landshipping or Blackpool Mill before setting out on the long walk ahead of them. Some had the luxury of a donkey, not to ride but to help carry the load, though most carried their wares on their backs in a willow weed pannier made by the men of the household. This was supported by shoulder straps and a thick padded belt with extra padding on the back to bear the load of one hundredweight or more. At the same time they would carry a basket displaying a selection of the fish they had to offer. The women's dress was practical. A heavy skirt was worn over a thick red petticoat, not so long that it prevented easy movement, and a thick flannel apron went over the skirt with a warm waist length jacket and a brightly coloured shawl. A white cotton head square under a flat black hat covered their heads and on their feet they wore sturdy boots over thick woollen stockings.

During what must have been a very limited time in their homes they cooked and pickled the cockles and mussels which were stored in earthenware jars to be sent for sale in Bristol. In this community of hardworking women it is interesting to speculate on the reaction to any young bride who chose to rebel against this centuries-old tradition.

In Elizabeth Arthur's book, *Turning of the Leaves*, she recalls the Llangwm foreshore at the beginning of the 20th century crowded with men mending their nets and spreading them out to dry. But by the early '30s fishing was concentrated in Milford. The fisherwomen still continued on their rounds, but sold fish they had brought from Milford on carts pulled by donkeys which they left grazing at Burton when they crossed to Pembroke Dock.

It seems that these Llangwm women did not confine their marketing to fish, for Leo Cole of Newport, Gwent, writing in the *Pembrokeshire Magazine* in 1985 refers to butter from Llangwm. 'Seven decades ago', he said, 'the ladies of Llangwm complete with shawls brought their richly coloured and delicately flavoured farm butter for sale in Pembroke Dock. It was carried there in large wicker baskets which were empty on the return journey. Soon after the butter delivery crusty and crisp cottage loaves were received and in my recollection nothing excelled the flavour and enjoyment of this bread and butter. Little wonder that the local folksong (sung to the tune of the British Grenadiers) ended like this "But Pembroke Dock was best of all for bread and cheese and butter".'

With smuggling being one of the county's major industries it would be surprising if the canny Llangwm people did not also do their share and it is said there are smugglers' caves in the area and that a house in Black Tar had a cellar leading to the beach while work on old cottages has revealed hideaways presumed to be the resting places for contraband spirits hidden from the authorities after French vessels had landed their illegal cargo.

Chapter 8

Pirates, Smugglers, Invasion & Wreckers

While the small creeks and inlets were busy trading ports, not only for coastal traffic but also sending regular cargoes to La Rochelle and Brittany, they were also ideal havens for pirates, smugglers and wreckers. Piracy thrived, with many of the local magnates not above trading with the pirates, who were a mixture of French, Spanish and indigenous buccaneers.

Although he operated mostly in the West Indies rather than in his home waters, Pembrokeshire still takes pride in the county's notorious and flamboyant Black Bart — Bartholomew Roberts — who was born in 1682 in Little Newcastle on the Preseli Hills.

Daniel Defoe toured the county in 1724, the time when Black Bart was prowling the seas, researching for his book *A General History of Pirates* which records the stories and trials of many of the best known privateers of the age. Tales of Black Bart — Barti Ddu in Welsh — occupy 40 percent of the book for, says Defoe, Roberts ravaged the seas longer than the rest, 'having made more noise in the world than some others'.

The story of his involvement in the world of piracy begins with another Pembrokeshire man, a Milford born pirate, Howel Davis. Davis grew up with the sea and was 'in honest employ' as chief mate on a cadogan (the largest of all the two-masted vessels), the *Snow of Bristol*, when it was taken by the pirate, Captain England. The *Snow*'s captain was barbarously murdered by the raiders, some of them men who had turned pirate in revenge for being refused their wages when they served under him. Davis was appointed captain in his place but shortly afterwards joined forces with the pirate Captain Rogers who commanded two sloops, the *Buck* and the *Mumvil Trader*. Dramatically, Davis declared himself 'against the whole world' and went 'apirating' on his own account with 35 hands aboard the *Buck* taking many a prize and strengthening his force with fresh hands — many of whom, he said, entered his service voluntarily.

This may well have been true. Conditions on board ship were often horrendous. Large numbers of sailors were victims of the press gang, a random catch of conscripts, to form crews who were turned off as soon as they were no longer required, only to be pressed again and again as their services were needed. There was some consolation in the thought of possible prize money, but the largest share, inevitably, went to the officers.

Many were prisoners from the gaols who often brought with them the scourge of typhus to infect the whole ship. Life at sea was one of unremitting physical labour for low pay at the command of despotic ships' commanders, the food as bad as the discipline was inhuman. It is not surprising that they were ever-ready to mutiny or desert — though they must often have found that they had committed themselves to even greater distress on board the pirate vessels. As they spent days and nights on end at their posts, high on the rigging, wrestling with soaking canvas, fighting the wheel and with no means of drying their clothes the crews were particularly vulnerable to disease. Cooking over a fire on shallow trays filled with sand had to be restricted to calm weather because of the ever-present risk of fire aboard these timber-built vessels. The men (though there were two notable women pirates) slept where they could, often on the upper deck at the mercy of the elements and, as voyages grew longer, scurvy was the greatest cause of mortality. Supplies of fresh fruit and vegetables ran out after only a few days at sea, water — stored in oak casks — was a major problem for it became foul tasting after only a few weeks. (On one voyage by Magellan, the early 16th-century Portuguese navigator, all but 15 men in his fleet died of scurvy — tales of the discovery of uncanny 'ships of the dead' were far from unknown.)

Not confining his piracy to the seas, Davis and his men went ashore on James Island on the River Gambia, where they visited the Governor of Gambia Castle purporting to be merchants offering iron and plate in return for slaves. The pirate force then succeeded in taking the fort, dismantling the guns and demolishing the fortifications. When they returned to their ship they had with them '£2,000 worth of gold bars, a great many other rich effects, everything they liked which was portable'.

Continuing his nefarious scouring of the seas Davis joined forces with a 24-gun vessel and a French pirate ship of 14 guns with 64 hands on board. With this additional strength the three captains took a 30-gun Dutch vessel with a crew of 90 men and, after fitting it out for their own use, renamed it *Rover*.

This proved to be a fateful time for Bartholomew Roberts. He had started out as a ship's boy and had risen to the position of second mate on the *Princess*, then at sea in the West Indies. His ship was trading for gold, elephants' teeth and negroes (one of the vessels taken at this time had on board 140 negroes) when it was taken by Davis and his crew — and so began Roberts' days as a pirate. He joined Davis who, just few days later, made the foray ashore that was to end his life. On this occasion his story to the local Governor was that he was in charge of an English man-of-war in quest of pirates but, this time, his mendacity was discovered. He was ambushed and shot dead. The time had come to appoint a new captain, and six weeks after beginning his new career, Roberts was appointed captain of the *Buck*.

During his years of piracy Roberts had an encounter with another Welsh born seaman, William Davis, which may have changed that young man's already dissolute life. Davis, who had packed years of infamy into his 23 years, was serving aboard a galley (a type of low, flat-built, one-decked vessel navigated by sail and oars), the *Anne*, when he severely injured the ship's mate in a brawl. Rather than face the consequences he jumped ship at Sierra Leone where he 'consorted to the idle customs and ways of living among negroes from whom he received a wife'. Soon he repaid their hospitality by selling his wife in return for strong drink and sought safety from the outrage of the natives by putting himself under the protection (as he believed) of the Governor of the Royal Africa Company. This company had been founded in 1672 to ship slaves to the American planters in the West Indies who, it was said, could not subsist without them. The Governor promptly handed the young man over to his pursuers, saying that he did not care if they 'took his head off'. Seeking a more profitable outcome they sold their captive to a local Christian who accepted Davis on condition that he would give him two years' service. Davis did not wait to serve his time but seized the opportunity when Roberts sailed up the river to join forces with the by now notorious pirate.

In 1772 Davis was taken captive during an affray, possibly sacrificed without too much regret by his captain, for at his trial evidence was given by two deserters from the pirate ship the *Royal Forester*, that 'the pyrates did design to turn Davis away the next opportunity, as a good-for-nothing fellow'. In his defence Davis claimed that he had been pursued and held by Roberts because of his knowledge of the river. Roberts, however, always held that he never forced any man into piracy — a claim not upheld by other prisoners, many of whom said at their trial that he hectored and upbraided them and they dared not refuse his commands.

Black Bart from a woodcut made when he was at the height of his fame

Roberts was notable for his striking attire, being always dressed in scarlet from head to foot with his pistols carried in a gold sash. But it was surely his sternly pious Welsh upbringing that gave him his uncompromising principles — he was a strict teetotaller and would never take a ship on a Sunday! It was only after he had taken 400 ships, on weekdays of course, that his luck ran out. He was mortally wounded when he was shot during an encounter and, according to his wishes, his body was committed to the waters he knew so well.

More than a century before the days of Black Bart and his crew, the seas around Milford were described as 'the great resort and succour of all pirates and enemies in storms'.

Smuggling was a way of life in most coastal areas, where it was accepted or at least tolerated by the populace for people from all walks of life were involved. As the saying has it: 'whisky for the parson, baccy for the clerk'! The Pembrokeshire standard of living was supplemented by this illicit 'free trade' which flourished along the county's long coastline. The Milford Haven waterway was particularly notorious for the smuggling of salt, the principal import of mediaeval times. This was brought in from the Continent by Spanish, Portuguese and French ships and was greatly prized for its importance as a preservative. But the duties levied on a range of goods — at one time the tax on wine reached 3s. per tun (around 250 gallons) and ran at well over 100 per cent on tea — made smuggling of these commodities as well as sugar, tobacco, spirits and French brandy, also a profitable enterprise. It compensated in some way for the low agricultural income, indeed this 'trade' was said to be third in value only to farming and fishing in the county.

Under the early Tudors much was done to establish law and order in Welsh maritime affairs. The defences of the Welsh coast were improved and vice-admirals with subordinate officials were empowered to deal with marine matters. Strong measures, which included surveys of ports, creeks and possible landing places, were taken in the hope of suppressing piracy, together with greater supervision of local trading activities, but the very geography of the coastline and the complicity of the landed classes made policing almost an impossibility.

Many of those in high office in the county (Sir George Devereux, a one time favourite of Queen Elizabeth who lived at Lamphey Palace, formerly a palace of the bishops of St. David's; Sir John Wogan, a sheriff of the county; his relative Sir John Perrot, and Henry Lort, sheriff in 1619, to name a few) profited in some way from the nefarious activities of pirates like John Callice, known as 'the king of the western pirates', Robert Hicks and John Perrot's former servant turned pirate, Halbert. With Admiralty and Customs officers, the mayor and local priest in Haverfordwest as well as the mayors of Tenby and Pembroke all involved, the pirates were able to deal openly from the quayside. They sold their misgotten wares — particularly salt, wheat, rye and dried fish — to the townspeople and to the merchants who were also happy to supply the pirates with the provisions they needed for their vessels. Rye was eagerly bought by the peasants while much of the wheat went to merchants who sold it on to northern Spain.

The Bristol Trader on the quayside at Haverfordwest, one of the many inns reputed to be involved with smuggling

Robert Hicks once spent five weeks anchored off Pembroke Quay selling his cargo from the large prize the *Jonas*, a Prussian vessel which he had captured off the Scilly Isles. On board was Jourdain, a Frenchman from St. Malo who was imprisoned at Newcastle Emlyn after the pirates handed him over to Sir John Perrot, (a man widely believed to be the natural son of Henry III by Mary Berkeley, wife of Sir Thomas Perrot). Perrot had been appointed under the 'Greate Seale of the Admiraltye' to suppress the pirates but clearly had a foot in both camps and there was many a tale of his clandestine dealings.

Jourdain escaped from Newcastle Emlyn but was recaptured and brought back to Carew. Perrot negotiated with his relatives for his release, demanding a cargo of Gascon wine in return for his freedom. The family agreed, but before the vessel arrived with its cargo Jourdain had escaped once more and, with the assistance of Erasmus Saunders, mayor of Tenby, made his way to London.

Control was almost impossible and the activities of the pirates and their accomplices seriously hampered legitimate trade. A feud had developed between the deputy Vice-Admiral of South Wales, Richard Vaughan of Whitland, and Perrot whose Admiralty commission gave him an authority independent of both the Vice-Admiral of Wales, Sir William Morgan of Abergavenny, and of Vaughan who constantly found his authority flouted by his enemy. When the Huguenot privateer Luke Ward put into Milford with a cargo of dried fish from Newfoundland on the captured French ship the *Greyhound*, Vaughan attempted, unsuccessfully, to buy both the vessel and her cargo. In revenge he had Ward and his men arrested and thrown into prison, but they were set free by Perrot who then allowed the fish to be sold on Pembroke Quay 'cried by the bellmen' (the town criers of the day). Even more determined on revenge, Vaughan next attempted to have the case heard at the Assizes in the certainty that Judge Fitzalan, his friend, would return the men to jail. Again he was foiled because, before the case could come to court, Ward and his crew had come to an 'understanding' (doubtless of a financial nature) with Perrot and had been allowed to return to France.

Perrot also found himself in difficulties over his involvement with the notorious John Callice. Callice was originally a merchant skipper employed by Sir John Berkeley but appears to have decided on a career change in 1574 when he attacked and took the *Grace of God*. He took her into Cardiff and there, and in Bristol, disposed of the cargo before continuing his nefarious activities and successfully dodging the authorities for some years. In 1576 he and his fellow pirate and friend 'Brother Battes' took another prize, the Spanish vessel *Our Lady of Conception* laden with wool for a Bruges merchant. The merchant complained to the Court of the Admiralty and an order was issued for the recovery of the wool from those to whom it had been sold by the pirates. The two men who had been charged with carrying out the order refused to do so and with the assistance of officials in Cardiff and Glamorgan, including the sheriff of Glamorgan (the complicity of the local dignitaries was not confined to Pembrokeshire) Callice departed for north Wales where he was able to sell the wool.

His activities continued over a wide area, taking vessels as far afield as in the Straits of Belle Isle and including French, Danish and Breton ships, often evading capture with the aid of his friends in high places. In 1576 he took a salt ship belonging to Peter

Chamberlain and openly sold her cargo and gear in Haverfordwest, an action which resulted in an enquiry involving Sir John Perrot (then a commissioner with responsibility for general surveillance of the coast) and Jenkin Davids who had succeeded Perrot as mayor. One entire meeting of the Privy Council early the following year was devoted to Callice's misdeeds and an angry letter was sent to Perrot: 'Whereas their Lordships are given to understand that one John Callice, a notable pirate frequenting that country [Pembrokeshire] and arriving lately at Milford, was lodged and housed at Haverfordwest, and being there known was suffered to escape, their Lordships do not a little marvel at the negligence of such as are Justices in those parts that knowing the said Callice to be so notable an offender would suffer him to depart in that order.'

As a gesture — 'for a show and colour of justice' — the authorities captured six of Callice's crew who were under lock and key in Pembroke gaol while Callice himself had indeed been allowed to escape after buying a horse from Roger Marcroft, whose Quay Street inn the pirate was known to frequent. Jenkin Davids denied that he and his fellow magistrates had any involvement with the pirates admitting, however, that he was aware that Callice had stayed with Marcroft whom, he said, he had believed to be a reputable merchant of the town. Perrot claimed not to have been aware at the time that Callice was being entertained at Haverfordwest and wrote that 'very few here knowe him, for I never heard that he was ever in this town before'. Possibly to give credence to his protestations of innocence Perrot, who was a ship owner, added that over the years he and his neighbours had suffered personally by losing wines to the value of £1,000 from the activities of pirates.

Just a few months later Callice was indeed captured and lodged in the Tower of London to await trial, but secured a pardon after petitioning the queen, begging forgiveness and bewailing his former wicked life:

> If she will only spare my life and use me in her service by sea with those she can best trust, either to clear the coast of other wicked pirates or otherwise, as I know their haunts, roads and maintainers so well, I can do more therein than if she sent ships abroad and spent twenty thousand pounds. I send herewith particulars of the partakers of my piracies and the maintainers of and victuallers of me and my companions.

Shortly afterwards his long time friend, 'Brother Battes', and a number of his old associates were captured and hanged. What eventually became of Callice is not known, but the last information of his activities came in 1584 when Peter Chamberlain complained to the Admiralty that he had been robbed at sea by two pirates, one of whom was none other than the John Callice who had seized his cargo of salt in 1576.

During the same period that Callice was active, Halbert was selling large quantities of Gascon wine from his pirate ship the *Elephant*, and while it was too expensive for the ordinary townspeople of Haverfordwest there was a ready market among the local dignitaries. Kift, the local sergeant of the Admiralty, claimed he had found some casks hidden at Pembroke Ferry and that he sold them to Perrot for £7 a tun, but it seems likely that the truth of the matter was that he had bought them from Halbert on Perrot's behalf.

Halbert was clearly doing a good trade in this much sought after wine. Sir John Wogan was among those accused of being a customer when he was 'reprimanded' for pocketing the proceeds of the sale of this pirate's cargo. Another tun of the Gascon wine was discovered at Lamphey Palace, which the owner Sir George Devereux claimed he had received in settlement of a debt. In 1537 Phillip Gibbys of Tenby gave evidence that 'a ship of Sainct Malowes robbed an english ship upon the coast of Cornewaill of certain wynes and sent iij [three] bottles thereof to Tynbye which was there taken by the Mayre and as yet remayneth in his handes'. He also stated that a number of French ships had been lying off the coast of Wales near Tenby and had taken a fishing boat from Milford and robbed all vessels in the vicinity 'wherewith they were hable to medle'.

Many Frenchmen, he said, were watching for Englishmen, Irishmen and Welshmen who were accustomed to attend the St. James' Fair in Bristol. Further evidence was given by Morgane Taillour of Tenby who said 'the diverdse and many ships of Ffraunce and Brytayn have byen upon the cost of Walys for the most part of this yere, and robbed and spoiled as many Englisshe ships as they were hable to medle with and many time have goon on lande and taken many shepe, and of diverse of such as they hade left behynde theym they have cut off their legges.' The captain of the French ship, *John du Laerquerec*, confessed that he had taken from the Englishmen 'roopes of ships, amryneres apparrell, v pieces of wyne, ffisshe, vone crowne of gold, and xj [eleven] half pens or pens in sylver, iiij [four] daggers and a couverture called in frenshe "ung port de Raye".'

In May 1543 Arnold Butler, gent, of the county of Pembroke was charged in recognisance of £100 (money that would be escheated — forfeited — if he failed to carry out the order) to restore and re-deliver to the king all gold and other treasure that had come into his possession from a French prize at Milford Haven. At the same time the Mayor of Pembrokeshire (*sic*) was required to submit an inventory of a ship which had taken shelter from the weather and Roger Barlow was subsequently requested to provide information about items which were thought to have been embezzled out of the ship by the mayor.

In his *History of Pembrokeshire* (written in 1909) the Revd. James Phillips refers to a Dutch ship which Halbert's men had taken and brought up to Pembroke Ferry intending to sell the cargo of salt. The vessel was recaptured by Perrot who then claimed a share of the prize. More prize money was claimed by the mayor of Pembroke, and by Customs, and by Vaughan on behalf of the Admiralty. 'Very little could have been received by the unfortunate captain' Phillips comments. 'The Dutchmen must have come to the conclusion that there was little to choose between the English pirates and the English officials.'

In the mid-16th century, when the country was at war with Spain, George Clerk was a Customs officer based at the Custom House in Pembroke and proved to be a good friend to the local merchants who were loath to lose their trade with the enemy. Cargoes of leather and grain left the port unimpeded as Clerk turned a blind eye to this trade

— which was in fact a treasonable offence. At the same time his inn in the village of Angle provided sanctuary for many a pirate, including the notorious Callice.

For many years his influence and position kept Perrot at liberty despite his clandestine dealings and though he was once sent to the Tower to account for his actions he was soon freed. Though he had been one of Haverfordwest's great benefactors and as such was greatly admired, his activities had also produced rivals and enemies who were eager to pass on derogatory comments he subsequently made about Elizabeth I to where they could do the most damage. So, it was the Tower once more. By this time he was far from well and suffered greatly from the appalling conditions of that dankly vile prison. He died there in 1592 before sentence of death could be carried out, or he could be pardoned by the queen.

Some years before his death Perrot had endowed Haverfordwest's earliest charity, the Perrot's Charity, 'in consideration of the love which he bore towards the burgesses of the town and county'. The rents and profits from 34 properties were to be used for the improvement of the town and the repair of streets, bridges, walls and conduits of water and for rebuilding a new quay and other necessary good works. Subsequently much of the property was sold and the proceeds invested in securities administered by the Trust which still holds some dwelling houses in the town, including 12 almshouses in Perrot's Terrace.

Pirate landings were often made by large and ruthless gangs under cover of darkness so that policing the creeks and inlets was a highly dangerous occupation. In the latter part of Elizabeth's reign oxen were not used for ploughing on Caldey Island for fear they would be stolen by pirates who were in the habit of provisioning there — according to Laws in his *History of Little England beyond Wales,* 'commonly to the good content of the inhabitants'.

News in 1625 that Barbary corsairs had landed on the Cornish coast and captured a congregation at worship in their church quickly reached Pembrokeshire and the people were not reassured when they learned of a landing by the Moors in Baltimore in Ireland where the pirates carried off the majority of the population. This was altogether too near to home and their fears were fully justified when a pirate vessel, probably with some local co-operation, raided Ramsey Island carrying off livestock, cheese and other goods on which the islanders were dependent. The livelihood of the seatraders was also greatly at risk as the menacing presence of the pirates prevented them from bringing in or shipping out their goods.

A particular instance occurred in 1630 when the mouth of the Haven was blocked by a 50-ton Biscayer which prevented the local traders sending produce to Bristol for the annual St. James's Fair. Bristol, described by Daniel Defoe in 1724 as 'the largest town and the richest and best port of trade, London only excepted', held a great attraction for merchants from west Wales, which it retained well into the 19th century. It was to Bristol that the well-to-do sent their sons, by sea, to be educated. (A record remains of the accounts for the schooling of one Pembrokeshire youth, Richard James of Goodwick, who attended a private school, Mr. George Pocock's Academy. The bill in 1848 totalled £16 9s. 10d. including £13 2s. 6d. for the half year's Board and Education, 5s. for a cap, 1s. 6d. for gloves and an item 'shoemakers 5s. 9d.'. But, offset, was the sum of £12 3s. 9d. for butter supplied by the James family, leaving Mr. James Snr. with a bill of only £4 6s. 1d.)

Earlier, William III's dispute with France had landed the country in considerable debt (by the end of his reign the National Debt had reached £11,000,000) which led to the imposition in 1694 of the Salt Tax. In *The Journal of the Pembrokeshire Historical Society* (issue 12) Alan G. Crosby writes of the loss of Mersey salt vessels off Pembrokeshire between 1695 and 1715. He refers to records which indicate frequent voyages to the county by salt-laden vessels whose owners had been certified by the Liverpool Custom House to have paid their tax — 'a serious burden at around 3s. 4d. per bushel'.

Among them was the ketch *Supply* carrying 1,035 bushels of salt 'for Milford or some other port in Wales where they could get a market'. The *Supply* was taken by a French Privateer on 8 December 1695 near St. David's Head. The pirate vessel was commanded by Richard Welsh and Thomas Fermly, and Alan Crosby comments that the commanders of the privateers were generally not French but Irish or disaffected English who supported the exiled Stuarts.

With the predatory pirate vessels operating in St. George's Channel the merchant ships were often forced further onshore than was safe, particularly during the violent winter storms. In May 1697 the *Recovery* of Dublin was forced ashore at Whitesands Bay where the water that cascaded into the hold dissolved 294 of her 1,023 bushels of rock salt, while the *Unicorn* bound for Fishguard in September 1702 sank near Holyhead with her load of 1,410 bushels and 6 gallons of white salt (refined and more valuable than rock salt) from the Lancashire Sankey Salt Works.

If the pirates were caught, they faced hanging, something which provided public entertainment for the townsfolk who flocked to the site in the vicinity of St. Martin's church and the castle in Haverfordwest to witness each spectacle. The pirates were joined there by other prisoners destined for the hangman's rope, many of them paying the price for crimes such as petty theft.

An eye-witness account of a hanging is contained in a letter from Captain Clegg, master of the *Reliance*, which forms part of the collection of Captains Letters in the Calendar of State Papers held in the Public Record Office:

> Hearing on board that several people were to be hung in the town the next day I agreed to accompany several of our seamen to see the execution. Therefore the next morning we got to the Gaol some time before the prisoners were ready to leave the prison. We kept close to the door round which a large concourse of people had assembled. We waited to see the prisoners put into the carts then made the best of our way to The Tree, passing St. Martin's Church where the passing bell was sounding its discordant notes in the ears of the poor criminals. We got near the gallows, in the midst of such an assembly of people as I have never witnessed before, nor ever wish to see again on such an occasion. The malefectors, consisting of a Jew, five or six other men and one woman, a servant who let her sweetheart rob the house of plate. He was also hung, by her side, and there was much cheering from the mob at this brave spectacle.

Piracy by large groups was gradually replaced by smaller gangs of smugglers, as an easier way to make a living. For those trying to enforce the law it was still somewhat less hazardous to intercept the smugglers while they were in the open sea and this was the responsibility of the Customs men on the Revenue Cutters. They patrolled the waters constantly, checking all the vessels they encountered and boarding and searching any they considered to be suspect. Prior to the development of the town of Milford the main Customs port was at Pembroke but by 1796, just six years after the foundation of the town with the introduction of the whalers, Milford had two locally based cutters, the *Speedwell* and the *Endeavour*. A third vessel, the *Diligence* — a 14-gun, 152-ton cutter with a crew of 44 — also patrolled the area under the command of Lt. William Dobbin who with other Customs men was to find fame at the time of the French invasion of Fishguard in 1797. It is suggested that it was Dobbin, out on patrol, who had the first sighting of the French fleet.

Britain had been at war with France for four years, following the execution of King Louis XVI in 1793, and the fleet was the result of a scheme laid by American born William Tate. Tate, a republican of Irish origin, had fought against the British in the American War of Independence after which he offered his services to the French, encouraging a belief that he could raise the Irish in an attempt to bring down prime minister Pitt and the British Government. An intended invasion of Ireland failed, and Tate's next plan was to take Bristol and march through Wales gathering the support of disaffected Welshmen on his way to Liverpool. This scheme, too, did not go according to plan and so it was at the North Bishop's Rock that the French fleet was first spotted on 22 February 1797 before they made what has now gone down in history as 'The Last Invasion of Britain'. With understandable discretion, Dobbin, recognising that although the *Diligence* was one of the largest Customs vessels he was heavily outgunned by the French, wasted no time in making for safety so that he could report his disturbing sight to his superior officer, John Adams.

The Pembroke Customs Officer John Adams put himself at the disposal of Lord Cawdor to assist with communications and Captain Longcroft, the Navy Regulating Captain for Haverfordwest took command of seamen drawn from the various ships in Milford Haven armed with guns from their cutters, as Dobbin and John Hopkins, the master of the *Speedwell*, mustered their own crews.

After the French landed at Carreg Wastad Point Colonel Knox first marched his men towards them, across Goodwick sands, then, deciding that his force was too small to confront the enemy he returned to Fishguard Fort, a decision his men accepted with considerable reluctance. Cawdor meanwhile had received instructions to lead the Pembrokeshire Yeomanry Cavalry to Haverfordwest together with the Cardigan Militia who were on guard duties at Pembroke, and to save time and avoid the long journey round by road the force crossed the river, ferried in a series of boats, at Pembroke Ferry. This force lost no time in making for Haverfordwest and so on towards Fishguard.

At daybreak Knox, realising how greatly he was outnumbered by the French, decided to retreat and after first ordering the troops in the Fort to spike their guns and tip their ammunition over the cliff (an order they disobeyed) he led them towards

Haverfordwest, taking a rest at Treffgarne where he was shortly joined by Cawdor coming in the opposite direction. An argument ensued among Cawdor, his second-in-command Colby, and Knox as to who was in overall command. Eventually it was agreed that this belonged to Cawdor, Knox turned his troops around and the combined force marched on to Fishguard. Meanwhile, the well-to-do local people gathered together their treasures and fled, in panic, towards Haverfordwest and Narberth.

During the course of the next couple of days there were a number of skirmishes with the French during which Jemima Nicholas (a local cobbler and a very powerful lady) achieved lasting fame when she marched to the Pencaer Peninsula and, single-handed, captured 12 of the French invaders. For this act of heroism Jemima was awarded a life pension of £50 per annum.

Yet it was the after effects of a shipwreck that were to play a large part in the downfall of the invading force. Just a few weeks before the invasion a cargo of wine from a wrecked Portuguese coaster had found its way into almost every home in the area and was soon discovered by the marauding French (many of them convicts and desperadoes) who lost no time in drinking themselves into complete intoxication. They had never been a very orderly fighting force, and soon became a drunken rabble. It was not long before the invading troops, by now drunk and disenchanted, mutinied and the force surrendered.

The enmity that had been simmering between Knox and Cawdor now came to a head. Knox was asked to relinquish his commission because of his 'ignorance and incapacity' and the allegation that, because of his cowardice, he had left Fishguard undefended. When he protested, Cawdor replied that he would resign his own commission rather than risk his character as an officer by serving under Knox. This so incensed Knox that he called out his fellow officer for 'satisfaction'. The two men arranged to meet, with their seconds, on 24 May 1797 'on the turnpike road between Pembroke Ferry and the road that turns off at Williamston'. There is no record that the duel ever took place although both men and their seconds kept the appointment. In his diary for that day Cawdor merely wrote: 'A very fine day. After breakfast rode to the Ferry. Met Jos there and Mr. Knox and Col. Vaughan near the Williamston road. Rode home, back by half past one.' Both certainly survived and later that year Knox left for London, where he died in poverty in 1825.

When the French surrendered they were first imprisoned in Haverfordwest, many of them in St. Mary's Church where they caused a great deal of damage. There was, however, some sympathy in the town for 'the poor starving wretches' and the townspeople, according to John Brown in his *History of Haverfordwest*, vied with one another in ministering to their necessities. It was then decided that over 500 of the prisoners should be marched to Milford where the cutters were used as a temporary prison. Thirty prisoners from a group imprisoned in Pembroke escaped with the help of local girls, boarded a boat belonging to Lord Cawdor — adding insult to injury — and made for the coast where they cast the boat adrift and took a brig on which they sailed to freedom. Others, it is said, escaped imprisonment and made marriages in the county. Later the remaining captives were removed to prison hulks off Portsmouth which had been brought into use when the American War of Independence had ended the practice of transporting convicts to North America.

In repelling the 'invasion' the Customs men had acquitted themselves with distinction. There was high praise from Lord Cawdor who wrote of the 'extraordinary efforts of the sea officers and seamen' who assisted him in marching the prisoners to Milford:

> I take the liberty of more particularly recommending to your honourable Board the conduct of Mr. Adams the Collector of Pembroke, who did me the honour of serving as a private in my troop of yeomanry cavalry, and who, with great intelligence and activity, had taken every measure in his power to obtain and communicate with despatch all information that might be important; of Lt. Hopkins of the *Speedwell* cutter, to whose extraordinary exertions in landing guns etc. from the vessel he commanded, the surprising expedition with which he brought them forward a distance of more than 27 miles and in short for the whole spirited and officer-like conduct; the conduct of Lt. Dobbin of the *Diligence* cutter, to whom I think the Service highly indebted for exertions that do credit to the profession to which he has the honour to belong and which will ever call for my grateful remembrance.

The Board expressed its gratitude by presenting Adams with a silver loving cup which bore a dedication from the Customs Commissioners and an engraving of the French surrender on Goodwick sands. Hopkins and Dobbin each received superbly engraved ceremonial swords.

Lord Cawdor was soon to become involved in a smuggling incident. In a letter written to Charles Greville in November 1801, Lady Caroline Cawdor of Stackpole Court describes an attack on her husband by smugglers who were unloading a cargo of spirits at Freshwater East. Cawdor had heard of the arrival of the vessel and rode, unarmed, with three men to accost them. When they arrived at the beach the smugglers dropped their casks on the shore and fled to their boat but returned when they realised that they faced only a small group of men:

> Lord C. and Mat [Cambell] were returning home when they were attacked by some of these horrible desperate villains. Two of them fell upon Lord C., one armed with a great bludgeon, the other with a large poker with which he hit Lord C. a violent blow on his arm. Lord C. jumped off his horse and tried to catch hold of him when another came behind and knocked him down with a blow to his head. In this situation, with both these men thumping him, it is most fortunate he was so little stunned as to be able to get up and twist the poker out of this man's hand, with which he hit one of them and then they both ran away.
>
> In the meantime Mat was attacked by two others, and you know how little able he is to make much resistance. Hand and Dio [the two other men who had gone ahead] came to his assistance. They beat off one of the men and the other they secured and carried him to Rogers' house in Trewent. A short time after, the house was surrounded by about thirty of the gang, people of the country armed with bludgeons, who immediately rescued their comrade.

Warrants are out for apprehending those men that are known but none are as yet taken. It was, to be sure, a most foolish business to think of going against smugglers without arms, and I trust they will act with more caution in future. I think it is most wonderful their escaping with their lives or, at least, without broken bones. Lord C. has been very ill in consequence. He kept his bed all day yesterday and was twice blooded but, thank God, he is so much better tonight I feel quite easy about him.

Wrecking was another way by which people could supplement their income. Stories abound of wrecking on the Pembrokeshire coast where it was said some isolated communities lived by displaying false lights to lure ships onto the rocks before the survivors were brutally murdered. Once every living thing on board, including animals, was dead the vessel could officially be declared a total loss, so belonging to nobody, and the wreckers were free to claim their prize. News of a ship in trouble spread rapidly and brought crowds onto the beaches in search of whatever cargo they could plunder before the authorities arrived on the scene. Bodies would be found washed up with the fingers broken where valuable rings had been torn off.

In 1894 Pembrokeshire created its own 'Whisky Galore' folklore when the full rigged iron ship *Loch Shiel* was wrecked after becoming stranded near Angle. It had been carrying a cargo of gunpowder, 7,500 cases of whisky and 7,000 of beer. Despite the prompt arrival of the Customs officers the greater part of the whisky soon found its way into hiding places around the village. It was reported that between 50 and 100 people were seen on the beach drinking and taking away all they could carry. The Angle lifeboatmen had carried out a magnificent rescue operation (for which they were honoured by the RNLI) but three deaths resulted from either excessive drinking or greed — a father and son drowned in their determination to take any risk to get their share of the booty and a young man died of exposure after collapsing in a drunken stupor and lying outside all night. In October 1999 members of the Adventurous Divers Club of Swansea recovered seven of the *Loch Shiel's* then 105-year-old bottles of beer.

There were, of course, genuine lights all around the coast to guide vessels to safety. Trinity House erected a light at St. Ann's in 1662 and 50 years later the local landowner Joseph Allen of Dale Castle was granted a lease to build and operate two coal-fired lights on the headland. He was permitted to collect the dues from the shipmasters at Milford Haven for the use of the lights, receiving dues of one penny per ton from British ships and two pence from the owners of foreign vessels.

The lighthouse was built on the site of what was possibly a mediaeval chapel and there is a suggestion that there was a light on the headland in these early times. It may be that, rather than this being a dedicated lighthouse, the monks or priests regularly kept a fire burning as a warning to shipping. The present lighthouse provides a waypoint for coastal traffic with a red sector light marking the Crow and Toe Rocks off Linney Head. It was built in 1841 and was manned until June 1998. Now it is monitored and controlled via a telemetry link from the Trinity House Operations Control Centre at Harwich. In 1996 it was converted into an observatory and holiday apartments, and early in the new century was put on sale at a guide price of £450,000 as a 'desirable residence with stupendous sea views towards Skomer and Skokholm'.

Chapter 9

Civil War

The fortunes, or misfortunes, of the county of Pembrokeshire have time and time again depended on its waterway. Undefended it was vulnerable to enemy attack (a point made by John Poyer, the Parliamentarian mayor of Pembroke as he sought aid in the defence of Pembroke Castle during the Civil War) but, at the same time, sea-borne reinforcements and provisions have played a vital role in countering siege and inland invasion.

At the outbreak of the Civil War Pembrokeshire was the only one of the 12 counties of Wales to support Parliament although its three Members of Parliament were divided in their loyalties. The county member, John Wogan of Wiston, and Sir Hugh Owen of Orielton, representing Pembroke Borough, were Parliamentarians while Sir John Stepney, M.P. for Haverfordwest, was a Royalist ('of a mild type' according to James Phillips in his *History of Pembrokeshire*).

While the local gentry tended to be divided it was the merchants of Tenby and Pembroke with their strong sea-borne trade links with Bristol and London who came out most vigorously in support of Parliament — most notably John Poyer who, with his supporters, held the town of Pembroke establishing it as a major Parliamentarian base on the edge of Royalist Wales.

The loyalty of the Haverfordwest mayor and corporation is difficult to establish as the church bells there were rung (at a cost of 2s. a time) and hospitality offered impartially to either side as victory swung between Cavaliers and Roundheads. It is unclear whether the town initially declared for King or Parliament, as Parliament claimed they held it at the end of 1642, yet the Royalist commander, Richard Vaughan, Earl of Carbery was able to visit in March 1643. Certainly Tenby and Haverfordwest were in Royalist hands in August 1643, Carbery receiving the same enthusiastic welcome in Haverfordwest later accorded to Cromwell. It all proved a costly business for the corporation who not only footed the bill for their impartial entertainment of friend and foe but were also made to pay the 'levies and exactions' of both sides, in addition, subsequently, to the cost of demolishing their own castle — the result of what Phillips and Warren describe in their *History of Haverfordwest* as 'their shifty tactics'.

Despite the Royalist threat, Pembroke remained the only town which never surrendered to the Royalists at any time in the conflict. The king's neglect of his fleet, despite choosing from 1634 to exact Ship Money from his subjects, had prompted the majority of the navy to declare for Parliament, encouraging Poyer to seek support from Bristol as the Carmarthen based Carbery pushed towards the Pembroke stronghold. He called on the mayor of Bristol to send men and arms to his aid but before help could reach him Bristol and its fleet had fallen to the Royalists. Two of the captured vessels were despatched to Milford Haven with guns and ammunition to arm the extensive earthwork fort which had been constructed by the Royalists at Pill in an attempt to seize supremacy over the waterway and break the military deadlock. The larger vessel, a warship, was recaptured while the other, the frigate *Hart*, escaped up river to Boulston where the crew landed and made their way to safety in Haverfordwest. Here they were entertained by the ever-hospitable mayor and were also provided with money to see them on their way back home to Bristol.

The Earl of Carbery. His leadership did not inspire his troops. He led them out of Tenby to assist in the defence of Trefloyne when it was being attacked by Laugharne, only to wheel 'about with all his forces and [run back] into the town' when he came under fire (Carmarthenshire County Museum)

Nevertheless, naval support did reach Pembroke in the shape of a squadron commanded by Admiral Richard Swanley. In early 1644, the Parliamentary military commander in Pembroke, Colonel Laugharne, a local man who was serving in the regiment of his uncle, Adjutant General Sir John Meyrick of Fleet, went on the offensive. He took Stackpole on 30 January and Trefloyne a few days later and then turned his attention to the Pill fort. Swanley was persuaded to land 200 seamen, 60 horse, two siege guns and four field pieces at Barnlake Pill, the guns being set up on the high ground on the east side of the entrance to the Pill. With these reinforcements the combined forces bombarded and then captured the fort.

After this success, Laugharne set out to cut off the Haverfordwest road, pausing at Steynton to leave 20 musketeers on guard in the church tower. The Royalist horse and foot approaching from Johnston took flight at the sight of the approaching horde, and turned back to Haverfordwest before pushing on to Carmarthen and taking with them the M.P. Sir Hugh Owen 'unbreasted and in his pantables' as their prisoner. The story was told, however, (particularly in Parliamentarian circles) that the Royalists'

Rowland Laugharne
(British Library)

hasty retreat was actually precipitated when they mistook a herd of black cattle stampeding towards them for an enemy attack. Two days later the Royalists had lost Roch Castle and Tenby, described by a writer of the day as 'the strongest hold in South Wales and of great consequence to the king'. Carew Castle soon followed, briefly returning the whole of Pembrokeshire to Parliament.

The Haverfordwest Common Council had meantime, during the recent Royalist presence, signed a deed of loyalty to the King, and as a reward the town had been charged with paying the expenses of the Royalist occupation for which a special rate was levied. However, with just over half of the money paid out, the town was now in Parliamentary hands and the remaining funds went towards the cost of Laugharne's re-occupation.

In the Spring of 1644 Charles Gerard replaced Carbery as Royalist commander in south Wales. Known for his brutality, he assembled a force of some 2,000 men and quickly counter-attacked the Parliamentary forces which had moved out of Pembrokeshire and into neighbouring Cardiganshire and Carmarthenshire, soon pushing them back into Pembrokeshire. Haverfordwest held out for a while, before Laugharne was left in control of only Pembroke and Tenby. However, in August Gerard was called away to fight in England, and towards the end of the year Laugharne was once more on the offensive, finding the countryside more ready to accept him as a result of Gerard's scorched earth policies.

1645 saw almost a repeat performance of the campaigns of 1644. Gerard returned and by May Laugharne was once more bottled up in Tenby and Pembroke, this time having hastily evacuated Haverfordwest as the Royalists entered at the other side, whereupon Gerard was again called away. Laugharne regrouped his forces and in July led his force forth from Pembroke, which included 200 men from Captain William Batten's frigate *Warwick* together with his own force of 500 foot, 200 horse and a party of dragoons.

In Haverfordwest the Royalists assembled their own army of 1,500 men, and the two forces met at Colby Moor on 1 August. In a total rout, Laugharne secured an historic victory leaving his opponents with 150 dead and 700 men taken prisoner while his own casualties amounted to a mere two killed and 60 wounded. The vanquished generals departed leaving behind a garrison in Haverfordwest Castle which Laugharne proceeded to take by firing the outer gate and scaling the battlements.

By September the Roundheads had regained the whole of the county and a Day of Thanksgiving was declared on 28 September — but the final battle had yet to be won. There was discontent everywhere in the kingdom with a bad harvest exacerbating anger at heavy taxation and the victorious leaders and the local forces were particularly vociferous in their furious demands. The locally recruited men, who were to be disbanded, asserted that they were owed considerable arrears of pay while both Laugharne and Poyer protested that they had used their own money (Laugharne said it had cost him the enormous sum of £37,000) in the conduct of the war for which they had been denied compensation. Poyer refused to hand over Pembroke Castle to the Parliamentary Col. Fleming who had been despatched to take over from him and, together with Laugharne and Col. Rice Powell, promptly changed sides, declaring for the King, one of a number of often isolated incidents that led to the Second Civil War.

It was a fateful move for the three men. They set out to take the whole of south Wales but were defeated in battle at St. Fagans to be driven back to Pembroke where Poyer's garrison prepared to be besieged by Cromwell. An early assault proved unsuccessful, for the castle was virtually impregnable, protected on three sides by water and high unscaleable cliffs and capable of being isolated from the town by the Barbican tower and Gate House. The arrival of heavy guns ordered from Gloucester was delayed when they sank at Berkeley on the Severn, not to be recovered until five weeks into the siege; an attempt to storm the walls failed because the scaling ladders proved too short and, to add to their difficulties, the Parliamentarians ran out of cannonballs and were forced to resort to firing pebbles while they awaited more supplies from the iron foundries in Carmarthen.

Eventually it was starvation that brought about the rebels' surrender. Morale was already low in the garrison and the town itself was in a sorry state — thatched roofs had been stripped to feed the horses of both sides, horses were stabled in the churches, property had been ransacked in the search for food and many of the houses were damaged during Cromwell's bombardment which had also killed 30 of the townspeople and around 100 of the garrison. Cromwell, too, suffered the loss of 30 men when Laugharne attacked with a troop of horse. Success came to Cromwell as a result of his strategy in cutting off essential supplies to the castle. Corn could no longer reach the garrison when the town mills on Dark Lane Bridge were bombarded and, at the same time, the pipes which carried water to the castle from a spring at Monkton were cut. Unaware that help was on the way as the Duke of Hamilton was making his way to Pembrokeshire with an army of 10,000 Scots, Poyer surrendered on 11 July 1648.

Poyer's, Laugharne's and Powell's estates were sequestered after which, in a bizarre lottery drawn by a child, it was determined which of them would be executed. Two of the lottery papers bore the words 'Life given by God', the third — a blank — was handed by the child to Poyer who was shot at Covent Garden in 1649, some months after the execution of the king. Better fortune smiled on Laugharne who was elected M.P. for Pembroke Borough in 1661 (after the Restoration of the Monarchy) a position he held until his death.

During the siege of Pembroke Castle the mayor and corporation of Haverfordwest sent a gift of 11 hogsheads and 50 barrels of beer to Cromwell's army, with a personal present for Cromwell himself of a cask of cider and $4\frac{3}{4}$lbs. of loaf sugar (at 2s. 6d. per lb). It is also recorded that when Cromwell arrived in Haverfordwest on 16 July 1648 after the eventual recapture of Pembroke Castle, he was welcomed, unsurprisingly, with 'a merry peal of bells' from St. Mary's church and was entertained by the family of the dyer, Richard Prust, at their home on the corner by St. Martin's church, known to this day as Cromwell's Corner. Each morning 'little Bobby Prust', the son of Cromwell's host, took their distinguished guest to Gwyn's Ditch (or Queen's Ditch) off Cokey Street (now City Road) 'that he might have his morning draught of the delicious spring water' from the well that became known as Cromwell's Well. (The Prusts were clearly significant townspeople. Robert Prust ['little Bobby'?] was sheriff in 1668 and mayor in 1673 and again in 1683, at which time Robert Prust junior was sheriff. Members of the Prust family — Stephen, Benjamin, Michael, Joseph, Charles and several more Roberts — feature in the list of town mayors until 1802, the reign of George III.)

Haverfordwest's hospitality didn't prevent Cromwell from ordering the slighting of both Pembroke and Haverfordwest castles. It had fallen to Thomas Barlow to consider which Pembrokeshire fortresses should be destroyed and a letter signed by him and by Roger, Sam and John Lort remains in Haverfordwest's extensive records. It was despatched to the mayor and aldermen of Haverfordwest saying:

> Wee being authorised by Parliament to viewe and consider what garrisons and places of strength are fit to be demolished, and we finding that the said castle of Haverfordwest is not tenable for ye service of the State, and yet that it may be used by illaffected persons to the prejudice of the peace of these parts. These are to authorize and require you to summon in the hundred of Rouse and ye inhabitants of the towne and county of Haverfordwest and that they forthwith demolish the workes, walls and towers, of the said castle, soe as that the said castle may not be possesst by the enemy to the endangering of the peace of these parts.
> Given under our hands this 12th of July 1648.
> To the Maior and Aldermen of Haverfordwest
> We expect an accompt of your proceedings with effect in this business by Saturday the 15th of July instant.

There then followed a footnote signed by Cromwell. 'If a speedy course bee not taken to fulfill the commands of this warrant, I shalbee necessitated to consider of settings a guarrison.'

The mayor, John Prynne, replied that demolition work had started but proved difficult and asked for powder from the ships and for the work to be shared by the whole county, with a levy raised to cover the costs incurred:

Lieftenant Gouerell —
Cromwells orders for
the demollishinge of the
Castell of Haverfordwest

Whereas vpon view, and consideration
with mr. Roger Loct mr. Samuell Loct [son]
and the maior and Aldermen of Haverford
west it is thought fitt for the present
ninge, of the peace of this County
that the Castle of Haverfordwest
should bee speedily demolished, Theis
are to Authorise you to call [together]
your asistant in the preformance of
this service, the Inhabitants of
the Hunderds of Dangleddy Dewisland
Kemis, Roose, and Kilganury. whoe
are hereby required to giue you asistance
Giuen vnder our handes this
14ᵗʰ of July 1648   Cromwell

to the maior and
Aldermen of Haver-
fordwest.

Sam: Loct
John Loct

The reply from Cromwell to John Prynne's request for help in demolishing Haverfordwest Castle
(Pembrokeshire Record Office, Haverfordwest)

Honored Sir,

Wee received an order from your honour and the Committee for the demolishinge of the Castle of Haverfordwest; Accordinge to which wee have this daie sett some workemen aboute it, but wee finde the worke soe difficulte to be broughte aboute without Powder to blowe it up, that it will exhuast an Immense some of money and will not in a longe time be effected: Wherefore wee become suitors to your honour that there may a competent quantity of powder be spared out of the shipps for the speedy effectinge the worke Wee and the Countye payinge for the same And wee likewise desire that your honour and the Comittee be pleased that the whole Countie may ioyne with us in the worke and that an order may be conceived for the levyinge of a Competent some of money on the severall hundreds of the Countie for the payinge for the powder and defreyinge the rest of the charge. Thus beinge overbold to be troublesome to your honour desiringe to knowe your honours resolve herein wee rest.

Your honours humble servantes

Haverfordwest 13th July 1648

Etheldred Wogan	John Prynne Maior		
Will. Bowen	Roger Bevans		
William Williams	John Harries	Jenkin Howell	Wm. Meyler

Cromwell, who seems to have been quite accommodating, replied (see opposite) '... it is thought fitt for the preservinge of the peace of this countye that the Castle of Haverfordwest should bee speedily demolished. Theise are to Authorise you to call unto your assistance in the performance of this service, the Inhabitants of the Hundreds of Daugleddy Dewisland Kemis, Roose, and Kilgarren whoo are hearby required to give you asistance ...'.

It has been noted, interestingly, that while the total levy amounted to £130 only £40 appears in the accounts for the work, suggesting, particularly in view of the less than total demolition carried out, (even now most of the keep remains intact), that the people of Haverfordwest had made a mere token gesture in response to the command and had found a better use for the money at a time when borough funds were at their lowest.

In Pembroke a charge of gunpowder raised the roof of the Barbican tower, which then settled again with little damage done. However, other parts of the castle were extensively damaged and it is believed that much stone from the castle was used by the local people as they set about restoring their own homes to the detriment of the once proud stronghold.

Yet, if Cromwell seems to have listened to the requests of the authorities in Haverfordwest, other petitions appear to have been less favourably received. The mayor requested relief from an assessment for revenue to fund the Commonwealth's campaign in Ireland, protesting that the £60,000 demanded was more than Tenby, Pembroke and Carmarthen had been called on to pay and pointing out (in effect) in a letter addressed to Cromwell, that times were hard because of the Irish 'frigetts' which barred them from trading with Bristol 'whereon all our trade dependeth'. The desperate situation is enlarged in a petition from the inhabitants of Haverfordwest to the Committee for the Army:

> Petitioners since the beginning of the war have been firm to the Parliament and in 1644 maintained a garrison upon their own charge against the late king's party, and for this have been plundered of their estates, and many taken prisoners and forced to redeem themselves by paying great sums of money. During the siege of Pembrooke, being nine weeks or thereabouts, they assisted the Parliament's forces, being under the command of Lieutenant General Cromwell and then on free quarter. Have been heavily burthened with the relieving of prisoners taken by the late king's forces, maintaining sick and wounded soldiers and demolishing the castle of Haverfordwest by the Lieutenant General's order and by paying the monthly assessment and the assessment for Ireland, being therein raised from £10 to £41 a month although the Army in August and September last in their march to Milford Haven to take shipping for Ireland were maintained by the petitioners for the most part upon free quarter and continued a long time there, and do daily quarter there as they go. Petitioners are brought very poor and most of the inhabitants not able to maintain themselves and families as many are forced to leave the town by reason of the heavy assessment, which if continued any longer will be to their utter undoing.

A further petition seeking relief 'out of the delinquents' [those who had fought for the king] estates in Wales or otherwise' added that the grounds around the town, which were the main means of their livelihood, had been ruined over a period of three years, plundered by Royalist forces. The inhabitants had built up bulwarks and other fences for the defence of the town and claimed that, at the rout of Colby Moor, many who were there in Parliament's service were wounded or killed. In the face of the latter apparent lie, it is perhaps unsurprising that the protests fell on deaf ears.

Early in 1649 Cromwell had been appointed by Parliament to lead the expeditionary force invading Ireland. Vessels assembled in Milford Haven, regiments were raised and on 13 August Cromwell sailed from the Haven, landing two days later, whereupon he sacked Drogheda and Wexford and seized Dublin from the city's Royalist defenders.

A hoard of coins discovered at Tregwynt Manor in 1996 provides a fascinating postscript to the story of the Civil War. There had long been a legend that treasure was buried at Tregwynt in north Pembrokeshire, a legacy, it was said, of the French invasion of 1797. The site was searched on many occasions without success until Roy Lewis of the Pembrokeshire Prospectors was invited back by the owners when a considerable amount of soil moving had taken place. This time he quite literally struck gold — and silver too. In all he unearthed 500 gold and silver coins and, nearby, a man's 17th-century gold ring inscribed 'Rather Death then Falce of Fayth', dating the hoard to the time of the Civil War. At this period the house was occupied by Llewellyn Harries and his family who were Catholics, and so almost certainly Royalists. A coroner's inquest deemed the hoard 'treasure trove' and it is now held by the National Museum of Wales and recognised as the most important hoard of Civil War treasure found in Wales.

Chapter 10

Milford Haven

During the closing years of the 18th century all that existed in what is now the town and port of Milford Haven was an old chapel and two farms, Pill Farm where the Whetham public house now stands and Summerhouse Farm at the rear of today's Robert Street.

Not too far away, though, were the small but bustling ports, a hive of industry at Hubberston (where the Norseman Hubba landed in 878AD), Hakin Pill and Priory Pill. Hubberston had extended along the shore line into Hakin as it developed into a busy fishing village with the mail packet for Waterford sailing from its anchorage in Hubberston Roads, some three-quarters of a mile away from the shore.

If they were lucky, passengers were ferried ashore in small boats — a potential lucrative earner for the local fishermen, although John Brown in *The History of Haverford-west with that of Some Pembrokeshire Parishes* records that in its earliest days, because of landing difficulties, there was little passenger traffic on the packet. 'The passengers', he said, 'had to submit to the inconvenience of being carried on men's shoulders over the mud when the tide was out. On one occasion two gentlemen, greatly to their amusement, were being thus conveyed when one of them incautiously burst out into a laugh and exclaimed to his companion "Well! if ever I expected to ride on a Welsh goat".'

'"Indeed then", said the testy Welshman, "and you shall see his tricks" — and with a simulated stumble deposited his load into the mud.'

The earliest packets (so named because of the mail packets they carried) were sailing vessels — the *Auckland, Freeling, Gower, Iris, Mansfield, Montrose* and *Camden* — which, under post office regulations of the day, would have been provided by their captains. In April 1824 the sailing ships were replaced by four steamers (each with a complement of 15 men including officers, engineers and seamen), but after only two months two of the best were transferred to Holyhead, an occasion for considerable resentment in Milford where it was felt that lower horsepower, smaller, inferior vessels had been substituted. Their captains, however, remained — experienced seamen and, it was said, notorious smugglers of salts, spirits, soap and glass.

Other vessels also used this little port and John Brown records extracts from the diary of a lady who travelled to Pembrokeshire from Liverpool in 1772:

On Tuesday morning, 1 o'clock, we were so happy as to anchor in Hubberston Bay. Happy indeed we were for immediately the wind shifted and had we lain to, which we first intended to, at the harbour's mouth, we might have been blown out to sea. At seven we landed in the village which is very small and irregularly built (the houses being all constructed of a rough stone) and consists only of a few little public houses ... After breakfasting and thanking God, who had been pleased to place me on dry land again, I took horse for Little Hoaten which is about seven miles, and arrived in time for dinner where I found my friends well.

Schooners sailed up Goose Pill off Priory Pill (also referred to as Hubberston Pill) to Havenshead, and up Priory Pill itself to unload cargoes of lime to be burned in the kilns of the two settlements. There was also a corn mill (mentioned by Charles Greville in 1779) and later a timber mill at Priory and these, too, were supplied by the vessels plying the waterway. Small scale shipbuilding was carried out at most of the settlements before the yards were built at Hubberston in the late 19th century and Hubberston and Priory were linked by a thoroughfare which ran through Havenshead — the route taken by men from the settlements as they made their way to work in the shipbuilding yards.

It was to the undeveloped tract of land on the Haven that Sir William Hamilton came in 1782. He was recently widowed and had inherited from his wife, one of the Barlows of Slebech, a substantial Pembrokeshire estate. He was accompanied on his visit by his nephew the Hon. Charles Greville whose vision and enthusiasm for the potential of the waterway inspired the older man. Through his appointment as Envoy Extraordinary to the Court of Naples, Hamilton was destined to become an absentee landlord and he appointed Greville as his agent with powers to develop the property as he saw fit. It is also suggested that, in a deal between the two men, Greville's appointment was in return for the 'gift' to his uncle of his mistress, Emma Hart — the notorious Emma who became the second Lady Hamilton and Nelson's mistress.

Greville worked enthusiastically on his waterway project and the Parliament Act of 1790 enabled him to 'make and provide quays, docks, piers and other erections and to establish a market with proper roads and avenues within the manor and lordship of Hubberston and Pill'. He set about building a Customs House (now occupied by the Milford Museum) with a quay in front of it to cater for the many vessels which were driven into the security of the Haven by bad weather. Another priority was building an inn to accommodate passengers from the Irish packet. But he also looked further afield.

During the American War of Independence the Nantucket Quaker whalers had remained loyal to the king with the result that it was becoming more and more difficult for them to pursue their calling on the high seas. Their ships were taken, harbours raided and supplies cut off and when Greville, with government support, offered them a new and better life in the embryonic town it must have seemed a God-sent opportunity. Letters giving a glowing picture of the area and its potential for their fishery trade encouraged them to make the momentous move. A Quaker, Thomas Owen, writing from Waterford, described the people of Pembrokeshire as:

rather comfortable in themselves, civil to strangers and hospitable in their houses having little or no propensity to trade farther than the verge of their respective farms, coal mines, slate or limestone quarry. Great number of hardy watermen employed at herring fishing, carrying lime, coal and culm round the coast dragging for oisters etc. wages small.

Manufactory stokings coarse and fine, all yarn made of wool made in the country, great quantity of coarse woolen cloth made in a neighbouring county Merioneth [!] sent to the London market undyed for clothing the Army, use of Slobb Shops [?] etc. etc.

Central situation of Milford Haven, about 18 hours sail to Bristol, same to Cork and Dublin, 10 to Waterford and about 24 to Liverpool. The first mentioned but more especially the last carry on a very extensive trade to the interior parts of the kingdom by the long rivers and canells, great advantage arising by getting to her mooring immediately from the sea ... its also well worth observing the contiguity of Milford with Ireland where the Newfoundland fishermen come from all parts of England to victual or man.

He also made reference to the Irish packet from Hubberston where it was said 'large men of war lyes off this pile'.

Pointing out what he described as a 'disadvantage', Owen added that the area had 'little or no oil', (which must surely have been an added inducement to a group whose business was oil), though he also mentioned that 'bone etc can be disposed of in the Haven'.

So great was the enthusiasm of both Greville and the government to bring the whalers to Milford that considerable inducements were offered. Each ship-owner lessee was to enjoy free accommodation for shipping at Hubberston and Castle Pill. There was to be 'easy accommodation, protection and preference to the Friends' with land at a peppercorn rent as a site for a Meeting House and burial ground plus exemption from ground rents for two years from Midsummer 1791. Their privileges, however, were not to preclude Sir William Hamilton from carrying out his plans for quays and docks on the Pills and the settlers would not 'embarrass themselves with agriculture' but depend on the markets which, said Greville in one of his many letters, 'the richness of the country can supply to any degree of increased population'. He also wrote that land could be rented in the neighbourhood for 7 or 14 years from 18s. to 30s. an acre according to quality, while the rent was less in more distant sites. Stone was available 'for the quarrying' and £1,000 worth of timber was ready to hand.

With so many assurances and promises ringing in their ears 25 families planned to make the journey in 13 ships (of an average tonnage of 75 tons) with a complement of 182 men. In the end it seems that fewer families set out, but in 1792 two of the most prominent Nantucket Quaker families, the Folgers and the Starbucks, had arrived in Milford. The main party followed shortly afterwards and the wealthy Benjamin Rotch joined them a few years later.

For some years the sperm oil trade prospered, but rather than continuing their own whaling activities many of the settlers imported the oil from the United States and

South-east view of Milford, reproduced by Jim McBrearty from a 19th-century lithograph

transhipped it in smaller vessels to London where its primary use was for street lighting. Evasion of import duty on these cargoes by passing them off as a local product later brought them into disfavour with the government. At least five vessels, however, appear to have operated from Milford.

In December 1799 the *Ann* sailed for Milford from New Bedford carrying a cargo of 681 casks of whale oil and 426 bundles of whale bone in addition to hard tack, raisins, chocolate and soap — a cargo destined for Benjamin Rotch and valued at £9,100. Just a few weeks later the *Whareham* arrived with around £7,000 worth of sperm oil and prime beef, pork, molasses, coffee, rum and wooden staves — another cargo which was addressed to Rotch. Similar imports continued over the years.

These settlers were not only seamen, they were also traders, well versed in commerce. Rotch's son, Francis, opened one of the town's first banks, the Milford and Haverfordwest Bank and without delay the Quakers set up a bakery to supply biscuits and ship's bread for their number, while a brewery started by Gayer Starbuck was established on the site which later housed the railway station, and Samuel Starbuck opened a mill at Priory.

However, by the early years of the 19th century the government had withdrawn the whalers' privileges on the grounds that they had not honoured an original agreement that their vessels would be fully outfitted at Milford Haven, and also that duty had not been paid on the oil imported into the country. At the same time the demand for spermacetti oil dropped dramatically with the introduction of gas lighting; whilst Greville, the Friends' major supporter, died in 1809. Many of the settlers began to return home. The end of Milford's brief whaling industry was in sight and by 1820, during the depression which followed the Napoleonic War, it was almost non-existent.

The coming of the whalers is recorded as part of a triptych in the small St. Thomas à Becket beacon chapel, a historic gem hidden from view by the houses on the Rath. The original chapel was built in 1180 AD and was a beacon chapel acting as both lighthouse and shelter to mariners, the only one surviving of three of these early lighthouses placed around the Haven. It acquired its name from the assassination ten years earlier of Thomas à Becket, Archbishop of Canterbury. That event is recorded as

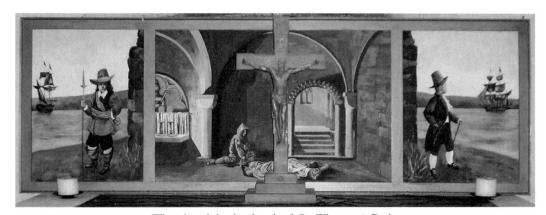

The triptych in the church of St. Thomas à Becket

part of the triptych, as is the Civil War battle which raged on the site in 1644 when the Parliamentarians under Swanley defeated the Royalists, capturing '7 captains, 300 men, 18 great ordnance and 6 field carriages'. After the Dissolution of the Monasteries the chapel became ruinous and was in use as a pig sty. It was not until 1935 that the building was restored using the original stones together with those from other religious houses. Although it is now less used it remains consecrated and is dedicated to quiet prayer. (The adjoining St. Thomas's Lodge is occupied by Franciscan Sister Gwenfryd, who has lived there since 1991 leading a solitary life after many strenuously active years of ministry and now uses the chapel for quiet contemplation.)

During the period when the whalers were actively in business the once successful businessman, Benjamin Rotch, had gone bankrupt, one of the many financial casualties of the development of Milford. At the height of his prosperity he had bought Castle Hall, a splendid and ornate villa which was built in the 1770s by John Zephaniah Holwell, the retired governor of Bengal who claimed to be one of only 23 survivors (out of 147 prisoners) of the Black Hole of Calcutta. In 1799 it was sold to a Haverfordwest wine merchant, John Warlow, who lived there until bankruptcy in 1804 forced him to sell. Rotch then abandoned his plans to build a house on Hamilton Terrace in order to buy this prestigious desirable residence.

However, it was not long before he too found himself in financial difficulties — three of his ships were sunk during the war with France even before the price of sperm oil plummeted. He was forced to sell his home and, a broken man, left the county. Castle Hall passed into the ownership of the Greville family, bought by Robert Fulke Greville who had succeeded his brother Charles.

By the time of his death Charles had fulfilled only a small portion of his plans for the new town. However, he had built the Customs House and quay and the French born 'Assistant to the Inspector General of Naval Construction', Jean Louis Barrallier, had been brought in to supervise the construction of the shipyard and the building of ships. The yard had opened and two men-of-war had been built and launched there before another bankruptcy in 1801 caused the suspension of the dock building scheme. The victims on this occasion were the London businessmen Harry and Joseph Jacob, who were contracted to the Navy Board to build ships at Milford and who had overstretched their finances in the interests of the scheme.

Men who had abandoned their own small scale shipbuilding and other employment to work in the yard were thrown out of work and there was considerable hardship and resentment.

The confidence of the backers was restored the following year when Robert Greville invited Lord Nelson (accompanied by Sir William and Lady Hamilton) to visit Milford. At a banquet in his honour at the two-year-old inn (named The Lord Nelson from that time onwards) the distinguished visitor proclaimed his own enthusiasm for the project and applauded the government's support for the naval dockyard. Work resumed and a total of seven vessels had been built there before Greville disastrously fell out with the Admiralty over terms for the sale of the dockyard, causing them to transfer it to Pembroke Dock.

He also lived to see St. Katharine's Church built and consecrated and work on his visionary College of King George III underway, though this was abandoned on his death and never completed. The building had been begun on high ground between Hubberston and Hakin, intended for 'classes in mathematics and then application to mechanics, military and naval and civil engineering, construction of ships, navigation and survey and drawing'. It was also to be equipped with an observatory and the remains of this building still stand, a ruin, in Hakin.

HMS Surprise, *built at the Old Dockyard, Milford, and launched in 1812.*
She was a 5th rate ship of the line carrying 46 guns

Remains of the Observatory at the College of King George III

The transfer of the dockyard to Pater in 1814 was another setback in the development of Milford. Robert Greville lacked his brother's drive and, possibly influenced by his wife who is reputed to have said 'Milford had better remain as cornfields', spent little time in Milford Haven dealing with the unresolved problems that Charles left behind.

Since 1787 mail coaches had departed daily on the 48-hour journey which took passengers and mail from Hubberston to London. The early introduction of this service, only two years after the first mail coaches were introduced, is an indication of the importance of the Irish Mail packet, but complaints were coming in about delays in the service. The lack of a pier and the system of passengers, luggage and mail having to be transported from the packet in small boats was becoming less and less acceptable. Equally problematical was the coaling of the packets from an old store ship used as a floating dock — something that was both difficult and dangerous in stormy seas.

A government Select Committee was convened in 1827 to report on Milford Haven's communications. Over a period of several weeks expert evidence was given: during the period between 1 January and 31 December 1826 the packets had made a total of 355 voyages in each direction between Milford and Dunmore, the journey time averaging 12 hours, but with very much longer times recorded on a number of specific dates. The crossing on 6 January took 36 hours and that on 27 October 31 hours and numerous occasions were cited of late arrival of the mail causing it to miss the mail coach. Sailing was delayed for four hours on one day when bad weather had made it impossible for the engineer to reach the packet's distant anchorage.

The solution it seemed was indeed to build a pier and the road engineer, Thomas Telford, was called in to report on road communications, make recommendations for new stage coach routes and for piers and landing facilities for passengers. While he suggested that Newton Noyes was a suitable site for a pier, representations were made for the establishment of a floating dock at Hubberston Pill, something recommended by local engineer Henry Edwards in 1814, whilst John Mirehouse, the Angle landowner, put the case for building the pier at Angle. In his 'bid' he volunteered to donate the land and to pay for the construction (employing the firm which built the dockyard at Pater) in return for a charge on the postage, and pointed out that there was a house on the land which would be suitable for use as a large inn.

The most damning evidence — from Milford's point of view — came from the Commissioner of the Navy, the Honourable Courtenay Boyle, who spoke of the problems experienced by the now all-important big employer, the dockyard, which was paying an average wages bill of between £500 and £600 per week. He stressed the importance, particularly in the event of war, of a direct service to the dockyard in order to receive urgent communications, plans and models from the Navy Board. The mail coach from London to Milford deposited the dockyard mail at Cold Blow (14 miles from Pembroke Dock) as it passed through at around 4am. It was taken by a post office employee to Pembroke to be collected by a messenger from the dockyard and finally reached its destination at about 11am. Outward post had to leave the dockyard by 4pm to catch the mail at Cold Blow. The decision was duly reached, to the dismay of the people of Milford Haven, to move the packet's berth across the water to Hobbs Point. Milford Haven had lost the dockyard and then, in 1836, the packet. The town was indeed falling on hard times.

The terminus of the Royal Mail coaches from London had been Point Street along the western shore of Hubberston Pill, a busy area of houses, many public houses plus small businesses involved in sail making, boatbuilding and repair. It had its own post office and Customs House — even a pair of stocks said to be large enough to accommodate

three offenders. It was home to harbour pilots, shipbuilders and shopkeepers. With the removal of the Packet, then the abandonment of plans to extend the dry dock the street lapsed into decay. It had long been overshadowed by the dock wall and many properties were condemned, others were compulsorily purchased and demolished. One of the casualties of this spate of demolition was one of Hakin's oldest pubs the *Wexford and Waterford Packet*. All that remains today as a reminder of this once prosperous area is a small plaque marking the end of Point Street, erected on the wall of the *Heart of Oak* which survives and prospers at the foot of Lower Hill Street.

In September 1821 the Haven had been able to provide refuge for an unscheduled royal visitor when George IV, returning from Ireland, sought shelter from a severe storm. On this occasion he did not land but set out for Portsmouth the following day, only to be driven back once more by renewed storms. This time he did come ashore to be greeted with suitable enthusiasm and the firing of

The Wexford and Waterford Packet, one of Hakin's earliest hostelries in Point Street, Hakin shortly before its demolition. The Heart of Oak survives (John Stevenson)

salutes from ships at anchor in the Haven and from the battery in Hakin. He then completed his journey to London by road. The event is recorded on a memorial tablet originally sited on the warehouse near the steps where he landed and, after being moved to several locations, is now on the Milford side of the wall under the Victoria bridge. Unfortunately this historic record is in poor condition with parts of the lengthily detailed inscription illegible though enough still remains to work out its content. This reads like a 19th-century newspaper report but does not record where the king spent the night:

> This tablet records the memorable and interesting event of Milford Haven having through the blessing of providence, twice afforded refuge and security to King George the Fourth and to his attendant squadron from violent and succeeding tempests which beset them in St. Georges Channel on his majesty's ret----g from Ireland in Septemb--
>
> The first storm was encountered in the night of the 1st September, the second on that of the 11th of Sept. On both these occasions the Royal Squadron happily made Milford Haven. Its first entrance into this haven was on the 9th of Sept.1821 and its second on the 12th of the same month. The kings squadron anchored in Hubberston Roads opposite the town of Milford on its first entrance into Milford Haven and on its return to it after an ineffectual attempt to proceed on the voyage, it a second time experienced refuge and security in the capacious and safe anchorage of Hubberston Roads. On the 1-- -eptember 1821 at half past five a.m. the king

> under a royal salute from the ships and from the battery on Hakin Point disembarked from his yacht the *Royal George* and thence proceeding in his barge with the Royal Standard at its bow, he landed by the adjacent steps at Milford cheered by continued acclamations and shouts of welcome from Welsh Subjects who from distant parts had hastened to the spot and now zealously united with the inhabitants of Milford and its neighbourhood in marking on this joyful occasion a d-i------ -nd affectionate homa-- to their beloved king.
>
> This tablet was placed here by the honourable Robert Fulke Greville on whose property near this spot King George the Fourth made his first landing in South Wales.

Memorial to the landing of George IV when seeking shelter from storm and tempest in 1821

Despite its problems, the facilities that existed at Milford were much in use. One vessel calling there in 1831 was the *Frolic*, a wooden-hulled two-masted paddle steamer with 80hp engines which belonged to the General Steam Navigation Company of Bristol. The owners advertised that it ran to Bristol twice weekly carrying passengers and goods from Tenby,

Milford Haven, Pembroke and Haverfordwest. It had a female steward, and horses and carriages were shipped with care. Its last voyage, setting out at 7am on Tuesday 15 March 1831 for the ten-hour journey to Bristol, is detailed in George Harries' *Early Bristol Paddle Steamer Shipwrecks.*

Captained by a Haverfordwest man, Edward Jenkins, and with a crew of 13, nothing was heard of the *Frolic* after she left Tenby with passengers from the other Pembrokeshire ports. Although her arrival at Bristol was overdue there would not have been immediate concern for in storm conditions vessels would lay up in shelter waiting for the weather to improve, and the following night was 'dark, dirty and tempestuous, blowing a gale with hazy visibility'. Two days later, however, the captain of the *Bristol,* the Swansea steam packet, reported floating wreckage at Nash Sand, off the Glamorgan coast. Further sightings of wreckage, bedding and stores followed and eventually bodies were washed up on the beaches. The body of the captain and that of a young boy were found lashed to the rigging and a young woman was discovered with a child still wrapped in her arms.

A full passenger list was never established but those on board included people from varying walks of life — there were three seamen from Fishguard, two servants from Picton Castle, Mr. James Lloyd, butler to R.J. Ackland of Boulston, a currier, a leather seller, three runaway apprentices from a Pembroke shoemaker, a butler and housemaid who were leaving the employ of Captain Robert Fulke Murray Greville of Castle Hall, and a number of children. It is thought that 23 passengers joined the ship at Tenby, among them General McLeod of the 1st Royal Regiment of Foot, with four servants, Mrs. Boyd, a colonel's wife with three servants, and a Colonel Gordon, late of the Queen's Bays with one or two servants. In total it is believed there were around 78 people on board, none of whom survived to solve the mystery of what happened to the *Frolic* on that ill-fated journey.

A month after this disaster the 100hp *George IV*, a paddle steamer of 260 tons, resumed the service advertising the following fares: Best cabins £1 1s. 6d.; Steerage 14s. 6d.; Children under 12 half price; 4-wheel carriage £2; 2-wheel carriage £1 5s. 6d.; Horses £1 5s.; Dogs 3s.; Fat cattle 15s.; Store 10s.; 2-year old 7s. 6d.; Yearlings 5s.; Pigs 2s.; Sheep 1s.

A rival service was set up a few months later by a syndicate of businessmen, including a cabinet maker, drapers, a maltster, watchmaker, several 'gentlemen', a sail maker and shipbuilder with one woman — Ann Morse ('spinster'), who came variously from Haverfordwest, Pembroke, Pembroke Dock, Milford and Bristol. Among their number was the Quaker merchant Gayer Starbuck. Their vessel, the 110-ton *County of Pembroke* provided a service from Haverfordwest, Pembroke and Milford to Bristol, leaving the Tenby route to the *George IV.*

After the death in 1824 of Robert Fulke Greville, his son Robert Fulke Murray Greville initially paid as little attention to his Milford estate as his father had before him. It was not long before he was seriously in debt and his decision in May 1831 to fight the election against the sitting M.P. plunged him ever nearer bankruptcy. It is possible that he was cutting down his household expenses in March when two of his servants were leaving his employ and lost their lives on the *Frolic*. Even in an era when it was normal for bribery to play a role in the campaign, this election was described as 'scandalous'. Voting was disrupted by both sides in every way possible; disorder ruled and Greville set out to buy votes by giving his supporters the run of nearly every inn in Haverfordwest, offering free drinks, meals and accommodation. His bill at the Hotel Mariners amounted to £1,878 10s. 7d.; at the Black Horse £750 4s. and at the Wellington £513 19s. — none of which, or those incurred with other hostelries, was paid. He lost to Sir John Owen by 99 votes but with so much evident corruption the election was declared void and a second poll took place five months later. Owen was again successful. After becoming involved in a duel with John Jones of Ystrad whom, he claimed, had insulted him and in which neither man was injured, Greville left the country and thereby his debts and his responsibility towards the Milford estate. It was to be 20 years before he returned to play his part in the development of Milford Haven.

Milford had fought and lost the battle with Paterchurch, now it faced a threat from Fishguard. In 1837 a Bill was promoted in Parliament for the construction of harbour works in Fishguard with a view to securing the Irish traffic. Shipbuilding and repairing was still being carried out in small private yards on the shore off Hubberston Pill — Hogan's Yard with its small graving dock was at Hakin Point, the Roberts Brothers had a yard on the east side of the pill and Watson and Wimshurst operated on the site of the old dockyard. Sail makers, rope walks, foundries and ships' chandlery businesses were there to serve the many different classes of vessels using the Haven. The very life of the town revolved around these services. Corn, coal and other goods were still exported to Bristol. In 1832, 43 per cent of the corn shipped to Bristol went from Milford and, in 1845, 66,100 tons of coal was shipped from Milford. Such prosperity as it enjoyed depended on its sea connections and a bitter fight ensued when the Fishguard Harbour Bill was proposed.

Milford's harbourmaster, David Propert, a former captain of one of the Irish packets, led the campaign, writing many letters to the *Pembrokeshire Herald* and the *Carmarthen Journal* with fierce replies emanating from the pens of some of Fishguard's master mariners. At the same time he enlisted the support of the president of the Board of Trade, Alderman Poulett Thompson, and the strength of this and other opposition eventually led to the Bill being dropped. This success, however, was soon overshadowed when, in 1845, the alarm sounded again as the respective claims of Milford and Fishguard as the western terminal for the railway to serve transatlantic traffic were at issue. The fierce battle of the written word recommenced with letters in the local press reproduced in pamphlet form by Haverfordwest printer William Perkins, while two years later another pamphlet, printed in London, reiterated Milford's claims. The strength of argument and the resistance by Milford again won the day and both the plans for a new harbour at Fishguard and the laying of a railway to it were to lie in abeyance for some years.

There had long been hopes that Milford could be established as a transatlantic port rivalling Liverpool, particularly in its trade with America, as a base for importing raw cotton for the manufacturing areas of Manchester. As early as 1845 a scheme for a

Hogan's Yard in the late 1850s

Manchester and Milford Haven Railway was registered and a prospectus was issued for a route from Llanidloes, via Llangurig, Tregaron and Lampeter, down the Teivy valley to Penybont and then 'by the most favourable route to Milford Haven'.

The scheme did not materialise at this time and despite being revived on occasion with degrees of success the line was never completed — however the line from Pencader to Aberystwyth retained the name Manchester and Milford Railway for some years. The South Wales Railway reached Haverfordwest in 1854 and, running via Johnston, was extended to Neyland two years later but it was not until 1863 that Milford had its much needed rail link.

As part of the bid to attract traffic using the western and south-western approaches an ambitious 20-year project, the West Dock and Floating Basin scheme, was mooted under which plans were drawn up for a line of docks extending from Hubberston Pill to Castle Pill and on to Newton Noyes. Like so many of Milford's projects, the scheme never came to fruition.

Hogan's Yard, Hakin Point in c.1860

The 'tube' at Neyland that connected the floating pontoon to the railway station can be seen on the far right

In the meantime, the absentee landlord, now Col. Greville, had returned. Stories abound of his 'missing' 20 years: he was said to have been involved in the delivery of the liberation papers for the West India slaves, to have been a Major in the Lancers fighting in Spain between 1835 and 1837, and to have spent time in France. In any event, he was now fired with enthusiasm for developing his Milford estate. The establishment of Neyland as the terminus of the South Wales Railway (selected for its proximity to the dockyard and the Irish packet terminus, both across the water at Pembroke Dock) had been a blow to his plans and worse was to come. Neyland, at least short term, was prospering at the expense of Milford. Jetties and cattle sheds had been constructed as part of the railway company's plans and in January 1856 the cargo ship *Transit* docked in Neyland to take on a cargo of 900 tons of coal and iron ore from Port Talbot and destined for Australia. Sailings to Ireland followed.

Not to be put off, Greville introduced his Milford Improvements Bill which was designed to bring gas lighting, sewerage and water to the town, something which called for capital borrowing and the imposition of special rates. The local businessmen were not impressed, for they had watched with mounting concern Greville's profligate spending and ever increasing debts. However, the Bill became law on 27 July 1857 and 15 commissioners were appointed with powers to levy a sewer rate not exceeding 1s. in

The first Hakin Bridge, built in 1859, which lasted 27 years.
This view is looking upriver towards Priory before the opening of the dock in 1888 (Sarah Whitfield)

Laying the foundation stone for the Milford Docks, most likely that in 1864

the pound, an improvements rate not exceeding 2s. 6d. in the pound and enabling them to borrow a sum not exceeding £7,000.

As part of the terms, Greville built bridges over Hubberston Pill and Castle Pill, and a 750ft wooden pier (off Pier Road) making it possible for passengers to land without having to be ferried ashore. They were to be accommodated at Pier House and the adjacent cottage served as toll house for the pier.

More plans followed — for docks at Castle Pill (a plan abandoned in 1864) and for docks at Hubberston Pill, a scheme which went ahead, eventually. The foundation stone was laid with much ceremony in 1864 and, with no work carried out in the meantime, another foundation stone was laid ten years later under the provisions of the Milford Docks Act.

Greville was suffering severe financial problems, first having to sell much of his estate in Pembrokeshire and then Castle Hall on which he had expended large sums of money, adding a tower and elaborate Ionic pillars. When he moved to Pier House where he died in September 1867, he was on the verge of bankruptcy. Soon little of what he had achieved remained — the wooden bridge (Blackbridge) over Castle Pill became rotten and dangerous and was replaced by an iron bridge, Hakin Bridge (over Hubberston Pill) was replaced in 1887 and his wooden pier was dismantled. The track of his Milford Junction Railway was changed to standard gauge in 1872 and Castle Hall itself was demolished in 1939. He did not live to see the completion of the pier at Newton Noyes nor the building of the docks at Hubberston Pill.

Once again Milford was looking to transatlantic trade but the 900ft pier at Newton Noyes with its connecting rail link to Johnston was not in use until 1872 when guano for the Phosphero-Guano Company of South America was unloaded there. Special storage sheds were to have been constructed for storage of the fertilizer but had not been completed when the cargo arrived. Overall several thousands of tons reached Milford but the project was not a success and in 1883 the guano was sold, at a loss, to a French company for re-export — via Milford's pier — to France.

Subsequently the pier was in use to import cattle from Ireland, an unsuccessful venture by a steamship company operating between the United Kingdom and New York and it was bought by shipbreaker, T.W. Ward, when he set up his yard at the entrance to Castle Pill early in the 20th century. Immediately prior to the Second World War it was acquired by the Admiralty as they set about establishing the Mine Depot at Castle Hall, and later it became the property of oil companies operating from the Haven.

Greville had died owing the National Provident Institution nearly £500,000, other sums were owed elsewhere and, as a result, the ownership of the Milford estate passed into the hands of the trustees of the Institution. This gave them ownership of the new town itself, the land on which the docks were to be built and the pier and railway link at Newton Noyes.

Milford was again in the doldrums. The Milford Improvement Commissioners' mortgages were put in the hands of the receivers because they had failed to meet their commitments on the money they had raised, the long established shipbuilding yard of Watson and Wimshurst was destroyed by fire, throwing scores of men out of work, whilst the oyster fishery in Hubberston Pill which was to have brought in a quick return proved a disappointment.

The salvation of the town seemed to lie in the long overdue construction of the Hubberston Pill docks and the Milford Docks Act came into force in 1874 with a proviso that the work was to be completed within six years. It was claimed at a meeting of the Docks Company that the docks would attract ocean traffic and work began, providing employment for 150 men, but was dogged with problems, not the least of which were the ever present financial difficulties. It was not long before the construction company were not being paid and so sought and gained release from their contract on payment for the work that had been carried out.

The scheme was now well behind schedule and the presence for repairs in the uncompleted dock of the *Great Eastern*, the largest ship in the world at that time (see overleaf) — something which was intended to provide positive publicity for Milford — impeded progress to such a degree that the vessel had to be moved to the Hakin side and later out into the Haven.

The census of 1881, carried out during the *Great Eastern's* stay here, showed that the Haven itself was busy. Over 150 vessels of British and Irish origin were berthed with crews originating not only in this country but also in Spain, Denmark, Germany, Sweden, Prussia, New Zealand, France, Austria, Jamaica, Norway, Canada and the

Wooden footbridge over the railway line from the dockyard in 1876

Channel Islands. The oldest crew members came from the Cardigan area with 75-year-old David Evans from Blaenporth on the *Ellen* and 77-year-old Thomas Evans from Aberaeron on the *Ruth* which also had on board a 13-year-old youth, Abraham Arthur Lloyd — not the youngest crew member in Milford on that evening. John Jones of Newquay, Cardigan — age 12 — is listed as the ship's boy on the *Syren* of which his father was master.

The *Great Eastern*'s links with Milford Haven

The *Great Eastern*, displacing 18,914 tons and measuring 692ft, had been designed by Brunel for the Eastern Navigation Company to carry cargo and passengers between England and India. She had cost £732,000 to build, twice the figure anticipated, and before her launching in 1858, had passed to the Great Shipping Company who put her on a New York trade route. It had been Brunel's subsequent dream that her maiden voyage to New York would be from his new town of Neyland but this was not to be and on 17 June 1860 she set out from Liverpool reaching New York ten days later. Although thousands of curious sightseers visited the vessel in dock there were less than 100 passengers on board the ship (with 403 hands) when she set out on the return journey to Neyland during which she suffered mechanical failure necessitating temporary repairs. A number of those on board were travelling only as far as Halifax, Nova Scotia and she was carrying just 63 passengers when she reached Milford prior to being piloted to Neyland for repairs, cleaning and painting.

The welcome, however, was tumultuous. There was already great jubilation, for vessels of the Channel Fleet — *Trafalgar, Edgar, Conqueror, Centurion, Royal Albert, Donegal, Aboukir, Diadem, Mars, Mersey* and *Algiers* — were gathered in the Haven in preparation for an exercise and the decision that, at the same time, this great ship should terminate her voyage there was seen as an added indication that Milford's future as a port was secure. 'Her arrival at low water with the harbour crowded with the Channel Fleet being effected without the slightest difficulties or disaster speaks more in favour of the resources of the port than columns of written or printed matter' exulted the *Pembroke and Dock News*. 'If this does not prove the capability and the eligibility and the superiority of the harbour nothing can possibly do so'.

Crowds gathered at every vantage point to see the vessel arrive. *The Haverfordwest and Milford Haven Telegraph* reported: 'At 12 o'clock the *Royal Albert* fired off one of the large guns and instantaneously the remaining ten ships boomed forth a tremendous volley from their ponderous iron throats, which shook the town to its very foundations ... each vessel simultaneously fired eleven guns, at the termination of which they were entirely enveloped in immense clouds of smoke which rendered them invisible to the gaze of the astonished and bewildered multitude.'

The crowds assumed the volley signalled the *Great Eastern's* imminent arrival but had, in fact, been fired in honour of Prince Albert's birthday. It was 6pm before she put in a spectacular appearance to what was an unprecedented compliment to a merchant vessel by vessels of the British naval fleet. As she made her stately progress past the ships of the fleet, dipping her flag to each in turn, vociferous cheering broke out from all the seamen on board the naval vessels and every yardarm was manned.

The passengers landed the following morning and those heading to London were carried by express train from Neyland, a creditably swift six hour journey.

Local businesses profited as thousands of sightseers (over 1,000 in one night from Merthyr) including soldiers and sailors stationed at Pembroke Dock flocked to the small town of Neyland to visit the ship as it wintered there, undergoing repairs on

The Great Eastern *at Milford Haven*

the specially constructed grid iron and wooden platform. The Great Eastern Hotel opened, while Ford and Jackson's river boats were kept busy. The officers of the vessel were invited to dinner at the Victoria Hotel in Pembroke Dock, an occasion for which 'an immense amount of beef' was provided by the butchers, Messrs Eastlake's.

Such was the enthusiasm of one party of sightseers crossing by boat from Pembroke that when their boat broke down at Pennar Gut they solved the problem by boarding and taking possession of another vessel. This act of piracy was observed by the boat's owner who, accompanied by a group of friends, set off in pursuit and took them in tow, intent on returning his captives to Pembroke and charging them with theft. The matter was resolved amicably with the payment of a 2s. ransom after which the group was allowed to go on its way.

Brunel himself was unable to enjoy this visit of the *Great Eastern* to Neyland, for he had died on board while supervising its trials.

Something of the ship's glory was tarnished as tales filtered through from America of the complaints of 'indignant excursionists' who had made a trip to Cape May during the vessel's stay in America. Headlines from the American papers were quoted: 'Sufferings of Passengers', 'The Noble Ship and her Ignoble Managers', 'Great Promises and Small Performances'. Accounts of the trip go on to tell of 'the most unseemly squabbles, of ladies dragged out of the berths by American "gentlemen", of fights on board, struggles for water, scrambles for mattresses, hopeless attempts to obtain refreshments, intoxicated stewards, bewildered ... waiters, fabulous prices for food and drink and disgusting scenes of rough practical jokes.'

One correspondent wrote saying 'All that man could do to make a noble ship odious and a grand experiment contemptible, the directors of the Great Eastern have most successfully done, while I can not now bethink me of a single means of annoying man, woman or child on a voyage of pleasure which the same ingenious gentlemen left untried between July 30th and August 1st'.

Further misfortune befell the *Great Eastern* as she left Neyland to sail to America in May 1861, an occasion which again attracted thousands of onlookers. As the vessel swung off the grid on a spring tide the hawser of a small sightseeing vessel fouled her screws and the small craft was swiftly wound towards the huge blades. The cheers of the passengers changed to screams of terror as they jumped for their lives and two were drowned. Before she could be moored once more the *Great Eastern* drifted away and crashed into the side of the frigate *HMS Blenheim*, removing the vessel's bowsprit, mainyards and mooring. Eventually she made the journey to Sandy Hook, near New York, a passage that took nine days, and while she was in port unsuccessful attempts were made by both Union and Confederate navies to obtain her services during the American Civil War.

After several years of operating at a deficit the *Great Eastern* was sold to the Great Eastern Steamship Company which, until 1874, used her as a cable-laying vessel. During this time she laid the first successful transatlantic telegraph cable and also, in a brief interruption to the service, made a voyage from Liverpool to New York to attract US visitors to the Paris Exhibition. On board was Jules Verne who wrote about the ship in his novel *Une Ville Flottante* (The Floating City).

In 1874, after laying the 5th Atlantic cable, she was brought to Hubberston Pill for a refit — the only oceangoing ship to be seen from Milford's still unfinished docks — but remained idle and deteriorating for the following 12 years, moving only to provide room for construction work to be carried out. There was hope in 1884 that she might be purchased for conversion into a coaling ship to be stationed at Gibraltar and again that she would be converted to carry slaughtered and refrigerated cattle from Texas to Milford, but neither sale materialised. This great ship which had held so much promise left Milford and was sold for £16,500 to be broken up for scrap.

The Great Eastern *stuck in the newly completed dock gates at Milford Haven around 1888.*
(12"x10" glass plate original, courtesy Roger Worsley)

Further trouble was in store for the Milford dock. One of the dock walls subsided and because of the increased size and draught of the hoped-for Atlantic steamships the docks had to be made deeper. A new contract was entered into with the accomplished engineer and remarkable character, and some say 'con man', Samuel Lake, who not only took on the building of the docks but also built breakwaters and piers using his own patented methods, and built houses near the old fort at Pill. It was his plan that the whole 600 acres of Milford — town, docks, railway, Newton Noyes pier and Castle Pill — should be run as one huge concern with himself at the helm.

Lake undertook to complete the dock in eight months for the sum of £80,000, neither of which he achieved. Work on the docks was soon once again behind schedule and another Bill was taken out to provide a further capital injection of £266,000 and extend the construction time to July 1883, increasing Lake's original eight months to 48 months. Foreseeably, before this time Lake's financial affairs were in total disarray. Work stopped on the docks and on 4 November 1882 he filed a petition of bankruptcy.

Lake had, however, set to work energetically establishing a three shift system for the workmen, bringing in electric lighting for night shifts. He had brought influential British and American businessmen to the town to see the work in hand and had set up the Milford Haven Railway and Estate Company which, with a capital requirement of £350,000, took over from the National Provident Institution the leases for the railway, pier and estate.

Nevertheless, Milford, which over the years had suffered many vicissitudes, was now at its lowest ebb — not only local men but artisans attracted from all over the country found themselves out of work. The closure of Hubberston Pill for the building of the docks had totally annihilated the shipbuilding and repair industry that had thrived there. It left Castle Pill as Milford's main yard where J. and W. Francis continued to build schooners and ketches until 1909 when their last major work was the building of the *Democrat* for owners in Braunton. Subsidiary businesses closed, rents remained unpaid to the property owners and the town's houses fell into disrepair.

After Lake's bankruptcy, the directors of the Docks Company had little option but to resign. The new board appointed contractors S. Pearson and Son to continue with the construction and as work resumed the Newton Noyes railway was used to transport soil from the excavation of the docks to the foreshore on either side of Castle Pill. At last this railway made a small profit — £151 7s. 1d. — on a year's trading. Work began on repairing houses and,

The Sybil, *the first vessel to enter Milford Docks, on 27 September 1888, built in Hull for London Trawlers Ltd (drawn by Steve Witham, reproduced courtesy of West Wales Maritime Heritage)*

167

The City of Rome, *an Anchor Line steamship, arriving in Milford Haven waterway in 1889,
escorted by two paddle tugs. She was built in Barrow for 271 passengers, and sold to
German shipbreakers in 1902*

in the 11 years from 1882 to 1893, the Improvement Commissioners claimed to have
spent £10,540 on repairs and maintenance out of the £45,086 rental received from the
tenants.

It was, in fact, not until 1888 that the docks opened, by then too late to secure the
transatlantic trade which was then securely established in Liverpool. The first vessel to
use the docks, exactly 98 years after Sir William Hamilton's Act 'to provide quays, docks,
piers', was no ocean-going vessel but the steam trawler *Sybil*, and although the Docks
Company was at first reluctant to accept the situation, it was to the fishing industry that
Milford was to owe its prosperity for many years to come.

One vessel, the *City of Rome*, on her way from America to Liverpool in 1889 did call
at Milford to land members of Barnum's Great American Circus. The 134 passengers

*Hakin Docks station on 24 October 1889. The train is waiting for the passengers
from the* City of Rome, *and took six hours for the journey to London*

168

with 378 pieces of luggage had to disembark six miles from the dock as there was no landing stage and they were transferred to the Great Western Railway tender *Gad* in Hubberston Roads (shades of the old packet service) to be landed on the quay at Milford docks. The resultant publicity would have been more beneficial to Milford's claims to be a suitable transatlantic port if the vessel had been able to offload at the dockside. This was not the thriving trade which had been the vision of so many entrepreneurs, which had caused numerous bankruptcies and for which the docks had been constructed.

Even so, still hoping for increased foreign trade the thoughts of the authorities turned to the protection of the health of the townspeople and the Port Sanitary Authority (later the Milford Haven Port Health Authority) was set up with its first meeting taking place in the South Wales Hotel in Neyland in January 1876.

Because of the prevalence of cholera in Mediterranean and European countries, as well as localised outbreaks of smallpox and typhoid, early discussions centred on the need for an isolation hospital. The Borough of Pembroke owned a smack, the *Betsy*, which was in use as a hospital ship but this was inadequate and initially the Authority used a cottage near Coombs at Marble Hall Road in Milford which they bought for £150. Shortly afterwards, to develop the hospital into an eight-bedded complex, a nearby house was converted by Messrs. Appleby and Lawton, one of the firms employed in building the docks.

However, considerable concern grew in the town at the possibility of infection being spread as patients were carried through the town to the hospital and the War Department was asked to lease Dale Fort for the reception of patients. The Medical Officer of Health (MOH), Dr. George Griffiths, was then authorised to buy a basket to lift patients from the landing stage into the fort but there is no evidence that the basket was ever used.

The old fish market before 1907

169

The situation was still unsatisfactory and, in *A Short History of Milford Haven Port Health Authority*, Councillor V.J. Lewis recorded the purchase of a hulk, the *Hoyle*, bought from Llanelli for £110 for use as a quarantine ship. It was stationed off Castle Pill and later moved to permanent moorings at Sandy Haven. The cottage hospital was sold for £300 and the *Hoyle* remained in use until 1910 when an inspection found conditions very unsatisfactory and a hospital was built on land near Sandy Haven. The *Hoyle* was sold in auction for £16 after all the equipment had been removed, whilst the new isolation hospital continued to function until 1948 when it was sold to a private buyer.

Not all infections were carried into the area by foreign vessels. An unexplained epidemic was rife in the town in 1885 and after investigation the MOH reported to the Improvements Committee that the cause lay in the stagnant pools of water lying in Hubberston Pill — 'a most noxious effluvia' — and the Docks Company was forced to remedy the problem.

As the fishing industry grew rapidly — as early as two years after the *Sybil* entered the dock some 1,660 fishing vessels had used Milford docks — it brought its own difficulties. An infestation of rats, lured by the thousands of wooden fish boxes stacked at the rear of the fish market, called for the attention of the MOH but this was a problem which remained unresolved until the boxes were removed at the end of the Second Word War.

Trawlers tied up at Milford's fish market before the First World War (Roger Worsley)

Rats also proliferated on vessels coming into the port, a matter which assumed political importance in 1952 when news of the fumigation of the Royal Armament Supply vessel *Amherst* with hydrogen cyanide brought the issue to the fore. Formal application was made for Milford Haven to be classified as a Designated Approved Port which meant that Deratisation Exemption Certificates could be issued once ships were declared rat free by an independent body, in this case Swansea Port Health Authority. They initially requested a fee of £200 *per annum* for the service, but eventually agreed to carry it out for the reduced price of £50.

Fishing had been carried out from Hakin and Pill long before there was any thought of the development of the area and fishing smacks from Brixham were already a familiar sight in the Haven. The waters were known to be good fishing grounds and with the rail link established to London and other prospective markets, trawler owners and fish buyers were quick to realise the potential of this new dock.

One fish buyer moved into the town in 1888, by 1904 there were 39 and in the mid-1920s nearly 100 buyers were operating from Milford Haven. The *Sybil* had arrived in September 1888, in January 1889 12 fishing vessels with a gross tonnage of 1,100 tons were using the port while in 1908 the number of vessels had risen to 323 with a gross tonnage of 46,132 tons. Within a few years of the docks opening 55 steam trawlers and 200 sailing vessels were fishing out of Milford, yet the Docks Company was still reluctant to accept that this was where the future lay. Large quantities of fish were being landed — 9,500 tons in 1890 and a peak of 18,245 in 1899 — and more trawlers were being built locally. In May 1896 a 20-ton trawler, the *Hit or Miss* was launched from William Wolfe's yard in Hakin, an event recorded in an eyewitness account of the day:

> Last Wednesday evening thousands of people lined the docks in the neighbourhood of Hakin to witness the launch of a steam boat which, if it were but a mite compared with the great *Hannibal*, [possibly a reference to the *Great Eastern* which had stood so long, nothing but an encumbrance, in the Haven] yet took to its baptism under more sensational circumstances. The steamer is named the *Hit or Miss* and was built by Mr. William Wolfe in his yard on the Hakin side of the docks. Her length is 56½ feet, her beam fourteen feet and her depth of hold seven and a half feet. She is a twin screw and was designed by Mr. Llewellyn as a 'long liner', the first of the kind that has been built at the haven. In fact she is the first iron vessel launched at the docks. This itself would have sufficed to draw a big crowd to the launching ceremony, but the ever-enterprising owner had arranged for a launch the like of which we have seldom, if ever, read of. Mr. Wolfe's yard stands at some height above the docks and at high tide the water is not within several feet of the top of his boundary wall. Over this wall the vessel had to fall ere it gained the water, and as undoubtedly a considerable element of risk attached to so novel a launch, there was naturally much speculation as to the probable result. With four workmen and a soldier on board, the *Hit or Miss* was slipped from her stays one hundred and eighty three feet distant, and as she rushed for her aerial flight the excitement of the multitude was intense. She flew from the dock wall and landed five and a half feet below as prettily as a duck. The men on board reeled a little and the soldier lost his equilibrium in the exuberance of his cheering, but no accident occurred.

The smart little vessel was thereafter moored to the dock wall where she will be fitted for sea. She will be capable of sailing eight miles an hour. Mr. Wolfe is to be congratulated on the success of his new venture and we trust the little *Hit or Miss* will fully justify the hopes entertained of her.

In fact she seems not to have justified those hopes, for whilst it is not known what befell the vessel, records show that she stopped fishing in December 1899.

William Wolfe, who lived in Gorseinon, Swansea, registered the *Hit or Miss* as 'builder and engineer of Hakin, Milford Haven' and also owned the steam fishing trawlers *Nile* and *Essex*. He later traded under the name Essex Trawling Company which he started up with an outlay of £7,200. But this enterprise was not a success and the firm went bankrupt at which the bank sold its vessels to Spanish buyers, in 1925, for the sum of £1,500.

Eventually the Docks Company accepted its role as a fishing port and set about providing some essential facilities. Initially there was no fish market and no ice factory, ice being imported from Norway and broken up on the dockside, ready for loading onto the fishing vessels or for sale to the merchants. The Company now converted the storage sheds which were intended for the transatlantic traffic into a fishmarket and built an ice factory. This produced 50 tons of ice a day, a quantity which soon proved inadequate, and although a second was built in 1901 there was still a shortfall (partly due, it was said, to a shortage of water) and some ice was still being imported as late as the 1930s.

Unloading block ice on the dock from the Norwegian sailing vessel Evviva, which carried 500 tons of block ice, on 26 June 1901, prior to the building of the second ice factory (Roger Worsley)

A trawler preparing to load with ice (Roger Worsley)

These were Milford's good years. Phrases such as 'fish was king', 'every day was a pay day' and 'what is good for Milford is good for the county' were used over and over again in the euphoria of the days of the port's unaccustomed prosperity. Rope walks, sailmaking lofts, ship's chandleries, braiding rooms (for making nets) flourished and the dry dock was busy with the repair and painting of fishing vessels on a timber gantry which remained in use until 1909, when it was replaced by a patent slipway. This improved slipway could accommodate vessels of up to 60 tons at any state of the tide

Trawler and ice wagons by the ice factory, 1920 (Roger Worsley)

Dock entrance and Milford Haven from Hakin Point in the early 20th century

and, in a much faster turn-round, the bottoms would be scraped and painted in just a few hours.

Fish was landed at Neyland before the opening of Milford's docks and, as far back as 1871, had been carried in refrigerated vans filled with Ash's Patent Ice Apparatus which kept the contents down to a maximum temperature of 55 degrees. The vans were conveyed by passenger and mail train until the late 1880s when special fish trains were run to cater for the increased volume of fish leaving the area. At first the service depended on each day's landings, the details passed on daily by the station masters at Neyland and Milford, until the need for a regular service was established. One train left

View of Hamilton Terrace, 'front' street', from Hakin showing the fine 19th-century houses, most of which remain today (Sarah Whitfield)

174

Milford at 2.45pm for stations *en route* to Billingsgate, the Midlands and the north, and an hour later a second train set out for London and the eastern counties. By 1905 three fish trains left Milford daily, two to Paddington and one to Cardiff.

As they prospered the owners replaced their old ships with larger and more up-to-date ones, including drifter trawlers for mackerel fishing. There was an abundance of good quality mackerel in the grounds off St. Ann's Head and around the Smalls, and the drifter trawlers trailing their shallow nets rapidly caught large quantities of the fish as they fed near the surface. The prime movers in introducing the mackerel trade to Milford Haven were two of the biggest owners, Thomas Jenkerson and John Pettit and, in one year at the turn of the century, 120 drifters landed 3,500 tons of fish. Herrings, too, were prolific and the docks were used constantly by vessels from other ports. The Docks Company had little choice but to provide more facilities. Mortgages were taken out to extend the fish market and to install a 400 ton slipway with a 350ft mackerel market alongside it, while over the years five smoke houses were built to service this trade. While the fishing industry was delighted with the smoke houses the townspeople were not. Their protests at the nuisance they caused was countered by a leaflet from the representatives of the trawler owners and the fishermen themselves which stressed the damage that would be caused to the people whose living depended on the industry by anything that hampered the development of the herring trade. This trade, they said, was growing to such a degree that Milford could become one of the greatest centres of it in the country.

Charles Street, Milford Haven, early in the 1900s with a DE registered car,
an early Pembrokeshire registration (Sarah Whitfield)

People suffering the 'offensive, poisonous and unwholesome smoke vapour' were not reconciled. John Warlow of Marine House (now the Royal British Legion Clubhouse) took court proceedings in 1928 seeking damages against the three firms — Wilson Smith, Standard Kippering Co. Ltd and J.D. Clark — which operated the smoke houses on the foreshore on Milford Beach below his house. The

Milford Fire Brigade in 1909

judge, however, ruled that the smoke did not constitute a nuisance in the legal sense and that people who chose to live in a fishing town must expect inconveniences of this kind.

Increased expenditure meant increased charges for the use of the docks which brought the Docks Company (never very popular) into further disfavour, and this was followed by a dispute between the Company and the ice factory companies which, in 1912, signalled near disaster for the port. The Docks Company's proposal to build a third ice factory enraged the existing ice companies and the trawler owners Sellick, Morley and Price, who had a controlling interest in one of the companies as well as owning nearly half of the port's modern fleet. The ice companies were paying the Docks Company 5s. per quarter per square yard, a royalty of 1s. per ton on all ice manufactured and hauling charges of 9s. per ton on all the coal they used. Water was also costly and their 21-year lease made it uneconomic to invest further capital in the plant. They held that under better terms they could produce all the additional ice that was required in the port and after a legal battle the Docks Company proposal was withdrawn, but relations had become strained and Sellick, Morley and Price transferred seven of their most up to date trawlers to Fleetwood.

Today fishing quotas and the establishment of fishing limits are an unending bone of contention in the industry but, prior to the First World War, similarly inequitable problems existed. In 1912 and 1913 foreign trawlers were allowed to fish right up to a three mile international limit off the British coast but, (it was said, to conserve stocks) British trawlers had to keep outside a limit defined by the Fisheries Board — and this could be ten miles or more off the coast! This left the plentiful grounds in Galway Bay in the area refused to the British, but accessible to foreign vessels.

In the early months of 1914 a new fishmeal factory had been established at Milford and despite the move by Sellick, Morley and Price, a spirit of optimism prevailed with some of the trawler owners investing in new boats. Mr. Birt bought one boat, the *Norman*, and was negotiating for another, the *Saxon*. Mr. Brand had just received a new boat, the

Nairana and was planning to launch the *Noogana*. Mr. Curzon, a newcomer to Milford, and said to be a most enterprising owner, had already accumulated eight boats and planned to increase the number of his fleet to 15. Mr. Thomas had ordered the *Maristo* and Mr. Podd was in the process of purchasing the *W.H. Podd*. Two boats were on the stocks for Mr. Pettit while other owners were taking steps to increase the number of boats owned or managed by them. Everything now seemed to promise great hopes and a bright future for the fishing trade, hopes, however, to be dashed by the outbreak of the First World War.

Sixty of Milford's fleet of 70 trawlers were requisitioned by the Admiralty for mine sweeping and patrol duties, some of the boats then under construction being lost at sea before they had a chance to catch a single fish. To a limited degree their place was taken by the arrival in September 1914 of around 700 Belgian refugees who had fled from German invasion and who brought with them 24 trawlers and began fishing from Milford. This friendly invasion of the town, which then had a population of something in the region of 7,000, was made welcome by the local people. Accommodation was found for the refugees in their homes and special provision was made for educating the children — throughout the war an average of 60 Belgian children attended the Catholic school in Priory Road.

In gratitude after they returned home, though many stayed, the refugees erected a memorial at the junction between Slip Hill and Hamilton Terrace. The inscription, in English and Flemish reads: 'Erected by Steam Trawler Owners and people of Ostend who were resident in this town during the Great War. 1914-1918 as a mark of gratitude to the British nation in general and the people of Milford Haven in particular. For the hospitality received here during the period of exile from Belgium.'

The Europa *in dock in 1906, with some coal wagons on the Hakin side*

Memorandum paper of I.J. Jenkins who was a trawler owner in addition to being an engineer, cast iron founder and ship's general smith

At the time the Belgian refugees toiled from their boats up Slip Hill to the security of Milford Haven, the town was already established as a Naval Base due to the imminence of war and became a prohibited area which could not be entered without a permit. The docks were guarded by the 4th Welch Regiment and a number of the Haven forts, including Hubberston, Scoveston and Dale, were brought into use as training bases for service personnel. The waters of the Haven had long provided anchorage for vessels of the fleet — men-of-war, battleships, torpedo boats and a cruiser squadron involved in an exercise on the Western Approaches were all familiar sights in the period between 1898 and the outbreak of war. Many of the local fishermen were trained members of the Royal Naval Reserve and were rapidly called into service on the minesweepers.

The townspeople became accustomed to seeing the aftermath of U-boat attacks, with both survivors and the bodies of the dead being brought ashore at Milford. The dry dock was busy repairing vessels damaged in action whilst the Haven was host to large numbers of merchant ships — sometimes as many as 120 vessels at one time — assembled as they awaited safe passage in convoy to distant parts of the world.

Vickers' Newton Noyes depot was chosen to test the otter anti-mine device. This was a torpedo-shaped float attached by rigid wires, one on either side of the bows of a minesweeper, so that the wires drew out to a wide 'V' under the surface of the water. When the anchoring wires of a mine came into contact with the otter's wires they slid along them and were severed by the cutters fixed near the otter at the end. The mine then rose to the surface where it was destroyed by gunfire.

During the war the Admiralty made full use of the docks and dry dock but naval vessels were not required to pay dues except as a concession. Times were hard for the Docks Company which had ceased paying interest to shareholders in 1916 and their hopes were pinned on a prompt settlement from the Admiralty after the end of the war. But it was not until several years after the armistice was signed that the claim was settled, at a disappointingly low figure that left only £17,428 after disbursements.

For a few years after the war the fish trade enjoyed a boom, the yield in grounds which had been rested for four years was prolific and demand was good, calling for special trains running daily to all parts of the country.

Many of the smaller fishing boats were sailing smacks and Hancock's Milford Engineering and Ship Repairing Works was one of the firms engaged in installing marine engines, among others, on the fishing boats *Avance*, *Avola* and *Arravale*. On the test run off Bantry Bay fire broke out on the *Avance* because a wooden casing had been built too close to the diesel exhausts. The fire was put out and, despite heavy weather which caused a steamship to limp into Milford with her deck-works wrecked, the *Avance* made port under her own power. *Unity*, belonging to Mr. L. Cobb was the first sailing smack to have twin petrol engines and a diesel engine was installed in the *Result*, an Eynon owned coaster used for transporting sand around the harbour from Angle.

In the 1920s Milford was the largest fishing port on the west coast, with over 100 steam trawlers (the most up-to-date fleet of any fishing port in the world) owned and engaged in the fish trade. These vessels burned around 250,000 tons of coal a year, nearly 50,000 tons of fish were handled at the market and about 1,500 men were regularly employed in the docks to deal with the fish.

Publicising the advantages of Milford over other ports, the Docks Company issued a report in 1922 in which they claimed that during the previous August to September over 124,000 barrels of herrings were landed, amounting to 50 million fish. (There were three spells of herring fishing during the year — off the Irish coast at Christmas, off the Smalls in June and 'bottom fishing' [as opposed to the shallow net fishing] from August to September.) 'In addition', the report continued, '3,850 tons of beautiful herrings were sent from Milford Haven to the East Coast and were pronounced super-excellent by rival merchants and fishermen.'

The report also claimed that 'owners, fishermen, salesmen and merchants work as one unit and are in constant touch with buyers all over the country' choosing not to mention the unhappy industrial relations of 1919 when the Milford fishermen went on strike. Wages had been reduced to meet increased running costs and there was also discontent at the slack stock control which allowed large quantities of fish to disappear in unrecorded sales. The fishermen of Milford and Swansea joined forces in an eight-week strike before arbitration resulted in compromise.

Fishing in Milford had become a way of life and businesses were handed down the generations. One of the first owners in 1888 was David Pettit and when his daughter married Fred Ingram, the founder of Norrard Trawlers, a dynasty was founded. One hundred years later David Pettit's grandson (also Fred Ingram) was a leading trawler owner and for some years president of the Trawler Owners Association, and still running the family firm until ill health forced his retirement.

Changes were meanwhile taking place in the town itself. After Lake's bankruptcy Castle Hall was managed by the National Provident Institution and occupied, until he left the county in 1903, by T.R. Oswald, a Southampton shipbuilder who had moved to the area to re-open the old Castle Steel and Iron Works. Castle Hall then remained empty until 1911 when a party of Anglican Benedictine nuns leased it and converted it into an abbey which they named St. Brides. Soon afterwards the community were received into the Roman Catholic church and, in 1920, they moved to Talacre Abbey in north Wales.

T.R. Oswald's Castle Pill Works in 1882

Castle Hall and the Milford estate was then bought by Major Hugh Thomas (knighted in 1922), a Haverfordwest estate agent and landowner who set about becoming a local benefactor. He contributed £1,000 to the cost of a permanent road bridge over Castle Pill (Blackbridge — retaining the name the early wooden bridge had acquired for its coating of black preservative), presented Market Square to the people of Milford and freed the Hakin Bridge of tolls. He also offered the leaseholders the right to buy the freehold of their properties and it was a great misfortune for the town when he died suddenly in December 1924 at the age of 45.

At his death the family left the area and Castle Hall was never again occupied. A caretaker ran a market garden business from its extensive gardens until 1934 when the property and surrounding land was bought by the Admiralty as the site of the Royal Naval Mine Depot. The hall and its attractive bath house were demolished in 1939.

By the early '30s electricity was replacing gas lighting and many firms were modernising. Electricity was installed at the Fish Meal Factory at Newton Noyes, near Mr. 'Box' Lewis's factory which was making fish boxes. This box factory transferred onto the docks but was gutted by fire and had to move again, this time to Thornton to the site once occupied by Maconochie's Smoke Houses. When Hook Colliery closed Lewis bought the disused Lancashire boiler from the pit head and a local electrician, William Edwards (widely known as 'puffer Edwards'), set it up at the box factory, coupling it to a steam generating set bought from T.W. Ward's shipbreaking yard after it had been removed from the *Seapro*, a fishing vessel. The generator was then fuelled by sawdust, waste timber and cheap coal.

Between the wars the Docks Company indulged in some speculative proposals, for example obtaining permission to build a railway (estimated cost £120,000) to St. Brides Bay for the

Seven trawlers were built by T.R. Oswald between 1889 and 1903 at their Castle Pill Works

development of the Pembrokeshire anthracite field. Although the mines were developed the railway was never built. It concentrated, however, on making improvements to the docks. New coal tips which could handle 20-ton wagons speeded up bunkering, the dry dock pumps were modernised and there was a great innovation in the handling of fish and cargo with the introduction of one-ton Lister trucks to replace scores of wheelbarrows — Milford is believed to have been the pioneer of this form of mechanisation. Rail tracks were renewed and more powerful locomotives obtained, a new tug was built and a dredger purchased. Besides fish there was a steady trade in fertilizer, cattle food, timber and cement for local use.

In 1935 the Company was given Parliamentary approval to invest in other trades and set up a subsidiary company, Milford Steam Trawling, with a fleet of eight vessels. This helped to maintain revenue for some time but Milford now had great need of alternative employment. The fish trade on which it was almost totally dependent was in difficulties. There were hundreds of job losses as the industrial depression in south Wales and the Midlands brought a sharp decline in the demand for fish. A strike by the fishermen in 1932, again over pay, did not help the situation and cost an estimated £100,000. This time 120 vessels were laid up and before the disagreement was settled by arbitration 5,000 men became unemployed. The owners' attempts to get some of their vessels to sea, manned by strike-breaking crews, were foiled when nearly 2,000 fishermen blockaded the docks. Shortly afterwards one of the port's finest fleets, that belonging to the Iago Trawler Company, was transferred to Fleetwood where the LMS railway gave more support than the GWR, and in 1934 the entire fleet of one firm — 19 first class trawlers — was sold for £21,000 due to bankruptcy. Four years later the receivership

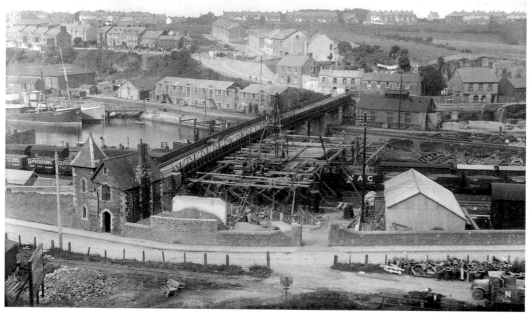

Building the bridge between Milford and Hakin in August 1931. Note the toll house in the foreground

of another major firm, Brand and Curzon, who owned 12 trawlers and other ancillary businesses including the ice factory, was yet another blow to Milford's economy.

When the industry seemed at its lowest ebb the Docks Company and a group of entrepreneurs, with the support of Barclays Bank, bravely formed what proved to be a highly successful joint company, Milford Fisheries. The bank had loaned the whole of the capital on condition that the new money was used for rehabilitation. Managed by Owen Limbrick the new company was a fully integrated business with repair shops, supply stores and a fish sales section to back up the fleet which had been purchased from the failed firms. Over a period of four years the Docks Company had received 105 per cent in dividends and, after selling its shares to the other partners, made a capital profit of 425 per cent. With the outbreak of the Second World War, all the Docks Company trawlers were requisitioned but Milford Fisheries managed to retain a few ships.

By this time the Mine Depot was a major employer operating on the Castle Hall land where the Admiralty had acquired the Newton Noyes pier, the railway beyond the swing bridge over Castle Pill, and also the land to the east of Castle Pill. Large underground storage areas had been constructed, and cranes for loading and offloading vessels were established on the lengthened and strengthened pier. There was also on-site housing for some key employees but the majority travelled to work from Milford and many other parts of the county. At its peak, during the war years, the Mine Depot provided work for more than 1,000 employees.

The Air Ministry too had acquired land in Milford for a petroleum depot and constructed 64,000 tons of underground tankerage with a pipeline through the docks to moorings in the Haven where tankers discharged by means of a flexible connection. Over 100,000 tons of aviation spirit were pumped through the docks each year and the dues on this provided the Company with a valuable source of revenue.

Privately owned yards staffed by skilled men in reserved occupations were also kept busy. A detachment of Seabees (United States Naval Construction) was based in Milford, and Wards Yard was used for the fitting-out and loading of United States' landing craft.

Once again convoys assembled in the Haven, taking their orders from the Naval Base headquarters in St. Peter's Road, and now with protection from Sunderland patrols based at RAF Pembroke Dock. In the 'Naval Activity' section of the *Pembrokeshire County History* Ted Goddard records that a total of 11,670 ships, totalling 36,897,252 gross tons, sailed from Milford Haven during the Battle of the Atlantic. More than 5,000 warships and thousands of fishing vessels also used the anchorage. 'Yet', he says 'on only one occasion did the port have to close to sea traffic for more than a few hours because of mines — a tribute to the work of the small minesweeping force, which at one time consisted of just two vessels, the trawlers *Courtier* and *Courgette*.' After the Normandy landings there was a constant stream of supplies going to France escorted by Milford ships.

The contribution of the mine layers is commemorated in a plaque on Hamilton Terrace dedicated to the 'Port of Milford Haven and HM Fast Minelayers *Abdiel, Apollo, Ariadne, Latonia, Manxman, Welshman*, in operational support of HM Minelayer *Adventure* operating extensive offensive minelaying against the enemy 1941-1945'. The workforce of the Royal Naval Mine Depot is also remembered 'without whose effort minelaying operations would not have been possible'.

As during the First World War, Milford saw its share of tragedy, though, because of censorship, it was only after the war that many of the facts became known. The greatest disaster was in April 1943 when 72 men of the Royal Navy and Royal Marines, with six rescuers from the escort sloop *Rosemary*, were lost with only three survivors. Two landing craft had foundered in a full onshore gale off the harbour entrance and when members of the crew of the *Rosemary* attempted to take a line across their boat was swamped and they too were swept to their deaths.

The fishermen went to sea in what vessels remained to them, braving the hazards of U-boat attack, mines and bombardment from the air. Some were armed with Lewis guns and steel helmets and did not hesitate to indulge in a shoot-out with enemy aircraft. The story of one encounter in April 1941 is told in the Ministry of Agriculture and Fisheries report *Fisheries in Wartime:*

> Skipper Bray [a well known Milford fisherman] was fishing south-east of Ireland when a German plane approached his ship, very low over the water. The man on watch gave the alarm to the skipper and others of the crew who were below aft.
>
> The skipper who had turned in, jumped from his bunk, and ordering the crew to remain below, himself proceeded on deck in his bare feet. Making his way forward, where the Lewis gun was mounted, with a total disregard of bombs and machine gunning, with bullets hitting the wheelhouse, funnel, rigging and deck casing, he uncovered the gun and awaited the plane which was turning to carry out another assault. Allowing the plane to approach near, and disregarding another stream of bullets, Mr. Bray trained the gun and fired several bursts. These silenced the rear gunner and forced the plane to give up the attack.
>
> Knowing that two planes had participated in the attack and that another trawler was in the vicinity, Mr. Bray steamed towards the place where the other trawler the *Whitby* was last seen. First he had to chop away his loose warps because one bomb had blown his trawl away.
>
> He found that the *Whitby* had been sunk and that the *Whitby's* crew had taken to their small boat which had been riddled with bullets and was sinking. Well knowing that the German planes were still circling in the vicinity and liable to renew their attack, Mr. Bray went alongside the small boat, picked up the crew of the *Whitby* and brought them safely back to Milford.
>
> On a later occasion Mr. Bray endeavoured to perform a similar service in respect of the Milford trawler *Westfield* but this vessel had vanished without trace.
>
> Mr. Bray fished consistently and regularly throughout the whole period of the war and was eventually awarded the M.B.E.

Surprisingly, while Pembroke Dock bore the brunt of bombardment from the air, Milford Haven with its many potential targets — most particularly the mine depot, but also the very many vessels in the harbour and the army and navy personnel based in the town — was almost free from attack. During the summer of 1941 an enemy plane made its way in, masked by a group of Sunderlands returning to base in Pembroke Dock, and dropped a stick of bombs which fell harmlessly in fields at the top of Priory Road. Later the same year a 50kg 'bomb' crashed through the roof of a house in Brook Avenue causing some damage but without inflicting any casualties. The 'bomb', which was about two feet long with a six-inch diameter, mystified the ARP until it was inspected by a Bomb Disposal squad who identified it as a type of flare. Dropped by parachute a small explosion should have cracked open the outer casing releasing magnesium or phosphorous which was then chemically ignited to produce a flash which would illuminate a 10 square mile area which could then be photographed from as high as 50,000 feet.

As a part of the defence from Luftwaffe attack airfields sprang up all over the county. RAF Pembroke Dock was already operational at the outbreak of war; the First World War airship station at Milton became RAF Carew Cheriton; land near Angle was developed to house fighter squadrons while Talbenny and Dale operated Coastal Command Wellington bombers. The Fleet Air Arm which had operated for a short period from Lawrenny Ferry later used Angle and Dale and, for 25 years after the end of the war, controlled *HMS Goldcrest* at Brawdy.

Ward's jetty was built for the ship-breaking firm, Thomas W. Ward, in 1935 and benefited from the wartime vital need for steel. During the 1940s the firm employed 120 men on highly paid piece work, dismantling ships at a rate of 500 tons a week, the metal then being sent by rail to Llanelli for re-smelting. Post-war, ships unsuitable for civilian use came to be scrapped and among their number was *HMS Faulknor*, the destroyer in which Field Marshal Montgomery had embarked from Portsmouth on his way to Normandy, landing to take command of his troops on the morning of 8 June 1944. Between the end of the war and 1958 a total 116 vessels were dismantled at the yard, after which it became uneconomic to transport heavy steel to Llanelli and shipbreaking then concentrated at Wards Yard at Briton Ferry, with the Milford yard working on old cars and machinery.

By 1950 Milford Haven as a fishing port was going through a severe period of depression. In March that year 25 vessels, about a third of the port's fishing fleet, were laid up. Harold Rossant, Secretary of the Trawler Owners Association, later added that 300 fishermen had been thrown out of employment and that a large number of shore workers were also workless. Three months later 40 skippers were said to be without ships and after 71 of the workforce of the Pembroke Dock ship repair yard — men from Pembroke Dock, Pembroke, Milford, Saundersfoot and Tenby — were laid off, a local councillor said 'It is imperative that we find employment for them to keep our men in the area. We don't want to see wholesale migration as when the dockyard closed in 1926.'

A *Western Telegraph* leader article blamed the dumping of foreign fish, especially Icelandic and Danish, for the destruction of the home market for British trawlers. The editor called for immediate Government action.

There was considerable concern, too, at Pembroke Dock when a Milford Haven based Admiralty ocean-going tug, the *Netta* was sent to Cardiff for re-fit when the local firm of Hancocks which had on two previous occasions overhauled the tug, had two dry docks empty and had not been asked to tender.

There was worse to come for Milford's fishing community during the 1950s and early '60s with the loss of four trawlers and 39 men. The mystery of the disappearance of the *Milford Viscount* with all hands in April 1950 has never been resolved. No trace of the vessel was ever found despite a search by about 100 British and foreign vessels. In February 1953 the 290-ton *Richard Crofts* ran aground on a reef off the Hebridean Isle of Coll with the loss of eight lives and only three survivors, while the *Robert Limbrick* went down with all 12 hands in February 1957 off the Isle of Mull, just 12 miles from the reef that brought disaster to the *Richard Crofts*. All the bodies from the *Richard Crofts* were recovered and they were buried side-by-side in Milford Cemetery. It was the area of the coast off the Hebrides that once again took its toll of the lives of Milford fishermen when the *Boston Heron* ran aground on the uninhabited Glas Island off the coast of Harris in the Outer Hebrides in December 1962. The Stornaway lifeboat and the Fishery Protection cruiser, *Brenda*, went to the rescue in what were described as the worse seas ever seen on that notorious coast. Two members of the crew were taken off by breeches buoy, three others struggled to a deserted beach and the bodies of five of the remaining crew were later recovered from the sea. It is believed that the *Boston Heron*'s boiler exploded when the vessel hit the rocks. On the 50th anniversary of the loss of the *Robert Limbrick* a memorial service took place at the cemetery in remembrance of the fishermen of the four vessels and this is now an annual event.

After the war the Docks Company had chosen to enter the ship-repairing business through a subsidiary, the Milford Haven Dry Dock Company (now under the aegis of the Milford Haven Port Authority as Milford Haven Ship Repairers) which eventually proved to be a profitable enterprise and the foundation of an important and flourishing business. However the Docks Company pronounced 1949 to be 'one of the worst trading years ever'. Although schemes were put forward for the construction of piers and dry docks and Acts of Parliament were obtained for massive new works involving an authorised capital from £1.1 million to £13 million, as had so often happened in the past, few of these projects materialised. Nevertheless, the dry dock was re-equipped and the workshops were improved with the incorporation of the long established Milford works of Peter Hancock Ltd. But the Docks Company was in difficulties. In 1956 they had a bank overdraft of over £200,000, by the first half of 1957 they were reporting a loss of £42,000 and at the and of the year all their reserves had gone. There was a debit balance and the outlook was described as 'hardly bright'. In an unsuccessful attempt to redress the situation the Company repurchased the oil tank farm at Goosepill which they had sold to the Air Ministry in 1939 and leased it to Esso. They also converted old buildings on the docks into a bonded warehouse but to the dismay of the stockholders, neither brought in much in the way of return and in 1963 an Extraordinary General Meeting was called at which the board was ousted and a new board elected.

The newcomers suggested new ideas and drew up plans for the construction of an Iron Ore terminal which would enable large bulk carriers to be discharged at the pier in deep water, after which the ore was to be conveyed on special trains to feed the

The northern end of Point Street, Hakin, in the foreground was demolished in the 1950s to make way for a proposed Docks Company scheme (John Stevenson)

south Wales steel works. The steel companies, however, were less than enthusiastic and the plans were shelved in 1965, by which time the Company's finances were in such straits that the bank and the Board of Trade were asked to appoint a receiver. It was only the complexity of the financial and legal issues which made it doubtful that anything could be recovered that saved the company from bankruptcy.

The area now had one of the highest rates of unemployment in the country for hundreds of workers were dependent directly or indirectly on the docks for a job. Problems were also faced by the flax factory which had opened during the war and employed a workforce of 205. The staff were employed deseeding and scrutching (beating) the excellent quality crop which was grown on some 3,000 acres of land in the county. The product was then despatched by rail for final processing, but as other types of crop replaced flax, the volume of work reduced and by the early 1950s the factory and its staff were redundant. The unemployment situation had been exacerbated, too, by the decision of the Admiralty, on the grounds of the imminent insolvency of the Dry Dock Company, to cancel their contracts with the Company and, as a result, the ship repair industry remained at a standstill for almost three months. To stave off total disaster the local M.P., Desmond Donnelly, persuaded the stockholders, creditors and other interested parties to join him in a salvage operation and slowly the Company re-established itself.

In the next few years substantial profits were made, largely from Admiralty work. Milford had become a recognised port for explosives and this traffic soon became a most important source of income for the Company. It was a period when there was great national interest in dry docks because of the Korean War and by 1959 commercial shipping in the Haven consisted almost entirely of cargo liners calling to load government and commercial explosives. The port also benefited, in 1967, from General de Gaulle's decision to order United States forces out of France. Because Milford was one of only a few ports ready to handle explosives a substantial part of the ammunition which had to be evacuated came there. Resources were fully stretched to deal with this unexpected boost and high wages were paid for long hours of overtime as trains and road convoys were continually to be seen leaving the docks.

The landings of fish in the first year after the war had reached an all time high as nearly 60,000 tons of fish were landed but, from that time on, there was a steady decline in the number of trawlers using the port and in the quantity of fish landed.

However, as fishing declined, the promise of better things was once more on the horizon. The oil industry was to come to Milford bringing with it a dramatic increase in commercial shipping using the port. In 1959, before the oil companies began operations, approximately 700,000 tons of commercial shipping entered the port. Two years later, in 1961, the first full year of operation as an oil port, the figure had risen to 4,700,000 tons and by 1973, when 3,886 ships entered the port, they were carrying 53,000,000 tons of cargo. The size of the tankers had also increased and 152 of these vessels were large crude oil carriers of over 200,000 tons dead weight, over 1,000ft in length and with a loaded draught of over 60ft.

The oil boom was not to last however; a number of the oil giants moved away. The hey-day of Milford indigenous fishing industry has long gone, but in the late 1990s and despite the limitations imposed by fishing quotas there was some resurgence in the industry. Some 7,000 tons of fish were landed in 1998 and the following year there was an increase of around 30 per cent. There were great hopes for the Electronic Fish Auction which opened on the docks in 1999, the first in the UK. Fish landed there were sold via internet auction to buyers throughout Europe, giving the trawlers the benefit of higher European prices, but within four years the decline in fishing activities, affected by decreasing fishing quotas, precipitated the closure of the loss-making auction. In 2007 landings of fish were down to 4,000 tons.

The port is, however, visited regularly by trawlers, most of them Belgian, French or Spanish-owned, with the greater part of the fish landed being transhipped to the markets of the home ports. There is also concern that foreign beam trawling ploughs up the seabed and sterilises it for between 12 and 36 months, leaving the areas around the North Sea rigs where the beam trawlers are unable to fish as the best preserved.

Better news came with the significant improvement in the Milford dockyard port facilities with the opening in June 2008 of a pontoon for the use of inshore fishing boats.

Since its main campus opened in Haverfordwest in 1990, Pembrokeshire College has been involved in providing training for work in local industry. The Port Authority collaborated with the college in creating a Community College which is sited in a converted stone-built Docks Company warehouse and offers courses in marine engineering, boatbuilding and design. This annex to the college, which opened in January 2000, has full time students from all over the country as well as a number who are already employed in the fishing and shipping industries and are undertaking flexible part-time courses. It is a Royal Yachting Association recognised teaching centre with both yacht and leisure boat related courses included in the range available.

The Port Authority continues to think about Milford's future. In 1990 it bought the Milford Docks Company and within three years, with the support of EEC funding, had completed a £10.2 million regeneration programme. In time to provide a fitting setting for the Cutty Sark Tall Ships Race in July 1991, it had breathed new life into the docks, clearing away derelict buildings and structures, creating walkways and pontoons, providing a road system and a range of services. The event brought around 500,000 visitors to the Milford area and even inspired some to set up business there. Further investment in the leisure industry followed with a 320 berth marina within the dock basin which quickly attracted the sailing community. Work has since begun on improving operational facilities for tugs and commercial vessels.

The bi-centenary of Charles Darwin's birth in 1809 is being celebrated by the Lawrenny-based *HMS Beagle* Trust which has plans, when funds allow, to build a replica of the vessel in which Darwin explored his theory of evolution. The £5 million replica is to be built on a site provided by the Port Authority and will be crewed by scientists, students and researchers as it sails in the wake of the voyage in which Darwin explored the theory of evolution. The new *Beagle* will be equipped with laboratories and equipment for contemporary research and, in a link with the NASA International Space Station, there will be an interchange of information between the astronauts and the sea-going scientists.

The co-founder of the Beagle Trust, David Lort Phillips, is a director of the Pembrokeshire College-based Darwin Centre and is a descendant of John Lort Stokes of Scotchwell, Haverfordwest who served on the *Beagle* for 18 years, sailing on all three of the surveying voyages and who was the vessel's last commander.

Over 100 years ago the Docks Company unsuccessfully sought to attract cruise ships but the past few years have seen Milford become a port of call for ships from as far afield as Germany and America. A rapid growth in cruising in the Irish Sea has resulted in Milford Haven being added to their itinerary and in 2007 over 2,700 cruise ship passengers and crew came ashore in Pembrokeshire, boosting the local economy by an estimated £1¼ million. The following year one of the seven visiting cruise ships was the transatlantic cruise ship *Maasdam* of the Holland America Line, one of the largest passenger ships ever to enter the Haven. It anchored on Milford Shelf with more than 2,000 passengers on board. During its stay 17 coaches took the passengers to St. Davids, the castles at Carew and Pembroke and across the county's border to the National Botanic Garden of Wales.

Currently large ships and cruise ships using the port anchor off the entrance to Milford docks, and passengers and crew are tendered ashore. Aware that the cruise companies would prefer an alongside berth, the Port Authority has long term plans for a dedicated berth with capacity for commercial vessels and cruise ships of up to 300 metres in length.

In 2007 the port was crowned Port Operator of the Year by Lloyds List. With a staff of nearly 200 it handled the highest level of gross tonnage of shipping in its history — the 51.4 million tons shipped during that year made it the busiest port in Wales.

In a world of economic recession at the beginning of 2009, Ted Sangster, chairman of the Port Authority still feels the future looks bright for Pembrokeshire's economy.

Today's Milford is very different from the vision that was never quite within the grasp of the pioneers — the Grevilles, the Quakers of Nantucket, Samuel Lake, the Rotch family, Brunel and all the unknowns who invested their lives and put their hearts into building Milford and its waterway settlements. But they all had in common the optimism which remains today, that tomorrow something better is waiting to happen, and, in fact, is already happening.

Chapter 11

Oil & Liquefied Natural Gas

It was in the 1950s when Milford Haven still came under naval jurisdiction as the dockyard port of Pembroke that both the British Petroleum and Esso Petroleum companies turned their thoughts to the extensive waters of the Haven because of the steadily increasing size of ships in their tanker fleets. Both companies planned to build deep water terminals for vessels up to 100,000 tons, later considerably increased after the closure of the Suez Canal during the Suez crisis of 1967. The long voyage round Cape of Good Hope was uneconomical for small carriers so ships' tonnage increased from 65,000 tons in 1960 to over 200,000 tons in the 1970s by which time Milford Haven was Britain's major oil port, indeed was second in overall tonnage to London.

In 1958, with the prospect of this much greater usage of the port, a new civil port authority, The Milford Haven Conservancy Board, (from 1986 it became the Milford Haven Port Authority) was set up, its area of jurisdiction bounded by the high water mark on the shores of Milford Haven and its approaches. This brought within the Board's jurisdiction the Cleddau river as far upstream as Haverfordwest and Canaston Bridge, the Cresswell and Carew rivers as far as Cresswell and Carew and the Pembroke river as far as Pembroke, and by 1960 effective control of the navigation in the whole Haven had passed to the Board.

First in the field, Esso obtained permission to build a refinery and ocean terminal on the north side of the Haven in 1957, only the second oil refinery to be built in the UK since the Second World War. Three years later British Petroleum built a deep water terminal on the south shore and linked this by a pipeline to their refinery at Llandarcy. Regent (later Texaco which itself merged with Chevron in 2001) followed in 1964, Gulf in 1968 and Amoco in 1973. Their construction created hundreds of jobs, though many of them could not be filled by the local labour force. That built for Esso provided short time employment for around 3,500 construction workers and later 2,000 were employed on the Gulf Oil Company site. The refineries themselves were not labour intensive but in 1980 the three that were then operational had created around 2,000 direct or indirect jobs and generated somewhere in the region of £6m in direct and indirect salaries — money which, for the most part, was spent in Pembrokeshire.

By 1960 the Esso jetty was ready to receive tankers and the first, the *Esso Portsmouth*, berthed at the terminal in July of that year, assisted by two tugs belonging to R. and J.H. Rea Ltd (later part of Cory Ship Towage Ltd). The occasion, however, was marred when there was an explosion followed by a fire on the tanker while she was still alongside. Fortunately, however, the tugs, equipped with firefighting equipment, were soon able to extinguish the blaze.

The initial design capacity of the installation (opened by the Duke of Edinburgh) was 100,000 barrels of crude oil a day and in 1973, after the expansion of the refinery, this almost doubled to a daily capacity of 180,000 barrels. However, by 1979 there had been a considerable downturn in the demand for oil products due to the great excess of refining capacity in Europe. Refineries were already closing elsewhere in the UK and in 1983 Esso closed the Milford refinery to concentrate on its Fawley refinery which had been their first in the UK. The impact of the Esso closure was a considerable one for the port, for the refinery had accounted for approximately 25% of the Haven's oil traffic.

British Petroleum, too, were discovering that Britain had an excess refining capacity. Their ocean terminal at Angle Bay had been built to meet an increasing demand for crude oil and also to accommodate the larger tankers of the mid-1950s. Their jetties at Queen's Dock, Swansea, which fed the nearby Llandarcy refinery were unable to cater for tankers carrying more than 28,000 tons of crude oil and the cheapest option lay in enlarging the refinery and building a terminal at Angle Bay. Popton Fort and the surrounding land was purchased for the construction of a tank farm at Kilpaison with a jetty with two berthing heads. From here the oil was pumped 62 miles to Llandarcy.

In April 1985 BP announced that their Llandarcy Refinery was to be reduced to a facility for producing specialised oil products and that their operations at the Angle Bay Terminal were to come to an end. The jetties were then leased to Texaco who took over the supply of BP requirements for petroleum products in south Wales, the Midlands and the west of England.

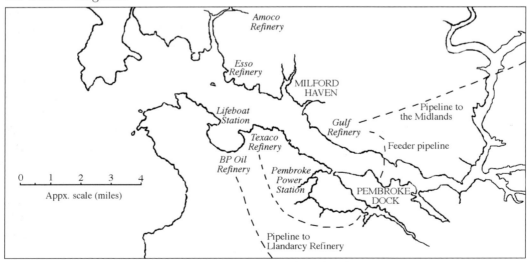

Map showing early oil refinery locations

The feeling of hope engendered by the proliferation of oil companies in Pembroke-shire had been clear in the comments of the local Member of Parliament, Desmond Donnelly, at the sod-cutting ceremony of the Regent refinery in 1963 when he said: 'This is the rebirth of Pembrokeshire, I only wish the men who were discharged from Pembroke Dockyard during the dark depressing days were here today to see it taking place.' He was not to know how relatively short lived this oil boom was to be, but Texaco, like Total Fina, has survived the many closures, although both have been involved in mergers losing their familiar names and becoming Chevron and Murco respectively. Chevron covers an area of 550 acres at Rhoscrowther and plays a vital role in the county, employing a workforce of hundreds and putting about £29 million into the local economy each year through salaries, rates and local labour.

The company made history in 1975 when the first cargo of North Sea oil (rather than the then usual Middle East import) to arrive in Milford Haven came in at its jetty. Today 75 per cent of the refinery's crude oil comes from the North Sea coming in on as many as five tankers a day. In one week it will receive about a million barrels of crude oil (a barrel equals almost 159 litres or 35 gallons) and produces 3.5 million gallons of petrol daily.

There had been fears as the new century dawned that Texaco was planning to close the Pembroke refinery, its only 100 per cent owned refinery in Europe, but these were allayed a few months later when plans were announced for a £44 million investment to upgrade the plant. A new low sulphur process unit enabled the company to meet the European Union's sulphur specification standards ahead of the 2005 deadline and at the same time safeguard the future of the 450 full time and 300 contract workers.

By 1968 the Gulf refinery was in production at Waterston, two miles east of Milford Haven, its jetty from Weir Point four miles further from the open sea than the Esso jetty. Originally constructed as a simple hydro-skimming refinery for production of a range of fuel products, it also included facilities for the manufacture of petrochemicals but these were closed down in 1982 and later demolished. By 1993 the refinery had been upgraded so that the daily throughput increased from 85,000 to 115,000 barrels per day. In 1977 Gulf, in partnership with Texaco, formed the Pembroke Cracking Company to build and operate a fluid catalytic plant alongside the Texaco refinery, Texaco holding the largest interest in the company. ('Cracking' increases the yield of petrol from crude oil by intense heat and pressure and further breaking down the oil by the introduction of a chemical catalyst, eventually producing a higher grade, high octane petrol.) The plant, sited on the Texaco site, was commissioned in 1981. A Vacuum Distillation Unit was also constructed to feed this 65,000 barrels per day joint venture, and in 1990 the cracker was upgraded to a throughput of 90,000 barrels per day.

Three years later an Isomerisation Unit was commissioned to enhance the Gulf refinery's production of unleaded petrol and investment in facilities for enhanced sulphur removal and the production of cleaner fuels followed. But in 1998, this apparently thriving company which had survived a disastrous explosion and fire in 1994, closed and was sold to the Dutch oil company, Petroplus, whose main area of activity is the storage of oil for third parties. Texaco bought out Gulf's share in the cracking company.

Amoco (a subsidiary of Standard Oil of Indiana) built a refinery which came on stream in 1973, the last to be built at Milford. As well as having large interests in exploration and production in the North Sea, Amoco was expanding its retailing and marketing activities in the early '70s and needed a suitable site for a UK refinery. The refinery was built two miles inland from Gellyswick Bay with a 715 metre jetty which accommodates three berths. The first can take crude oil tankers of up to 275,000 dead weight tonnes, and at the second and third berths refinery end products such as LPG, jet fuel, petrol, diesel and heating oil are loaded into tankers of up to a maximum of 30,000 dead weight tonnes.

During the construction of the jetty a total of 393 tubular steel piles, mainly of 30 and 36 inch diameter, were driven into the seabed to support the jetty. The project also required the dredging of approximately 550,000 cubic metres of rock and sand for the berth pockets and approaches. Thirteen pipelines connect the jetty to the refinery, passing beneath Milford Haven Golf Course, two of which carry the crude oil while the others carry refined products, water, electricity and telephone cables to the tanker berths. Its 69 tanks hold either crude oil awaiting the refining process, or the end products of the process itself.

In 1990 when the French oil company Elf was expanding its refining and marketing business it purchased Amoco's Milford Haven business. Then Elf was acquired by Total in 2000 after which the refinery was operated by Total as a 70/30 joint venture with Murco until late 2007 when Murco acquired the majority interest.

In an area of so much industry it is almost inevitable that there will be some incidents and the Haven has seen its share of accidents and oil spills, although the first 'spill' came in 1936, long before Milford became an oil port, when the oil tanker *SA*

The remnants of Rhoscrowther 'nestling' beneath the Texaco refinery in 2001

*Banda Sharpu*r became stranded on Dale beach and oil was discharged into the harbour. Further oil spillages occurred during the breaking up of vessels at T.W. Ward's yard at Pill Point and from time to time spillages were reported on various beaches, but as the source could never be traced the Port Health Authority was, at that time, powerless to take action.

A fire which raged at the Amoco refinery in September 1983 — exactly 43 years after the massive fires in the Llanreath oil tanks caused by the Luftwaffe — injured seven firemen and is remembered as one of the biggest peace-time fires ever known in the UK, burning so brightly that, at midnight, the sensors on the street lights at Herbrandston switched the lights off. The intense heat melted thick metal plates and black columns of smoke rose several thousands of feet high. The fire was thought to have been started when burning material from a flarestack landed on the roof of the largest crude oil storage tank in the refinery capable of holding 600,000 barrels of oil. Fortunately it was only half full at the time. As the fire intensified it 'boiled over', causing the flames to extend over a four acre area. During a 50-hour period 150 firemen from all over Wales fought the blaze attempting to blanket it with more than 120,000 gallons of foam brought in by sea and road. Twenty-five appliances were in attendance with 40 pumps, six hydraulic platforms, 14 foam tenders and 66 commercial tenders.

Today the dying village of Rhoscrowther is best known for lying under the shadow of the Texaco oil refinery and being the victim of two massive explosions at the plant, explosions which led the majority of the residents to flee the once peaceful area where they had lived all their lives.

These were the people who had bitterly opposed what they saw as the intrusion of the multinational company in 1964, indeed some of them people who had subsequently lost their childhood homes to the bulldozers as the refinery was built. Further local opposition came in 1979 when an expansion programme brought an influx of 2,500 construction workers, with little of the additional skilled work being available to the men of the village.

This long, uneasy relationship between the oil company and the people of Rhoscrowther came to a head on a January day in 1992 when the village was rocked by an explosion during maintenance work on the catalytic cracker. Twenty-six Texaco workers were injured and many of the people who had fled from their homes said they were too frightened to return, even for their most precious possessions. With angry protests ringing in their ears Texaco offered to buy every home in the village, an offer which 24 of the villagers took up and moved away at a cost to the company of £2.5m. The post office subsequently closed and over a period of 12 months all the unoccupied property was demolished.

Albert and Peggy Powell who had lived in Rhoscrowther for 57 years remained, together with brother and sister Merfyn and Gwen Lewis who were brought up in a cottage which had stood on the site of the refinery. Neither family wanted to make a fresh start but their resolve was severely tested two years later. Early one Sunday in July 1994 the county experienced one of the worst electrical storms in living memory. At 7.20am the first lightning bolt hit the ground and by 10am more than 400 bolts had scorched the earth in a 30 mile radius round the refinery. The Esso refinery was hit several times as was the fractioning column at Texaco which sparked small fires that appeared to be quickly extinguished. At Gulf one process plant had to be shut down because of the huge fluctuations in the electrical supply as the storm raged. Then, at lunch time, a hundred-foot fireball ripped through the cracking unit and produced the equivalent power of a force 11 wind. The blast caused tremors over a three mile radius shattering windows in Milford's main street, and could be heard 30 miles away. Subsequent investigation revealed that the storm had caused severe fluctuations in the temperature and pressure gauges resulting in the pressure inside a flare-off pipe building up until the metal could no longer take the strain. A 20-ton ball of boiling oil and gas escaped, exploding in the air and causing a series of further fires and explosions. Miraculously, though mostly because the explosion occurred on a Sunday with few staff on site, there were no serious injuries.

What were described as 'errors of judgement, faulty equipment [a rusty pipe] and inadequate training' caused millions of pounds worth of damage to the plant and cost the two companies — Gulf and Texaco, the partners in the cracking unit — not only fines but £180,000 in compensation to residents, claims for damages by oil workers plus 80 per cent of the considerable fire-fighting costs. They then spent a further £9 million upgrading the system, enabling Texaco to claim that their Pembrokeshire refinery had the most advanced monitoring and alarm system in the industry. In court a representative of the companies said that between them Texaco and Gulf had 'poured a billion pound investment into the Pembrokeshire economy.'

But it was an event that saw an end to Rhoscrowther as a village. More of the remaining residents departed, the pub closed, and by the end of the year the 14th-century church of St. Edmunds held its last service, and with the church closed its 71-year-old organist Miss Myfanwy Llewellyn also left her home.

The economic repercussions of this disaster had a particularly serious effect on Gulf. With Texaco's refinery shut down for a period of 18 weeks Gulf's production plunged from 60,000 barrels of gasoline per day to 30,000 and the company had to buy in both gasoline components and gasoline itself to meet the needs of its UK customers.

The Milford Haven Port Authority which levies charges on shipping using the Haven suffered losses of some £100,000 as a result of lost trade during the shut down with the drop in the number of tankers using the waterway. Cory Towage which provided 24-hour safety cover were also affected; while their crews continued to provide the cover there was no revenue coming in from their usual refinery work.

In a 1996 court case the two companies, Texaco and Gulf were each fined £100,000 and ordered, jointly, to pay costs of £143,000 after admitting serious breaches of health and safety legislation.

There were some benefits, however, for 1,750 men, many of them locally based, were brought in to get the refinery back into production and those who came in from outside the county brought a welcome boost to the B & B sector. Presumably the public houses also benefited, though possibly to a lesser degree than in the days of the 'navvies' who flooded the county at the time of the building of the railway.

Yet this 'benefit' was short lived for in 1996 came news of the impending closure of Gulf Oil Refinery as part of a merger with Elf/Murco. Gulf had a direct workforce of between 250 and 270 jobs, provided 100 contract jobs on the 450-acre Waterston site and 700 jobs in associated services and industry. Its spending on wages, rates and services mounted to an annual figure of £22-25 million. It was also a company known within the community as a good neighbour. Over a period of 25 years it had provided more than £55,000 to Pembrokeshire undergraduates through its scholarship awards and had invested hundreds of thousands of pounds in sponsorships, charities and voluntary organisations. The Gulf closure in 1998 followed that of the Royal Naval Armament Depots at Milford Haven and Trecwn, the closure of RAF Brawdy and US Brawdy, cuts in the Pembroke RN Dockyard and the departure of the Rescue helicopters and the German Army from their training base at Castlemartin — a combined loss of 1,500 civilian jobs and 2,000 servicemen. At the same time Pembroke power station had been mothballed (eventually to close with demolition begun in January 2001) and the Port of Pembroke was in receivership. Local incomes were reported to be 30 per cent below the UK average and among the worst in the European Community even before the Gulf closure. On top of all this, it was also estimated that 60 fewer ships would use the Haven.

In amongst all this came the *Sea Empress* disaster, as a result of which 226 operators in tourism claimed £46m in compensation. It had long been appreciated that the activity of massive tankers in the busy oil port which brought prosperity to the area, also brought the threat of a disaster waiting to happen. That disaster occurred on the night of Thursday 15 February 1996.

As the 147,000 tonne supertanker *Sea Empress* was being piloted through the treacherous rocky entrance to Milford Haven on the final stage of her three-day voyage from Grangemouth to the Texaco refinery, the pilot lost control in the strong tide and she ran aground on rocks in Mill Bay just off St. Ann's Head.

The vessel was carrying a full cargo of North Sea light crude oil and on that initial grounding she suffered immediate and extensive damage as her oil tanks ruptured. It was not realised at the time that the tanker immediately began to lose a significant quantity of her cargo, a flow which continued over the course of a week until 72,000 tons of oil had been released into the waters of the Haven. In the meantime, Haverfordwest aerodrome was opened and salvage equipment was rushed to the scene.

Two days after the initial grounding the vessel was pulled clear of its original position but when the holding cables snapped the engine room flooded, the Russian crew was evacuated and, as the gales grew in intensity, the tanker hit the rocks again, sustaining more damage as the hull was holed. The salvage team which had been landed on the vessel was hampered by the risk of explosion, a danger created by oxygen being sucked into the damaged cargo and ballast tanks, and during the Saturday afternoon the team was helicoptered from the ship for personal safety.

Weather conditions deteriorated still further and the tanker grounded for a third time after drifting across the Haven and it was not until Wednesday 21 February that she was refloated and towed to Herbrandston berth at Milford Haven. It is greatly to

The Sea Empress *aground (Martin Cavaney)*

the credit of the salvage team, working in extreme conditions, that the ship was saved and the remaining 70,000 tons of oil was removed and pumped into tanks. Despite the attempts to control the spillage with floating booms and spray from specially fitted aircraft, around 200 kilometres of the Pembrokeshire coastline was polluted. During the course of the clean up operation 445 tonnes of dispersant was used in the battle against pollution.

In this, the third worst oil spill in British maritime history (after the *Torrey Canyon* off the Cornish coast in 1967 and the *Braer* off the Shetlands in 1993) several Maritime and Nature Reserves, 35 Sites of Special Scientific Interest and 20 National Trust properties were affected. It is thought that tens of thousands of seabirds died (the *Sea Empress* Environmental Evaluation Committee estimated that 3,500 skoda duck had been killed and the cushion star fish in West Angle Bay were almost decimated). Fisheries as far afield as the rivers Taf and Tywi were closed for nearly six weeks at the start of the 1996 season, while it was said that commercial fishing suffered losses of up to £10 million. The clean up work, which continued intensively over a period of six weeks cost a minimum of £60 million.

At the court hearing in January 1999, when the Port Authority admitted a charge (brought by the Environment Agency) of causing pollution by allowing oil to enter the water, it was stated that the Liberian Registered *Sea Empress* was built in 1993 with a single skinned hull — prior to the report on the *Braer* oil spill which recommended that tankers should have double skinned hulls. It was also revealed that the port's radar did not meet international guidelines. The system had been in place since 1986 and had gradually deteriorated until by mid-1994 it was known it would need replacing. Evidence was given that at the time of the *Sea Empress* grounding the existing radar would have been incapable of providing any observation of the ship's entry to the west channel, precluding the possibility of the duty officer identifying the danger the pilot was sailing into and warning him accordingly.

Although the fine of £4 million was welcomed by environmentalists as befitting the seriousness of the oil spill it was greeted with dismay by many in the Pembrokeshire community as a double whammy for an area which had already suffered greatly from the spill, and headlines such as 'Job hopes of hundreds hit by £4m fine' proliferated in the local press.

Port Authority General Manager Mr. Ted Sangster wrote to the 200 plus workforce reassuring them that there would be no immediate job losses but adding that the fine would greatly impair the future viability of the business. In addition to the immediate staff which includes pilots, marine staff who operate the launches and port control, administration staff, staff at Milford docks and marina, the Ro-Ro ferry terminal, ship repair business, crane hire company and Pembroke Port, the work of the Authority supports thousands of spin-off jobs in west Wales. In addition, a turnover of over £1 billion from companies making use of the waterway depends on the continuing and successful operation of the facilities provided by the Port Authority.

Once again the outlook seemed bleak for Milford Haven. Major job creating projects scheduled to contribute significantly to Pembrokeshire's fragile economy were put on hold. But again, as so often in the history of Milford, there came a respite when, on appeal in March 2000, the fine was slashed to £750,000.

No longer restricted by the heavy debt burden of a £4 million fine the Authority launched plans to spend that sum constructively over a several year period on a variety of projects, with their first priority improving the safety of the port which is now the fifth largest in the UK. The building of a new pilot boat went ahead, the navigation buoys were upgraded and closed circuit TV cameras have been installed in the radar station to feed visual links back to the control centre at Hakin. The lesson of the *Sea Empress* was truly learned.

Following renewed calls for increased protection for the sensitive coastline skirting the oil terminal at Milford Haven, more good news for the safety of shipping in the Haven came early in 2001 when the government announced that the emergency heavy duty towing vessels which protect Britain's coastline in winter will be on duty all the year round. The need for an extra tug positioned in the Irish Sea had been highlighted by a near miss on Christmas Eve 1999 when the 1,500 tonne *Blackfriars*, carrying 1,800 litres of fuel oil, had to be hauled off a Pembrokeshire beach by the St. David's lifeboat. While lengthy negotiations were taking place to secure the services of a rescue tug (which finally arrived from Falmouth, seven hours after the tanker grounded) the vessel had been re-floated. The Marine Accident Investigations report into the incident recorded that the local tug's response was restricted because of its contractual agreement with the oil companies that in bad weather it will look after vessels already in the Milford Haven

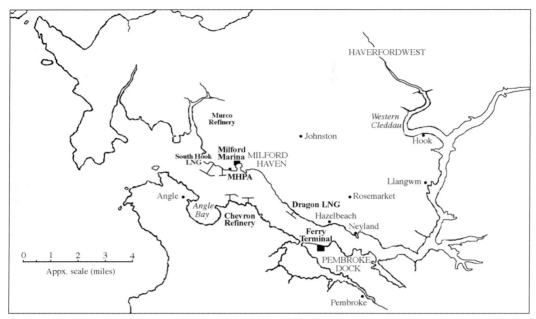

*The Milford Haven waterway showing the location of tanker berths and associated facilities,
with details of recent developments at Pembroke Dock (below) and Milford Haven (opposite)*

waterway. Had a tug responded it would have left only one tug available to cover any
major emergency that might arise at one of the oil terminals.

With Milford's unfortunate experience of oil pollution it seems only fitting that it is
here that the greatest expertise in dealing with oil spills may be found. The D.V. Howells
company, (now Braemar Howells as a part of the Braemar Shipping Services Group)
has over 50 years experience in oil spill response, and is one of only 20 organisations
worldwide accredited to undertake International Maritime Organisation Oil Pollution

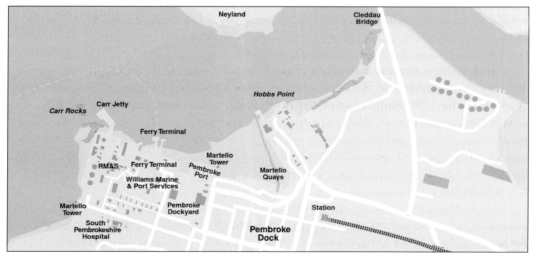

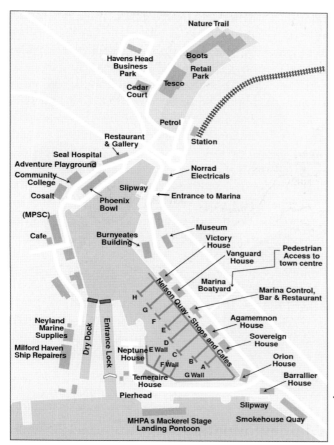

Nature Trail

Havens Head Business Park

Boots

Retail Park

Cedar Court

Tesco

Petrol

Restaurant & Gallery

Station

Seal Hospital

Adventure Playground

Community College

Norrad Electricals

Cosalt

Slipway

Phoenix Bowl

Entrance to Marina

(MPSC)

Cafe

Burnyeates Building

Museum

Victory House

Vanguard House

Pedestrian Access to town centre

Marina Boatyard

Marina Control, Bar & Restaurant

Nelson Quay - Shops and Cafes

H

G

F

E

D

C

B

A

Agamemnon House

Sovereign House

Orion House

Barrallier House

Neyland Marine Supplies

Dry Dock

Entrance Lock

Neptune House

E Wall

F Wall

G Wall

Milford Haven Ship Repairers

Temeraire House

Pierhead

Slipway

MHPAs Mackerel Stage Landing Pontoon

Smokehouse Quay

Preparedness, Response and Co-operation spill response training. The company's purpose-built Marine Pollution Salvage Centre on Milford docks contains the UK government's stockpile of national response oil pollution and salvage equipment, ready to be deployed at an hour's notice in time of emergency. The company assists governments, oil companies and UK and overseas ports to review their oil and chemical spill preparedness and response plans, either in the UK, hosting representatives at Milford or travelling to the client's own facility. This has included places such as Chile, Nigeria, Azerbaijan, Namibia, Tanzania, Angola, Mozambique, USA, Kenya, Ireland, China, Japan, Hong Kong, Singapore and Brunei.

In 2001 Marathon Oil were given permission to drill a second exploratory well for gas in the Dragon field 21 miles off the Pembrokeshire coast. A well had been drilled in 1994 in 315 feet of water and the request then for a second well was refused on safety grounds due to concern over the risk to shipping. Drilling eventually went ahead with stringent restrictions. Although gas had been discovered in 1994 giving rise to hopes of oil being found in the area, current thinking is that the reserves are not economically viable for reclaiming.

Today the waterway has taken a giant leap forward with developments that are destined to make Milford Haven — the area which has seen so many vicissitudes in the years since the 1790 foundation of the port — the new energy capital of the UK. The port is the biggest port in Wales, the fifth largest port in the UK and one of the largest oil and gas ports in northern Europe. The two refineries run by Chevron and Murco provide around 20 per cent of the UK's petrol and diesel, while the new and refurbished tankage and berth improvements provided by Semi Logistics make it the largest area of oil tanks in the UK.

Until recent years the UK was self sufficient in gas, for the most part due to abundant supplies from gas fields in the North Sea. Now, however, the output of the off-shore fields is decreasing while demand increases daily, making the country potentially more and more dependant on imported gas. Delays in getting new sources into the system have also sent prices soaring.

As a substantial contribution to meeting the demand, Liquefied Natural Gas (LNG) will be imported to this country from the Middle East and brought ashore at terminals at Herbrandston and Waterston. The natural gas, obtained from the off-shore fields in the Arabian Gulf north of Qatar, will be chilled to minus 160°C and liquefied, reducing its volume by 600 to one. The liquefied gas is then loaded and transported to the Milford terminals in specially built 216,000m³ and 265,000m³ double-hulled tankers through the Red Sea and Suez Canal. Here the cold LNG will be discharged from the ship into insulated tanks at South Hook on the former Esso Refinery site for the product to be passed through vaporisers to be re-gassified, ready to be sent through a pipeline network to the customer. Over a period of three years, 1,300 workers, half from south-west Wales, worked on the construction of the two new pipelines which run from Milford Haven to Aberdulais, near Neath, and from Velindre, near Swansea, to Tirley in Gloucestershire.

Phase 2 of the LNG development is underway at the Dragon LNG site at Herbrandston, the former Gulf refinery land.

The choice of the port of Milford for the LNG terminal was determined by its strategic position on the west coast of the UK with the shorter shipping distance than to other potential ports being a significant factor in reducing transport costs. When the system is fully operational, a potential 30 per cent of the country's gas requirements will be processed through the port.

In response to public concern on safety issues, Port Authority General Manager Ted Sangster said: 'We are confident that we can handle the LNG ships safely and efficiently. Through LNG the future looks brighter for the port and Milford Haven, for the Pembrokeshire economy and for the UK's strategic need for secure energy provision.'

Work in progress on the South Hook LNG terminal (Martin Cavaney)

Bibliography

Archer, Michael Scott *The Welsh Post Towns before 1840*, 1970

Arthur, Elizabeth *Turning of the Leaves*, Clifford E. Collins, Pembroke Dock

Blacklaw Jones, Richard *Pembrokeshire's Past — lost and found*, Pembrokeshire Prospectors, 1997

Brinton, Piet and Worsley, Roger *Open Secrets*, Gomer Press, 1987

Brown, John (writing as Christopher Cobbe Webbe, gentleman) *History of Haverfordwest and Some Pembrokeshire Parishes*, 1882

Brut y Tywysiogion

Carradice, Phil *The Book of Pembroke Dock*, Barracuda Books
The Last Invasion, Village Publishing, Pontypool
Pembroke for King and Parliament, Pembroke Town Council

Cathcart King, D.J. 'Pembroke Castle' in *Archaeologia Cambrensis, 127*, 1978

Charles, B.G. *Calendar of the Borough of Haverfordwest*
Record of Slebech

Children, George and Nash, George *Neolithic Sites of Cardiganshire, Carmarthenshire and Pembrokeshire*, Logaston Press, 1997

Clarendon, Lord *History of Rebellion*

Cole, Leo 'Family Cameos of Yesteryear' in *Pembrokeshire Magazine, 37*, 1985

Crosby, Alan G. *By Tempest and Piracy the Loss of Mersey Salt Vessels off Pembrokeshire 1695-1715*

Dale Womens Institute *Dale, an Illustrated History*, 2000

Davies, Desmond N. *The End of the Line*, Pembrokeshire County Council Cultural Services

Davies, Peter B.S. *Pembrokeshire Limekilns*

Davies, Robert L. and Nelson, Jane *A River Never Sleeps*, SPARC
Flow Gently Sweet River, Teg Fin, 2003

Davies, Wendy *Wales in the Early Middle Ages*, Leicester University Press

Defoe, Daniel *A General History of Pirates*

Dickman, H.J. *History of the Council 1894-1974*, C.I. Thomas and Son, 1976

Edwards, Sybil *Haverfordwest in Old Picture Postcards*, European Library, 1997

Evans, John 'Military Aviation' in *Pembrokeshire County History, Vol.IV*, 1993

Fenton, Richard *A Historical Tour Through Pembrokeshire*, 1811

Forder, Phil and Oram, Peter *The Encircled Cross*

Fraser, Maxwell *Introducing West Wales*, Methuen, 1956

Gaunt, Peter *A Nation Under Siege - The Civil War in Wales 1642-48*, Cadw, 1991

Guard, John *History of Pembroke Dockyard*, 2004

George, Barbara *Pembrokeshire Sea Trading before 1900*, reprinted from *Field Studies Vol.2*, 1964

Giraldus Cambrensis *The Itinerary Through Wales*

Goddard, Ted 'Naval Activity' in *Pembrokeshire County History, Vol.IV*
Harris, George *Early Bristol Paddle Steamer Shipwrecks*
Haverfordwest Civic Society *Haverfordwest Plaque Trail*
Hickling, C.F. *Hake and the Hake Industry*, Edward Arnold, London
Historical and Municipal Documents of Ireland
Hodges, Geoffrey *Owain Glyn Dwr & the War of Independence in the Welsh Borders*, Logaston Press, 1995
Hogg, Ian V. *Coast defences of England and Wales 1856-1956*, David & Charles, 1974
Howells, Richard (ed.) *Where the River Bends*, Menter Preseli
James, David *Down the Slipway*, Peter Williams Associates, 2006
John, Terry *Sacred Stones*, Gomer Press, 1994
        The Civil War in Pembrokeshire, Logaston Press, 2008
Johnson, Keith *The Pubs of Pembroke, Pembroke Dock, Tenby and South Pembrokeshire*, Logaston Press, 2003
        The Pubs of Haverfordwest, Milford Haven and Mid-West Pembrokeshire, Logaston Press, 2006
Jones, Stephen K. *Brunel in South Wales Vol.2*, Tempus, 2006
Laws, Edward *Little England Beyond Wales*, 1888
Leland, John *Tour Through Wales*
Lewis, V.J. *Short History of Milford Port Health Authority*
McBrearty, Jim 'Thoughts on a Mountain' in *Pembrokeshire Magazine, 64*, p.12
McBrearty, Jim (ed.) *Accounts Rendered*, Pembrokeshire Publicity Service, 1987
McKay, Wing Commander K.D. *A Vision of Greatness*, Brace Harvatt/Gulf Oil
Miles, Dillwyn 'The Freemen of Haverfordwest' in *A History of Haverfordwest*, Gomer Press, 1999
Milford Docks Company *A History of the Milford Docks 1874-1974*
Morgan, Mrs. *A Tour of Milford Haven*
Morris, John *Railways of Pembrokeshire*, H.G. Walters, Tenby
Nicolle, Geofrrey *Rosemarket*, Gomer Press
Owen George *Description of Pembrokeshire*, 1603
Pembrokeshire County Council *County Development Plan 1953*
Pembrokeshire Herald *Sinking of Hirano Maru*, November, 1918
Pembrokeshire Life *Personality Profile, Ivor Evans*, August, 1991
Pembrokeshire Military and Maritime Heritage Group *A Guide to the Military History of Pembrokeshire*, PLANED
Phelps, Reg 'We Lived by the River' in *Pembrokeshire Magazine, 22*, April, 1984
Phillips. Revd. James *History of Pembrokeshire*, Elliott Stock, London, 1909
Phillips and Warren *History of Haverfordwest* - additions to original by John Brown (see above)
Rees, William *History of the Order of St. John of Jerusalem*
Richards, W.L. *Pembrokeshire Under Fire*
        Changing Face of Haverfordwest Haverfordwest Civic Society

Roche, John 'Roman Pembrokshire - a Personal View' in *Journal of the Pembrokeshire Historical Society*, 1992-3

Scott, Vernon *Inferno*, 1940

Smylie, Mike *Working the Welsh Coast*, Tempus Publishing, 2005

Speede, John *Treatise of the Empire of Great Britain*

Thomas, Flora *The Builders of Milford*, Western Telegraph

Thomas, W.G. *Llangwm through the Ages*

Timmins, Thornhill *Nooks and Corners of Pembrokeshire,* Elliot Stock, 1895

Walker, R. *Freemen of England*, York, 1915

West Wales Maritime Society *Secret Waterway*

Western Telegraph *Changing Sea Trade of a Village Port*, Then and Now No.339

Worsley, Roger *The Pembrokeshire Explorer Coastal Cottages of Pembrokeshire*, 1988
        'Railways Galore' in *Pembrokeshire Magazine, No.3*

Index

211

sailors 127-128
St. Ann's Head 1, 9, 175, 195
St. Botolphs 9
St. Bridges Bay 180
St. Brynach 10-11
St. David 21
St. David's Head 10
St. Fagans, battle of 144
St. Fagans, National Museum of Wales 55
St. Thomas à Becket chapel, Milford Haven
     152-153
salt trade 28, 130, 135
Sangster, Ted 188, 197
Saunders, Erasmus, mayor of Tenby 131
Saxon, trawler 176
Saxons Ford 6
Scourfield, Sir Owen 63
Scoveston Fort 75, 178
Scurlock's Yard, Westfield Pill 98
Seabees 182
Sea Empress, disaster 195-197, *196*
Seapro, fishing vessel 180
Second World War 36, 37, 64, 80, 83, 87,
     90-92, 105, 121, 182-184
Sellick, Morley and Price, trawler firm 176
Semi Logistics 199
Sherbourne, family 71
ship-breaking 88-89
shipbuilding 78-80, 83-85, 87, 97, 101, 122,
     154
ships, early types 13-14, *18*, 26, *44*, 58
'Shipping Gut' 97
shipwreck 137
Short Point 8
Simmons, David 50
     Thomas 50
Sisters House, Minwear 108, *109*
Slebech 41, 107, 109, 110
Smalls lighthouse 120
smuggling 32, 126, 130, 138-139, 149
Snow (of Bristol) 127
Society of Friends, *see* Quakers
Society of Sea Serjeants 118
Sonnegen, James 49
South Pembrokeshire District Hospital 85
Spain, trade with 26-27, 113
Speede, John 25

Speedwell, Customs cutter 136
Spillers and Bakers 60
Stack Rock 72
     Fort 74, *75*
Stackpole 142
staple ports 25, 47
Starbuck, family 151
     Daniel 51
     Gayer 152
     Samuel 51, 152
Stephens, Eddy *94*
Stepney, family 45
     Alban (of Prendergast) 29, 30
     Sir John, MP 141
Steynton 48, 114, 142
Stokes, John Lort 188
Stone Age 1-4
     finds *2*
Stonehenge 1-5, *3*, 9
Style, Dr. Hurrell 6
Summerhouse Farm 149
Sunderland flying boats 89-90, 92
Supply, ketch 135
Surprise, HMS, 46 guns *154*
Sutle, battleship 85
Swanley, Admiral Richard 142, 153
Swinburne, Sir Thomas 19
Sybil, trawler 167, 168
Syren 163

Taillour, Morgane (of Tenby) 133
Taliesin, tug 104
Tall Ships Race 187
Tancred, a Fleming 40
tanyards 27, 41
Tate, William 136
Taylor, George Ledwell 79
Taylor, Richard, mayor of H'west 45
Technium Centre 95
Telford, Thomas 120, 155
Temperance Tea Rooms, Broadhaven 68
Tenby 10, 25-26, 31, 33, 133
     Castle 15
     in Civil War 141, 143
     Hospital 24
Texaco 190, 191, *192*, 193-194
Thomas, David Edward 67